105870

D1647147

Born in 1941, Ian W͏_____ry
from Magdalen College, _____ ny
books including the bestselling *The Blood and the Shroud*;
Holy Faces, Secret Places; *The Columbus Myth*;
Undiscovered; *Shakespeare: The Evidence* and *The Bible is
History*. Ian Wilson also co-wrote the script for *Silent
Witness*, the BAFTA award-winning documentary on the
Turin Shroud, and his acclaimed book *Jesus: The Evidence*
was accompanied by a major television series.

BEFORE
THE
FLOOD

UNDERSTANDING THE BIBLICAL
FLOOD STORY AS RECALLING A
REAL-LIFE EVENT

IAN WILSON

ORION

An Orion paperback

First published in Great Britain in 2001
by Orion
This paperback edition published in 2002
by Orion Books Ltd,
Orion House, 5 Upper St Martin's Lane,
London WC2H 9EA

Copyright © Ian Wilson 2001

The right of Ian Wilson to be identified as the author
of this work has been asserted by him in accordance
with the Copyright, Designs and Patents Act 1988.

All rights reserved. No part of this publication may be
reproduced, stored in a retrieval system, or transmitted,
in any form or by any means, electronic, mechanical,
photocopying, recording or otherwise, without the prior
permission of the copyright owner.

A CIP catalogue record for this book
is available from the British Library.

ISBN 0 75284 811 9

Typeset by Selwood Systems, Midsomer Norton

Printed and bound in Great Britain by
Clays Ltd, St Ives plc

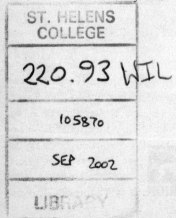

ST. HELENS
COLLEGE

220.93 WIL

105870

SEP 2002

LIBRARY

ACKNOWLEDGEMENTS

Fig 1: Map by Ian & Judith Wilson modified from data and a more detailed map in Frank Press & Raymond Siever, *Earth* (4th ed.) New York, W.H. Freeman, 1986, p.254; *Fig 2*: Based on a graph reproduced on the website of Claude Lantz, after Jacques Labeyrie, *L'homme et le climat*, Denoël, Paris; *Fig 4*: From a photograph of the 1920s in the University of Pennsylvania Museum Archives; *Fig 5*: Supplied courtesy of Prof. Ian Plimer of the University of Melbourne; *Fig 7*: From the web-site of the Institute for Exploration, Mystic, Connecticut, reproduction permission kindly granted by Dr Fredrik Hiebert, University of Pennsylvania Museum; *Fig 8*: Map by Ian & Judith Wilson based on data and a map in Tjeerd van Andel's scientific paper 'Late Quaternary sea-level changes and archaeology' *Antiquity* 63 (1989) pp.733–45; *Fig 9*: From a painting of the Henri Lhote Tassili expedition; *Figs 10, 13, 14, 15, 16, 21* (right*)*, *22* & *23*: Drawings and photographs supplied by kind permission of Dr James Mellaart; *Fig 11*: Drawing supplied courtesy of Dr Denise Schmandt-Besserat and the University of Texas; *Fig 12*: Drawing from Alastair Hull's *Living with Kilims*, Thames & Hudson, 1988, p.35, courtesy Thames & Hudson.

Fig 17: Map by Ian & Judith Wilson based on data and maps in William Ryan & Walter Pitman's *Noah's Flood*, New York, Simon & Schuster, 1998, pp.189 & 194;   *Fig 19*: (left) N.Vlassa, (right) Ashmolean Museum, Oxford; *Figs 20 & 26*: photos by Ian Wilson; *Fig 21* (left): Photo Mario Mintoff, courtesy M.J. Publications, Malta; *Fig 24*: Ankara Museum; *Fig 25*: Map by Ian & Judith Wilson based on a map in Keith Muckelroy (ed.) *Archaeology Under Water* New York, McGraw Hill, 1980, pp.162–3; *Fig 27*: Directorate of Antiquities, Baghdad; *Figs 30 & 31*; Heraklion Museum, Crete; *Fig 32*: Ekdotike Athenon; *Fig 33*: Max Hirmer; *Fig 34*: Archaeological Museum, Damascus.

Whilst every reasonable effort has been made to contact copyright owners, the author & publishers apologise in the case of any that have been untraceable and will be pleased to insert appropriate acknowledgement in future editions.

CONTENTS

AUTHOR'S PREFACE

'The days are long gone when one, or even two scholars, could master as many diverse fields as this book covers'.[1] With those words Mark Rose, managing editor of the admirable American journal *Archaeology*, dismissed the undeniably daunting hypothesis ventured in William Ryan and Walter Pitman's *Noah's Flood*.

Rose published his remarks in January 1999, and was not to know that by October of the same year Dr Robert Ballard of *Titanic* fame would find the first serious evidence of the truth of Ryan and Pitman's hypothesis. Or that this would be followed in September 2000 by Ballard finding the most astounding proof of this same.

This said, there is a very real sense in which Rose was right. Today archaeological work has become so specialised, so high-tech and so tightly focused on perhaps one site, the evaluation of which may become one or more scholars' life-time's work, that few professional archaeologists will dare to pull back and try to see a bigger picture.

But this is a catastrophe that happened eight thousand years ago, that affected huge areas of dry land, that touches on the work of climatologists, oceanographers, geologists, archaeologists and biblical scholars. It also spawned myths that have spread as far afield as Greece and India. Trying to see the bigger picture is then not only unavoidable, but also extremely important.

This book, which unashamedly follows Ryan and Pitman's most inspiring lead, is one such attempt. By training a historian, prehistory has frankly never had much appeal for me. Yet the task of a historian is to try to determine, from often very varied and conflicting types of evidence, what happened in the past, from mere decades ago, to several thousand years ago. And that is certainly the assignment here. In recent decades archaeology has made immense strides in being able to retrieve many minutiae from thousands of years ago that previous generations would have supposed gone for ever. But in writing about such matters archaeologists all too often speak in a technical jargon that loses sight of what their discoveries mean about the lives of people from the past. In order to make matters simple there are instances in which scholars may feel that I have gone too far in the opposite direction. For instance, rather than use the term 'Neolithic' I have opted for 'late Stone Age'. Rather than use the usual terms 'Anatolia' or 'Asia Minor' when referring to Turkey as it existed in ancient times I have kept it as Turkey, while making clear that this is its modern name.

The idea of writing this book came when researching my earlier *The Bible is History*, and my very special thanks are due to agent Daniela Bernardelle of David Higham and publisher Trevor Dolby of Orion for greeting it with immediate support and enthusiasm. In the course of my researching the book a mutual friend, Gillian Warr, kindly facilitated an introduction to Dr James Mellaart, excavator of Çatat Hüyük, and I am deeply grateful to Gillian for this, also to Dr Mellaart for reading the manuscript, granting many most helpful insights, and allowing use of several of his fine illustrations. Geologists Professor Ian Plimer of the University of Melbourne and Dr Edward Rose of Royal Holloway College, University of London also generously contributed further help and expert knowledge, likewise archaeologists Dr Fredrik Hiebert, John Romer and Denise Schmandt-Besserat. I am most grateful to Andrew George of London University's School of Oriental and African Studies, also to Penguin Books, for kindly allowing me to reproduce relevant portions from his excellent recent translation of the *Epic of Gilgamesh*. Special thanks are also due to Griselda Warr for helpful information-gathering; to Kay Macmullan for patiently tolerating some excessive authorial changes in the course of her copy-editing the manuscript; to Pandora White of Orion for most unflappably steering the book through to production; and above all to my ever-supportive wife Judith for spending countless hours unstintingly helping me on every aspect, including checking every word of the manuscript and preparing many of the maps and other illustrations.

Ian Wilson
Bellbowrie, Queensland, Australia
June 2001

WHAT'S IN A DATE?

If you had lived in the 19th century and had asked a well-educated member of the Church of England when Noah's Flood occurred, he would most likely have told you, with great confidence '2348 BC'. And he would have had every justification for such confidence. Opening up his 'King James Authorised Version' Family Bible, he could have pointed out to you in its introduction and margins the date of 4004 BC for the Creation, and 2348 BC for the Flood. Surviving copies of Family Bibles quote similarly precise dates for other momentous events. Many of them also include among their illustrations a finely etched but rather lurid artist's visualisation of the Flood, depicting the last scraps of humanity desperately clinging to mountain peaks moments before they are swept away by even more mountainous flood-waters.

Had you lived back in the 17th century you might have learned from Archbishop James Ussher of Armagh (1581–1656), the man chiefly responsible for such datings, that the task of calculating them was a simple one, scarcely needing anyone of his considerable erudition. Martin Luther's great disciple Philip Melanchthon had showed that the world would last just eight thousand years from Creation to Doomsday, four of these millennia before the birth of Christ, and four of them after. Ussher knew from the 1st century AD historian Josephus that king Herod (who tried to kill the infant Jesus),[1] had died in the 23rd year of the Roman emperor Augustus – by Christian reckoning, in 4 BC. So it followed that Jesus was born in 4 BC and the Creation must have happened in 4004 BC.[2] And since from the list of 'begats' in Genesis chapter 5 it can be calculated that Noah's Flood occurred 1,656[3] years after the Creation, then the date for this catastrophe has to have been 2348 BC.

Today, of course, only die-hard biblical fundamentalists and Creationists are wont to cling to such thinking. Scientists have shown convincingly enough for the great majority of individuals (including myself), that the earth began around 4.5 billion years ago, give or take the odd few hundred million. Likewise geologists have plainly and lucidly demonstrated that our planet has had its fair share of catastrophes, including an event of 65 million years ago which wiped out the dinosaurs. But during the mere hundred thousand years that humankind has walked it there has never been anything approaching a world Flood. The biblical idea that within the time that men have been making boats there was a universal Flood which rose so high that it covered mountaintops and swallowed up every creature of creation except for a selected few, is as patently absurd as it is untrue.

While the dismissal of this story is entirely proper in the interests of scientific truth, there was something very satisfying about Archbishop Ussher's 'hard' dates, which were widely accepted for some two centuries.[4] Despite modern-day scholars sometimes quoting with quite unwarranted authority exact years for ancient Egyptian pharaohs' reigns and happenings within them,[5] the fact is that historians and archaeologists lack the means of providing truly firm chronological pegs for any events of the ancient past prior to the 7th century BC. It would make the creation of timelines much easier if certain epoch-shattering events, such as the burning of a big city or a serious volcanic eruption, could be pinpointed to a particular year. But even the most promising archaeological tools such as radio-carbon dating and tree-ring dating have yet to be refined to provide this degree of precision.

Instead for the last two hundred years archaeologists have mostly relied on a system of setting the ancient past into a timeframe that is governed by whatever was the principal material used during that period. It was back in 1816 that Christian Thomsen (1788–1865), newly appointed as Curator of Denmark's National Museum, hit upon the not entirely new[6] idea of grouping the objects in his care according to whether, in his view, they belonged to the Stone Age, the Bronze Age or the Iron Age. Ever since, and right up to and including the present day, archaeologists have mostly tinkered with refining these classifications, inventing sub-groups such as 'Palaeolithic' (Old Stone Age), Neolithic (Late Stone Age) and Middle Bronze Age II, together with adding the odd extra 'Age', most particularly the Chalcolithic, or Copper Age, rather than inventing any replacement system.

Yet one serious problem to the Three-Age System is that, in the case of the Stone Age for instance, it creates what I would term the 'Fred Flintstone Illusion', that almost everything that anyone used at that time was made of stone. This makes it easy for the layman to forget that during this period stone was used to cut and shape wood for housing, furniture, utensils, boats and so on – particularly as such wooden objects will not have survived the millennia in anything like the manner of the stone ones.

Another problem is that while archaeologists will often quote fairly precise dates for any one sub-division of an Age, such as dating the Middle Bronze Age to 2200–1570 BC, these dates vary quite considerably between one culture and another. This is because one culture may advance to bronze or iron metallurgy significantly earlier or later than even its neighbour, let alone cultures further afield. Likewise the names and dates that are accredited to particular periods vary from one archaeologist to another, since there is no single, universally agreed method or chronology.

Yet another problem is that declaration of a chronological change from say, Late Bronze Age II to Iron Age I can convey the impression that almost overnight everyone shifted from using bronze to using iron. Logic should, of course, counsel that this is not the way that such things are likely to have happened in real life, in the past any more than today.

This is why the Archbishop Ussher's 'hard' dating system, hopelessly flawed though it undoubtedly was in relation to our present-day understanding, was so much more meaningful and comprehensible than anything that has followed it. When the biblical book of Genesis recorded a major event, such as the Flood, there, set down in black and white, was Ussher's authoritative determination of exactly when it happened, to an exact year. The rest of human history could then be seen as either before or after it.

So, what if, according to findings so recent that they are as yet far from assimilated, we now have grounds for believing the Bible to have been significantly more right in respect of the Flood than anyone bar Creationists and fundamentalists have been giving it credit for? What if, millennia earlier than Archbishop Ussher could have imagined (indeed, earlier than he believed the entire world to have been created), there actually was a Flood? A Flood that may not have risen anything like as high as the world's mountaintops, or so extensive as to cover the entire earth, but which certainly swept away a major heartland of civilisation as it existed at that time?

In fact there is no need for such 'what ifs'. For this book is the story of just such a Flood event actually having happened. An event that though we may not be able to date it to a single year, certainly occurred in or about 5600 BC, give or take a few decades. From what we know about it so far, it was an event that occurred in a most unexpected location, the environs of what is today the Black Sea. And it was also so massive and devastating that it arguably spawned not only the 'Noah' Flood story as this became preserved in the folklore of the Hebrew peoples, but also the Flood stories that have been preserved in a number of other cultures besides.

That such an event actually happened is now absolutely certain, accredited by scientists of international repute to the same degree of confidence with which, only a few years ago, the Noah story was being dismissed as nonsense. The first serious archaeological evidence has been found on the seabed of the Black Sea, with undoubtedly a great deal more to follow.

So recent has been our awareness of the actuality of this catastrophe that no one yet knows the exact population numbers, distribution and scale of advancement of those peoples who became overwhelmed by it. But opening up a better understanding of their world, as was lost in a terrible maelstrom 7,600 years ago must surely represent the biggest single archaeological challenge that our 21st century is likely to tackle. It also forms the topic that we are about to explore in this book.

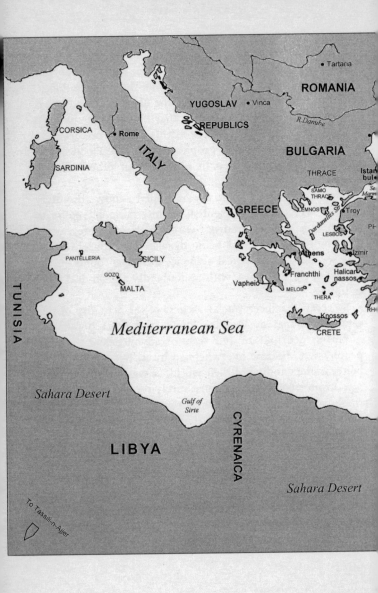

CHAPTER I

WHEN THE ICE MELTED

The ... rise in sea level, of the order of decimetres a year, must have caused widespread flooding of low-lying areas, many of which were inhabited by man.

Professor Cesare Emiliani, 1975

Scientifically it is quite certain that throughout humankind's existence there has never been any biblical-type Flood that destroyed everyone in the world except for a chosen few. Yet the great paradox is that all around the world there are quite an extraordinary number of peoples who remember some such event in their folk memories.

World Flood myths, some of them very similar to the Biblical one, have been recorded by the Sumerians, Assyrians, Babylonians, Chaldeans, Zoroastrians, Hebrews, Persians, Egyptians, Greeks, Romans, Celts, Hindus, Maya, Toltecs, Zapotecs and Incas. Likewise on every continent there are peoples who have preserved world Flood myths of some description in their folklore. These include, in Europe the Scandinavians, Welsh, Lithuanians and Germans; in Africa the Yoruba, Ekoi and Efik-Ibibio of Nigeria, the Mandingo of the Ivory Coast, also the so-called Pygmies; in North America several Eskimo tribes of Alaska and British Columbia, also the Yakima, Algonquin, Navajo, Mandans, Cherokee, Choctaw, Hopi and numerous other 'Indian' tribes; in South America the Arawak and Arekuna of Guyana, the Muysca of Colombia, the Yanomamo and Yaruro of southern Venezuela, the Yamana of Tierra del Fuego; in the Far East and India the Andaman islanders in the Bay of Bengal, the Loto of Southwestern China, the Chingpaw of Upper Burma, the Kelantan of the Malay Peninsula, the Batak of Sumatra, the Dyaks of Borneo, the Toraja of the Celebes; and in Australasia and the Pacific islands the Kabadi of New Guinea; the Gumaidj, Maung and Gunwinggu aboriginals of Arnhem Land, the Andingari and Wiranggu of south Australia, the Maori of New Zealand and the peoples of Fiji, Samoa, the Cook Islands, Tahiti and Hawaii.[1]

It is important to recognise that the territories where some of these peoples are living now are not necessarily where they believe their ancestors to have experienced their particular Flood. Also, many of their stories are very different from the biblical story – indeed some are so patently 'mythological' that it would be absurd to try to claim any sort of historical sense for them. And even where there are striking similarities to the biblical story – as, for instance, amongst the Flood tales of certain of the Pacific islanders – the indications are that these derived from Flood stories that were told to them by Christian missionaries and which were then assimilated into their own folklore.

But this said, the idea of a world Flood is undeniably so deeply ingrained in the folk-memories of so many different peoples that it raises the fundamental question of just how and why should this be so.

In fact there is no real mystery, as the answer to this question can be summed up in six words: the end of the Ice Age. For as has been scientifically established for over a century, the world has repeatedly suffered from Ice Ages, at the last count no less than 36 of these occurring during the last three million years. And although exactly why these happen is still not yet fully understood, the last Ice Age, and the melting that stemmed from it, was quite definitely well within the time that humankind walked the earth.

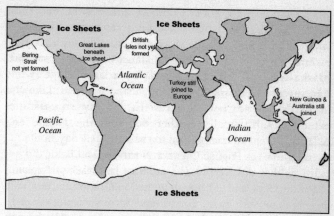

Fig 1 The world's coastlines as they looked at the height of the Ice Age
c.16,000 BC

Now anyone who has flown over Greenland on a clear
day will have some picture of what North America and
northern Europe would have looked like during this relatively recent but extremely inhospitable period. In North
America, from Portland, Oregon in the west to New York in
the east there were ice sheets up to a kilometre (half a mile)
thick that covered the entire landmass northwards, extending all the way to the North Pole. Northern Europe presented much the same desolate picture, its ice-cap extending as
far south as Dublin, Birmingham and Berlin, with snow covering much of the terrain immediately south of this.

What is rarely appreciated is that there was so much
water locked up in the ice sheets covering the land that the
world's sea-level was significantly lower than it is today.
Thus, if a cartographer had been around at the time, the map
of the world's coastlines as they then existed, though
broadly familiar [fig 1], would have had some significant
differences to our present-day world maps.

For instance, in the United States the major east coast

cities such as New York, Baltimore and Boston, had these existed at the time, would have been 120 to 240 kilometres (75 to 150 miles) inland, since the coastline of that time extended further east by those distances. On the west coast, Alaska was still joined to Siberia by a land-bridge, while Vancouver and its island lay some distance inland. Likewise in South America both the western and eastern coastlines extended substantially further out into the Pacific and Atlantic oceans in comparison to their present-day limits.

In Europe the English Channel, North Sea and Baltic did not exist, neither did Ireland as a separate landmass to England, Wales and Scotland. Although in the Mediterranean the straits of Gibraltar were open, Corsica and Sardinia were joined to each other, likewise Sicily to the Italian peninsula. There was a large extra landmass off what is today Tunisia. Much of what is today the Adriatic Sea was dry land. To the south of Greece there were fewer, but larger islands than those of the present day, while what is now the Black Sea was an inland freshwater lake, a land barrier preventing any joining of it with the Mediterranean and thereby with world sea-levels.

Across the other side of the world, Japan, although it had its own internal sea, was linked to the Asian mainland, with Russia to its north and Korea to its south. In South-East Asia what are today the islands of Sumatra, Java and Borneo were joined to Malaysia and Thailand by a landmass that geographers call the Sunda Shelf. To the south another landmass, the Sahul Shelf, joined New Guinea to the north Australian mainland, so that the present Timor and Arafura Seas, also the vast Gulf of Carpentaria which on maps appears as the bite out of Australia's top end, did not exist. Tasmania was joined to the Australian mainland and in my own state of Queensland you would have been able to stroll out to well beyond the farthest limits of what is today the Great Barrier Reef without getting your feet wet. The North and South islands of New Zealand were still joined to each other.

This is but the broadest sketch of the world as it is understood to have looked up to around 14,000 BC, but then the ice began to melt, and all began to change. And as is the way with climatic changes, these happened in stages that were far from regular or tidy. Thus after some gradual warming over several thousands of years there was suddenly a reversion to a short sharp mini Ice Age that scientists call the Younger Dryas. This event is dated, not always as consistently as historians might expect from scientists, to sometime around the 10th and 9th millennia BC. Only after this final part of the last Ice Age did the earth gradually become as predominantly free of ice as we continue to be at present. And even then there was the occasional minor fluctuation, as occurred as recently as the 17th century, when it was relatively common for London's Thames to freeze over.

When the ice was at its full height, it has been estimated that the total volume of its coverage of the earth's surface comprised some 70 million cubic kilometres.[2] That is, nearly three times the 25 million cubic kilometre volume that exists at the present day, mostly in the Arctic and Antarctica. And obvious though it may sound, when ice melts it turns to water. So glaciers became rivers which fed into the oceans. And since all the world's oceans are linked to each other, the huge influx of extra water increased the overall volume of the seas relative to the land. All around the world the sea-levels must have risen significantly, bringing with them a drowning of huge areas of what had formerly been dry land.

To put this in perspective, it has been calculated that if some uncontrolled global warming were to happen in our own time and as a result of this the last 25 million cubic kilometres of remaining ice were all to melt, the present-day world sea-level would be raised by about 65 metres (210 feet).[3] The inevitable result of this would be that most of the world's major cities, such as London, Paris, New York, Washington, Tokyo and Sydney, would be almost entirely inundated, together with the great bulk of the low-lying areas of the continents, where most of their populations live. Only a few rare exceptions such as Mexico City, at an elevation of 2,260 metres (7,415 feet) would stand clear of the flood-waters. The scale of such a catastrophe is so unimaginable that not the least of its effects would be the instant ruin of every insurance company world-wide.

Spare a thought, therefore, for our ancestors. Living only three or four hundred generations removed from us, they were around at the time when, as already estimated, nearly twice the amount of ice that is in our world at the present time was in the process of melting. The picture of sea-level rise that we have so far painted is but the broadest one, based on scientists' best calculations of recent decades. So it is important that we have at least some understanding of how scientists can have such confidence in its actuality, and how they are able to gauge roughly when the main surges would have occurred.

One of the great pioneers in this field was oceanographer the late Professor Cesare Emiliani, founder of the University of Miami's Marine and Atmospheric Science Faculty. Helping him obtain the necessary backing for this venture was the fact that the state of Florida, as the second most low-lying on the US mainland, has a particularly vested interest in promoting research into sea-level rise. For Emiliani a key principle to be pursued was that melted ice added to the ocean must mean the addition of fresh water to salt water. The effects of this, in unusually large volumes, are then bound to show up in marine micro-organisms.

Accordingly in 1971 Emiliani and his colleagues made a series of 11 core drillings deep into the seabed off Florida's West Coast. They arranged for radio-carbon dating to be carried out on the organic content of different levels of the cores obtained, thereby enabling them to be put into chronological sequence. They then selected certain micro-organisms amongst the cores which they knew to have special sensitivity to salinity, or the lack of it, and subjected these to isotopic analysis, a field in which Emiliani was specialist. This revealed that those micro-organisms that had lived (according to the current carbon-dating calculations), around the 9600 BC period had been in sea-water that had been significantly less saline than the previous sea-water salinity levels. The clear implications were that a particularly large surge of fresh meltwater had cascaded into the oceans around this time.[4]

Researchers in more recent years have developed further from Emiliani's findings. Thanks to improved radio-carbon dating accuracy, they have somewhat lowered the date he estimated for the sharp surge, without in any way undermining the fact that overall a huge melt occurred in the wake of the Ice Age. One of these researchers has been Rick Fairbanks of Columbia University's Lamont-Doherty Earth Observatory in the environs of New York. In 1988 he obtained temporary usage of the US Naval Under Sea Command survey ship *Ranger* to drill for cores of young coral (that is, less than 20,000 years old), in the seabed of shallow waters just off the island of Barbados in the Caribbean.[5]

The coral that Fairbanks concentrated on, the common Elk Horn variety *Acropara palmatta*, is one that lives in water only a metre or so deep. Drilling into the seabed, he found ancient samples of the same coral, which he then dated, and from this was able to gauge the level of the sea at that particular date when the coral was being formed. To carry out the datings Fairbanks used both radio-carbon dating and a new technique, Thermal Ionization Mass Spectrometry, for which he had the assistance of a young French specialist Edouard Bard.[6] From their researches and similar ones by other scientists, the current prevailing consensus is that between 14,000 and 5000 BC the world's

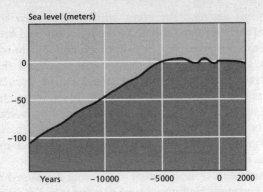

Fig 2 The sea-level rise from the end of the Ice Age to AD 2000, showing the steep rise up to 5000 BC. From Jacques Labeyrie, '*L'Homme et le Climat*'

sea-levels rose by no less than 120 to 130 metres (around 400 feet). That would be more than enough to drown two Nelson's columns set one atop the other, St Paul's Cathedral, London, St Peter's, Rome, to the top of its dome, and the entire Statue of Liberty.

Another way of expressing this spectacular historical sea-level rise is via a graph, as shown above [fig 2]. As can be seen, French scientist Jacques Labeyrie, who formulated this particular graph envisaged the rise as a steep but steady gradient between 15,000 and 5000 BC, then levelling off between 5000 BC and the present day. While this corresponds readily enough to the chronology broadly accepted among scientists, simple experience teaches us that nature's darker forces never conform to nice steady patterns. And as other scientific approaches have indicated, the true rise is likely to have been much less regular, most likely marked by major and potentially devastating surges at certain points, with by far the greatest proportion of these occurring during the 8000 BC–5000 BC period, a time when many human populations around the world were in the process of changing their lifestyles from nomadic wandering to creating more permanent settlements for crop-growing and cattle-raising.

Overall we can be sure that there were a whole series of major coastline changes during the immediate post Ice Age period, even though scientists remain vague about providing the detail of exactly how and when these occurred individually. Thus we know that sometime during the 8000–5000 BC period the sea must have burst through what had previously been a continuous landmass between Siberia and Alaska, thereby creating the Bering Strait. We know that sometime during these same millennia the sea must have flooded inland for several dozen kilometres all along North, Central and South America's western and eastern coastlines. We know that sometime before 5000 BC there was a major inrush of the sea, which caused the British Isles to break away from the main European continental landmass, in its turn fragmenting to form Ireland, the Orkneys, the Shetlands, and other offshore islands.

We can be sure that sometime within roughly this same period there occurred a sea-level rise in the Mediterranean. This split Corsica and Sardinia apart, tore Sicily from Italy, flooded what had been dry land to the east of northern Italy, reduced many Greek islands in size, and burst the former land-bridge in the Bosporus region, thereby joining the Mediterranean and the Black Seas. Sometime within this same time-frame the sea rose above Australasia's Sunda Shelf, creating the Indonesian islands. It flooded the Sahul Shelf, separating New Guinea from Australia, and also created what has become Australia's Gulf of Carpentaria. Again sometime within the same period, action by the sea split northern Japan from the Asian mainland, and then proceeded to split that country like the British Isles, into several islands.

It has long been natural for human populations to settle

on flat, low-lying land and to cluster along seashores. In my own adoptive Australia, for example, over 90 per cent of the population lives within just a few kilometres of the sea. So it stands to reason that when the above-mentioned breakthroughs of the sea occurred, quite possibly suddenly and unexpectedly, they were accompanied by serious localised catastrophes as people were unable to escape the waters in time. Although by the very nature of these events, any remains of human occupation would have been swept away long ago, this is not to say that they never existed or that the floodings never happened.[7] As the oceanographer Emiliani expressed it:

> The concomitant, accelerated rise in sea level, of the order of decimetres a year, must have caused widespread flooding of low-lying areas, many of which were inhabited by man.[8]

Equally it stands to reason that these events must have been responsible for at least some of the Flood stories that are commonplace in the folk memories of so many peoples around the world. Again Emiliani, for one, had absolutely no doubt of this, despite his words causing some eyebrow-raising among his scientific colleagues:

> We submit that this event, in spite of its great antiquity in cultural terms, could be an explanation for the deluge stories common to many Eurasian, Australasian and American traditions.[9]

In fact there can be little justification for scepticism on this point, as clusters of the stories occur precisely where, from completely independent geological evidence, we know there to have been large areas of land that were drowned due to the sea-level rise.

For instance in the case of the Bering Strait, created from what had formerly been a land-bridge between north-east

Siberia and Alaska, the Eskimos of Alaska's Norton Sound inlet recall that in ancient times:

> ... the earth was flooded, all but a very high mountain in the middle. The water came up from the sea and covered the whole land except the top of this mountain. Only a few animals escaped to the mountain and were saved; and a few people made a shift to survive by floating about in a boat and subsisting on the fish they caught till the water subsided.[10]

What is particularly noteworthy here is the phrase 'the water came up from the sea', attributing the flooding to water rising up from the ocean, rather than coming down from the sky, something repeatedly recurring in other accounts. The Chippewa Indians, also of North America, even ascribe the water specifically to melting snow:

> In the beginning of time ... there was a great snow. A little mouse nibbled a hole in the leather bag which contained the sun's heat, and the heat poured out over the earth and melted all the snow in an instant. The meltwater rose to the tops of the highest pines and kept on rising until even the highest mountains were submerged.[11]

Another case in point, in the Australasia region, is the drowning of the Sunda Shelf, already mentioned as the landmass that joined Malaysia and Sumatra to Borneo until the post Ice Age sea-level rises. According to Peter Bellwood, author of *Man's Conquest of the Pacific*, sometime before 5000 BC, more than three million square kilometres (one million square miles) of what had been land in this region subsided beneath the sea, and not necessarily in gradual stages.[12] And when we look to the folklore of those peoples of the present day who live on the mainland and islands that surround this drowned region, we find, for instance, the Benua-Jakun, a tribe on the Malay Peninsula, relating that:

... the ground on which we stand is not solid, but is merely a skin covering an abyss of water. In ancient times ... the deity broke up this skin, so that the world was drowned and destroyed by a great flood. However ... [the deity] had created a man and woman and put them in a ship of *pulai* wood ... In this ship the pair floated and tossed about for a time, till at last the vessel came to rest and the man and woman ... emerged on dry ground.[13]

On the Indonesian island of Sumatra the Bataks recall that their creator god:

... sent a great flood to destroy every living thing, The last human pair had taken refuge on the top of the highest mountain and the waters of the deluge had already reached to their knees when the Lord of All repented ... took a clod of earth ... laid it on the rising flood, and the last pair stepped on it and were saved.[14]

To the west of Sumatra on the island of Engano the native peoples tell how:

Once upon a time ... the tide rose so high that it overflowed the island and every living thing was drowned, except one woman. She owed her preservation to the fortunate circumstance that ... her hair caught in a thorny tree ... When the flood sank, she wandered inland ... and hardly had she taken a few steps when, to her great surprise, she met a living man. When she asked him what he did there ... he answered that someone had knocked on his dead body and in consequence he had returned to life ... Together they resolved to try whether they could not restore all the other dead to life in like manner ... No sooner said than done. The drowned men and women revived under the knocks and thus was the island repopulated after the great flood.[15]

What is notable about so many of these stories, exactly as in the case of their better-known biblical counterpart, is that to those who lived to pass them on to their descendants it had seemed as if the whole world had been destroyed. And this is a very understandable reaction given the scale of sea-level rises that we know to have occurred. But what is also remarkable about them – and it provides the clearest indication of the deep impression that the sea-level rises made at the time – is that the stories have been handed down with such a consistent and credible underlying thread to them throughout so many millennia. In view of their being around ten thousand years old, we are surely justified in calling them humankind's oldest collective memory.

But the question that inevitably now rises is this: how exactly does the Biblical story of Noah and his ark fit in with these sea-level rises? As we earlier noted, the fact that the world's oceans are joined together means that the sea-level rise, albeit occurring in surges, must have happened relatively evenly across the world. But this is not to suggest that the creation of the Bering Strait, the Baltic, the English channel, the splitting off of Sicily from Italy, and similar localised disturbances, all happened at the same time. Individual quirks of geography may well have meant that these events were separated by thousands of years in time. These occurrences, when they happened, were all at least partly due to the overall sea-level rise. But they may also have been triggered by individual localised circumstances such as seismic activities whereby the sea finally broke through into some hitherto unaffected area of low-lying populated land.

One particular curiosity of the Noah story, and other remarkably similar stories is that they emanate from a surprisingly inland region. The Indonesians, the Eskimos and others all have Flood stories, but they lived on the edges of the mighty Pacific ocean, so it is very credible that they might have been affected by sea-level rise. In the Noah story, however, the single geographical feature mentioned which is still identifiable today is Mount Ararat, on the slopes of which Noah's ark was said to have grounded. Mount Ararat is in northern Turkey, several hundred kilometres from any ocean and 320 kilometres (200 miles) from the Black Sea, which is its nearest link to any ocean. The Black Sea, however, is joined to the Mediterranean by the Bosporus strait, the creation of which is believed to have been triggered by the sea-level rises. And this, along with the creation of the Bering strait and the English Channel, remains one of a number of still poorly understood post-Ice Age events.

If the Eskimo and the Indonesian Flood stories had their origins in dramatic sea-level rises which affected their locality, could the Noah story also derive from true-life memories of when the Mediterranean broke through into the Black Sea? This is indeed a pertinent question, but first we need to explore whether the Noah story is one that originated on its own, or whether it belongs to a whole group of stories that all emanated from the one single, localised but momentous catastrophe.

CHAPTER 2

THE NOAH FAMILY OF FLOOD STORIES

I am going to send the Flood, the waters, on earth, to destroy all living things having the breath of life under heaven. But ... you [Noah] will go aboard the ark, yourself, your sons, your wife, and your sons' wives along with you. From all living creatures ... you must take two of each kind aboard the ark, to save their lives with yours; they must be a male and female.

Genesis 6: 17–19

The story is one that has enthralled umpteen generations of children for at least two millennia, and arguably, for several more besides. Aeons ago the entire world had grown very wicked and disobedient, so the creator god decided that every living person and thing should be destroyed. All, that is, except for a 'righteous' man called Noah who lived with his three sons and a wife (who is never named), in an unspecified location of the world, and upon whom the creator god took pity.

Noah was duly instructed to build a huge vessel, usually referred to as an 'ark', in which he was to accommodate his family and his sons' families, together with selected pairs of every living creature. When the creator god's Flood began inundating the earth, drowning all its inhabitants, it was this ark which kept Noah and all those with him safely above the rising waters until only they remained alive.

For many days the ark bobbed upon an empty, featureless ocean that had covered the world so completely that not a single mountain-top was to be seen. Even when the vessel grounded on what would later be found to be Mount Ararat, there was no landing place in sight, so that Noah had to send out first a raven, then a dove, as aerial scouts. Even then it was not until the dove returned carrying a fresh olive branch in its beak that anyone could be sure the floodwaters were receding. Whereupon at last they were able to step outside on to dry land, give thanks with animal sacrifices for their safe deliverance, and set about repopulating the world.

These are the essentials of the Flood story as this appears in chapters six to eight of the book of Genesis with which Jewish and Christian Bibles commence. But where did whoever compiled the book of Genesis get it from? And just how far back is it possible to trace the story?

Traditionally the authorship of Genesis together with that of the next four opening books of the Bible has been ascribed to Moses, the semi-legendary 'prophet' who is said to have led the Jews' ancestors out of Egypt. But as generations of scriptural scholars have determined, the Flood story, together with similar elements of the earliest biblical books, show signs of much more complex compilation. The scholarly consensus is that the written traditions of two or more Semitic tribes or groups have been skilfully combined to form the texts that have come down to us, their original separate strands still being distinguishable.

One of these strands was the so-called 'J' text, which is thought to have circulated amongst the Jews' Judahite ancestors. In this the deity was consistently referred to as *Yahweh* – 'He who is'. A second strand called 'E', thought to have circulated amongst the Jews' 'Israel' ancestors, consistently differs from the first in that the deity is regularly referred to as *elohim* – 'God', or more literally 'gods'. A third strand 'P', in which the *elohim* name is again used for God, is most notable for its interest in all things priestly, as if it had been composed and circulated chiefly amongst priests.[1]

In the case of the Flood story it is clear that someone at some stage in the text's history combined both 'J' and 'P' strands. Indeed their individual textual characteristics remain so distinctive that you do not need to be a scripture scholar to recognise them and to convert them back to their original forms. On the next page the opening parts of the Flood story have been separated into their theoretical original strands. The full texts can be found in the Appendix, part 1, document 1 (p.343). Even from a cursory perusal, it is evident that 'J' and 'P' are both perfectly comprehensible and self-contained on their own, even though each has been specially separated from the other from wherever they appear combined in the canonical biblical text.

Furthermore, the very process of separating the strands out in this manner makes it possible to discern some of the individualities of their authorship. Thus the 'J' version describes a surprisingly anthropomorphic deity, one who personally closes the door of the ark, and who gains great satisfaction from the savours he smells coming from Noah's animal sacrifices. The 'P' version, on the other hand, can be seen to have been the work of someone with a rather fussy mathematical interest in Noah's incredible longevity, in the ark's exact dimensions and in the dates of the year. 'P' has Noah load into the ark just one pair of each kind of animal, an act rather lacking in foresight, since his later animal sacrifices would thereby have wiped out whole species. 'J' represents him as rather more sensibly loading seven pairs of 'clean', or 'fit for sacrifice' animals, and one pair of 'unclean' (in Old Testament Hebrew writers' eyes, sheep were clean animals, and lions unclean). Whereas the 'P' version represents the Flood as lasting a year (370 days), 'J' has it lasting just 40 days and nights. According to 'P' Noah sent out a raven from the ark to check on how much the flood-waters had subsided, while according to 'J' the bird was a dove.

The Bible is in fact a comparatively young document. The earliest actual biblical manuscripts bearing any fragmentary written text of Genesis and its Flood stories have been found amongst the Dead Sea Scrolls. The oldest of these date from

J

Yahweh saw that human wickedness was great on earth and that human hearts contrived nothing but wicked schemes all day long. 6 Yahweh regretted having made human beings on earth and was grieved at heart. 7 And Yahweh said, 'I shall rid the surface of the earth of the human beings whom I created - human and animal, the creeping things and the birds of heaven - for I regret having made them.' 8 But Noah won Yahweh's favour. Yahweh said to Noah, 'Go aboard the ark, you and all your household, for you alone of your contemporaries do I see before me as an upright man. 2 Of every clean animal you must take seven pairs, a male and its female; of the unclean animals you must take one pair, a male and its female 3 (and of the birds of heaven, seven pairs, a male and its female), to preserve their species throughout the earth. 4 For in seven days' time I shall make it rain on earth for forty days and forty nights, and I shall wipe every creature I have made off the face of the earth.' 5 Noah did exactly as Yahweh commanded him. 7 Noah with his sons, his wife, and his sons' wives boarded the ark to escape the waters of the flood. 10 Seven days later the waters of the flood appeared on earth. 12 And heavy rain fell on earth for forty days and forty nights . Then Yahweh shut him in. 17 The flood lasted

P

Noah was a good man, an upright man among his contemporaries, and he walked with God. 10 Noah fathered three sons, Shem, Ham and Japheth. 11 God saw that the earth was corrupt and full of lawlessness. 12 God looked at the earth: it was corrupt, for corrupt were the ways of all living things on earth.

13 God said to Noah, 'I have decided that the end has come for all living things, for the earth is full of lawlessness because of human beings. So I am now about to destroy them and the earth. 14 Make yourself an ark out of resinous wood. Make it of reeds and caulk it with pitch inside and out. 15 This is how to make it: the length of the ark is to be three hundred cubits, its breadth fifty cubits, and its height thirty cubits. 16 Make a roof to the ark, building it up to a cubit higher. Put the entrance in the side of the ark, which is to be, made with lower, second and third decks.

17 For my part I am going to send the flood, the waters, on earth, to destroy all living things having the breath of life under heaven; everything on earth is to perish. 18 But with you I shall establish my covenant and you will go aboard the ark, yourself, your sons, your wife, and your sons' wives along with you. 19 From all living creatures, from all living things, you must take two of

Fig 3 The 'J' and 'P' strands of the biblical Flood story separated from each other, showing how each forms a coherent story in its own right, even though they became combined to form the 'received' biblical text around the 2nd or 3rd century BC, at which time scholars are confident that the 'J' and 'P' strands had already been combined for several centuries. So we have to accept that no actual early manuscript has yet been discovered with the Flood story either in its original 'J' or 'P' form. Nevertheless, other versions that can only derive from the same tradition have been found in documents from other cultures that date way back further into antiquity.

Back in the mid-1840s the British adventurer Austen Henry Layard (1817–94) created a great stir by travelling to what is today Iraq, where he uncovered the ruins of the ancient Assyrian capital Nineveh. Layard's finds were spectacular, including the 7th century BC Assyrian king Sennacherib's palace, its walls decorated with some two miles of bas-reliefs, the best specimens of which he duly sent back to a grateful British Museum. But it was Layard's lesser-known assistant and successor, Hormuzd Rassam, who later discovered Sennacherib's grandson Assurbanipal's palace, and with it the king's library containing thousands of cuneiform tablets. For us, the great significance of these tablets is that they included texts that Assurbanipal's scribes had copied from the archives of Mesopotamia's earlier Sumerian and Babylonian peoples, these dating back to the 2nd and even 3rd millennia BC.

Some time in the late 1860s Rassam sent a quantity of the tablets to the British Museum. Many were written in Akkadian, a Semitic language that was the common tongue of ancient Mesopotamia, and was also widely used diplomatically. The task of translating them fell to a young banknote engraver called George Smith, whose self-taught interest in Assyriology had led to his employment by the museum. One day in 1872 Smith was patiently translating a tablet catalogued as number XI when the familiar ring of its wording forcibly struck his attention. He read:

> The seventh day when it came,
> I brought out a dove, I let it loose:
> Off went the dove but then it returned,
> There was no place to land, so back it came to me ...
> I brought out a raven, I let it loose
> Off went the raven, it saw the waters receding,
> Finding food, bowing and bobbing, it did not come back
>   to me:[2]

As George Smith quickly recognised, here on this 7th century BC Assyrio-Babylonian tablet was an episode of an as yet unknown Babylonian Flood story that was strikingly similar to that described in the biblical book of Genesis:

> At the end of forty days Noah opened the porthole he had made in the ark and sent out the raven. This went off and flew back and forth. Then he sent out the dove to see whether the waters were receding. The dove, finding nowhere to perch, returned to him in the ark, for there was water over the whole surface of the earth. After waiting seven more days he again sent out the dove. In the evening the dove came back to him and there was a new olive branch in its beak.[3]

Reportedly Smith was so excited by the discovery that he even began to undress himself before his startled British Museum colleagues. In December 1872 he lectured on the subject at a meeting of London's Society of Biblical Archaeology that was attended by Britain's then Prime Minister, William Gladstone and other dignitaries. As Smith explained to this assembly, the Assyrio-Babylonian tablet belonged to a major epic, parts of which, conceivably containing more elements with a biblical ring to them, were still missing. This prompted London's *Daily Telegraph* newspaper to provide Smith with the princely sum of one thousand guineas with which he set off for Nineveh in search of further tablets at the site of Assurbanipal's library. Quite remarkably, he found some within only a few days, and returned with some 384 fragmentary clay tablets to add to the British Museum's collection.

As Smith was able to determine, tablet XI had belonged to a set of 12 cuneiform tablets that comprised the so-called Epic of Gilgamesh. This was the tale of a king of Uruk, who in the course of a quest for immortality met Uta-napishti, the Mesopotamian Noah, and the only mortal ever to have been granted eternal life.

As this story ran, Uta-napishti had been warned by the god Ea, or Enki (the Mesopotamian deity of water and wisdom), that the god Enlil intended to destroy the noisy and sinful human race by means of a universal deluge – recalling the words of Genesis 6: 17: God said to Noah, 'I have decided that the end has come for all living things, for the earth is full of lawlessness because of human beings'. As the Gilgamesh story went on (see Appendix, part 1, document 2), Enki, speaking through the wall of Uta-napishti's hut, urged Uta-napishti to tear his house down, abandon all his possessions, and build a large boat or ark which he should load with 'all living things' seed'. The Genesis version, of course, represented Noah as being similarly ordered to 'make yourself an ark out of resinous wood. Make it of wood and caulk it with pitch inside and out' (Genesis 6: 14), then 'from all living creatures' to take 'two of each kind aboard the ark, to save their lives with yours' (Genesis 6: 19).

In the Gilgamesh story Uta-napishti duly obeyed Enki's instructions, creating a huge seven-decked vessel which he caulked with bitumen and loaded with gold and silver, together with all his 'kith and kin, the beasts of the field, the creatures of the wild, and members of every skill and craft'. Though in Genesis Noah's ark has only three decks (Genesis 6: 16), his actions may be regarded as essentially identical to Uta-napishti's. As the Gilgamesh version described the ensuing events:

The Storm God ... charged the land like a bull [on the
    rampage]
He smashed [it] in pieces [like a vessel of clay]
For a day ... [winds flattened the country]
Quickly they blew, and [then came] the [Flood][4]
Like a battle [the cataclysm] passed over the people ...
For six days and [seven] nights ...
The gale, the Flood, it flattened the land.[5]

Only Uta-napishti and his family, together with the creatures they had loaded with them in the ark, were saved.
This readily corresponds to the Genesis equivalent: 'Every
living thing on the face of the earth was wiped out, people,
animals, creeping things and birds; they were wiped off the
earth and only Noah was left and those with him in the ark'
(Genesis 7: 23).

The Gilgamesh tablets refer to where the ark grounded as
Mount Nimush or Nisir, a location that remains geographically unidentified, though it is generally thought to have been in
Kurdistan[6], the very same region as that in which Mount
Ararat stands. At this point, as we have already learned from
George Smith's initial discovery, Uta-napishti sent out a raven
and dove as scouts, exactly as Noah does. On his being able to
step out of the ark Uta-napishti then offered up sweet cane,
cedar and myrtle as a thanksgiving sacrifice. And again
common to both the Gilgamesh and Genesis versions is that
the savour of the thanksgiving sacrifices delighted the nostrils
of those divinities to whom they were offered (Genesis 8: 21).

Some sceptics, after acknowledging such striking and
unmistakable similarities between the Genesis and
Gilgamesh stories, have dismissively argued that the compilers of Genesis must have cribbed the Flood story during
their time of enslavement by the Babylonians. The
Babylonians, after all, took over not only the old Assyrian
empire's subject peoples, but also its archives, and some of
the more intellectual Jewish captives are thought to have

worked on these during the reign of the historically minded ruler Nabonidus (556–539 BC). But such carping over who may have told the story first, besides being virtually impossible to prove either way, misses the far more important issue of where the story came from before it came into the hands either of the compilers of Genesis *or* of the Assyrians.

It is now certain that the 7th century BC Gilgamesh tablets found at Nineveh were far from unique, and by no means the oldest amongst those since discovered. Rather the story that they told was a widespread, popular and well-known one that is to be found right across the Near East. An Akkadian version dating from the 2nd millennium BC was found in the archives of the Hittite capital, Hattusas, at what is now Boghazköy in central Turkey. Versions in the Hurrian and Hittite languages were also found in the same location. Portions were found in an important ancient library excavated at Sultantepe in northern Syria, not far from the Turkish border. Sumerian language variants have been found at sites such as Ur and Nippur. Other ancient fragments have turned up at Assur and Nimrud in north Mesopotamia, Babylon, Sippar and Uruk in south Mesopotamia, also in Egypt, and at Megiddo in Israel.

The story of Gilgamesh, including his encounter with Utanapishti, is also commonly represented pictorially on the cylinder seals that the ancient Mesopotamian peoples used to make personal seals on their legal documents. As some of these seals date back to *c*.3000 BC it can be inferred that the story was already circulating at that time and must therefore have originated at some earlier time.

It is also evident that this Gilgamesh cycle was merely one of a surprisingly widespread and ancient 'family' of similar Flood stories. While the names of those involved in these stories vary, reflecting the differing cultures and their folk-heroes, their common underlying 'plot' has too many similarities to be dismissed as coincidence.

Thus for the Babylonians a version independent of the Gilgamesh epic but telling much the same story was their Atrahasis epic.[7] In this the gods were again named Enlil and Enki, but the Noah/Uta-napishti equivalent was now named Atrahasis, meaning 'exceedingly wise'. Exactly as in the case of Uta-napishti, the god Enki warned Atrahasis of the impending flood and told him to build a boat, which he did, loading it with his possessions and animals and birds. When the flood came all those in the boat were saved while the rest of creation was destroyed. Although the several versions in which the Atrahasis story has been found are rather fragmentary[8] – for instance, the story of the landing of the boat and release of the birds is missing from the discovered texts – the fact that versions survive from the Old, Middle and Neo-Babylonian Periods shows that it must have been copied and re-copied over the centuries. Again all the indications are of a very ancient story, dating in terms of extant texts at least as far back as 1900 BC, but probably originating much further back into the mists of antiquity.

Amongst the Sumerians, an even older people than the Babylonians, the equivalent of Noah, Uta-napishti and Atrahasis was a pious king called Ziusudra, whose name meant 'he saw life'.[9] In Sumerian literature Ziusudra's story was not part of the Gilgamesh epic, but an independent poem. Nonetheless, just like his Babylonian and Hebrew counterparts, Ziusudra was warned of the gods' decision to destroy all mankind, in his case by a mysterious 'voice'. Although the section of the story in which Ziusudra was given his boat-building instructions is missing from the again fragmentary text as found at Nippur (an ancient Sumerian city in what is today Iraq), when the text resumes its narrative is explicit. The Flood 'swept over the land', and even the 'huge boat' which Ziusudra had apparently built was being 'tossed about by the windstorm on the great waters'. Following the storm's abatement the sun reappeared, and

Ziusudra, just like his Akkadian, Babylonian and Hebrew counterparts, offered up a thanksgiving sacrifice.

If we look to the Kurdish region of what is now Turkey, an area that is repeatedly associated with where the ark came to rest, we find that the early Hurrian inhabitants, who are now thought to have moved into the area no later than the early 3rd millennium BC, had their Noah in the person of one Nahmizuli.[10] As has been pointed out by the Egyptologist John Romer,[11] this particular name very notably bears the Hebrew word for Noah, *Nhm* in its first three consonants. Furthermore the Hurrians particularly venerated Mount Ararat as the sacred centre of their kingdom.

The Armenians in their turn, as later inhabitants of the same region, had an equivalent story that was recorded by the 4th or 3rd century BC Babylonian priest Berossus in his book *Story of Chaldea*. Although Berossus' three-volume work perished, its Flood story survives at least in extract thanks to a reference quoted in the lost works of the 1st century BC Greek writer Alexander Polyhistor, which became quoted in the *Chronicles* of the 3rd century AD Bishop Eusebius of Caesarea. (This work has also been lost but the passage is preserved in the writings of the 9th century AD Byzantine chronicler George Syncellus.) In this version the Noah equivalent was named Xisuthros, a version of Ziusudra, and the god who ordered him to build the boat was Kronos, in Greek mythology the king of the gods before Zeus. In all other respects, however, there were the same familiar elements: a divine decision to destroy mankind with a flood; Xisuthros' instructions to build a boat, stock it with food and drink, birds and animals, and embark in it with members of his own family; a release of birds at the subsiding of the flood-waters; the return of the successful bird with a green leaf in its beak; the grounding of the boat in Armenia; and the offering up of a thanksgiving sacrifice.

The ancient Greeks are normally supposed to have been culturally distinct from Semitic peoples such as the Hebrews. Yet their version of the Flood story bears such striking similarities to that of Noah that the great mythographer Robert Graves, for one, has attributed a common Asian origin to both.[12] In the standard version as related by Greek writers such as Appolodorus (see Appendix part 1, document 4) and Romans such as Ovid,[13] it was the god Zeus who was intent upon destroying all mankind, while Noah's Greek counterpart was Deucalion, father of Hellen, the ancestor from whom all Greeks claim descent. Deucalion received his warning from his father Prometheus, whom the Greek myths geographically associate with the Caucasus, just to the north of Noah's Mount Ararat. Conforming closely to the versions told in other more eastern cultures, Deucalion is described as having built an ark, filled this with provisions and gone aboard with his wife Pyrrha, a name which means 'the red one'. Then as the whole world succumbed to Zeus' flood, everyone died except Deucalion and Pyrrha, who for nine days floated about in their ark until it came to rest on a high mountain of no definite location. Deucalion sent out a dove for reconnaissance purposes and then, following his and his wife's safe disembarkation, offered up a thanksgiving sacrifice, just like his eastern counterparts Noah, Uta-napishti and Xisuthros are said to have done.

These comparatively widely scattered examples of Flood stories far from exhaust the huge number of similar tales. For instance there is the Persian or Zoroastrian Flood story which tells of a hero called Yima who receives instruction from his god Ahura to build a *vara* or fortress. Into this *vara* Yima had to cram fire, food, and animals in pairs in order to protect them from the Flood.[14] There are also at least faint familial hints to be found in certain Indian Flood stories, particularly that told by the Hindus. In this version Manu, the first human, is warned by a friendly fish to build a boat in which to save himself from the impending Flood, also to tie this to a tree growing from a mountain. When Manu does this, he alone is saved, while everyone else is drowned. Manu, like all his counterparts, then offers up a thanksgiving sacrifice, following which a woman is created from his offerings with whom he couples to found the human race.[15]

Surely a real-life Flood must lie behind these stories. The collective memory, scattered over wide geographical distances, is too prevalent, too deep-seated for this not to have been the case.

Although the nature of the evidence is such that it is only possible to make the broadest of inferences, it looks as if the actual Flood must have happened some time before the 3rd millennium BC. By that time, the tradition had quite definitely become documented and scattered amongst different peoples. Indeed, for the Sumerians of Mesopotamia the event was so real that some of their king lists specifically distinguished certain of their rulers as having existed before the Flood.

We can also be reasonably sure that the Flood did not occur anything like as far back as the 10th millennium BC, since Noah is described in Genesis as a 'tiller of the soil' (Genesis 9: 20), and any agricultural expertise was still new as late as the 7th and 6th millennia BC and mostly confined to the Near East. Noah's counterparts are described as the rulers of towns, the earliest towns again appearing no earlier than the 7th and 6th millennia BC. Likewise the building of a substantial multi-deck boat, one of the most consistently reported elements to the Flood stories, is a technology that the 6th millennium BC might just have been capable of (despite no actual examples having survived), but which is quite inconceivable for any earlier period.

In terms of location, again only the broadest and most tentative inferences are possible. The main Noah family of

Flood stories point to a swathe of territories stretching from
Greece to Iran (allowing for the not infrequent migration of
ancient peoples). Yet if we look to where any serious Flood
might have affected them, there is no obvious body of ocean
– and it is in the oceans that the sea-level rise happens – that
is common to the cultures from which the stories emanate.
The most central body of water of any size is the Black Sea.
And this is hardly obvious as having been responsible for
the world's most enduring myth except for one key component to the stories – that so many of them describe the ark as
having grounded on mountains in the Ararat region, which
lies immediately to the south-east of the Black Sea.

Clearly there are grounds to suspect that what have often
been tossed aside as Flood myths have a considerable foundation in fact. But first we need to dispel certain Flood
'myths' that rather more richly deserve this name, myths
which have been created only as recently as the last century.

CHAPTER 3

MODERN-DAY FLOOD MYTHS

Of course, it's the Flood
Lady Katherine Woolley

If there was one 20th century individual who more convincingly than anyone else of his time seemed to have found *the* evidence for the biblical Flood this would have to have been the British archaeologist Sir Leonard Woolley (1880–1960). The son of a clergyman, and in his youth reportedly minded to follow in his father's footsteps, Woolley is best remembered for his excavations between 1922 and 1935 of a mound in southern Iraq known as Tell el-Mukayyar, a site that with characteristic éclat he publicised to the world as biblical Abraham's 'Ur of the Chaldees' (Genesis 11: 28).

My single personal memory of Woolley dates back to 1959 when at the age of 79 he was among the judges of an essay I had submitted, on the archaeology of Sumer, for the British public schools' G.A. Wainwright Oxford Near Eastern Archaeology essay competition. As Wainwright later confided to me, Woolley fiercely vetoed his fellow judges' inclination to award me the first prize, relegating me to runner-up. Nonetheless I cannot but admire Woolley's archaeological skills and the genuinely spectacular nature of the finds that he unearthed at Tell el-Mukayyar – even if in certain of the conclusions he reached I believe him to have been fundamentally wrong.

Inscriptions on cylinder seats that had been turned up before Woolley arrived at the site supported the suggestion that the Tell el-Mukayyar site had been called Ur in antiquity. And in its heyday, when it was located on the banks of the river Euphrates (the course of the river has since shifted), it was undoubtedly one of the great cities of ancient Sumer. Excavating its 'royal' cemetery Woolley opened up ancient tombs dating back to the 3rd millennium BC. In some of these the occupants had been buried not only with gold and silver objects of extraordinary richness and craftsmanship, but also accompanied by households of up to 70 attendants, charioteers, bodyguards and musicians. All of these appear to have died voluntarily in order to serve their dead master or mistress beyond the grave.

In terms of the 'Flood myth', Woolley's most pertinent discovery at Ur came about in 1929 when, in order to trace the stages of the city's development before the era of the lavish burials, he ordered the digging of a test-trench, cutting deeply through millennia of occupation layers all the way down to virgin soil. Three feet down the Arab workman assigned to this job reached what certainly appeared to be virgin soil, a thick layer of clean, water-laid mud that lacked human artefacts of any kind. Accordingly, the workman would have stopped digging at this point had Woolley not instructed that he continue. Woolley had calculated, with characteristic care, that this was not deep enough for where he anticipated the city's earliest occupation layer to be.

The workman continued to dig for no less than 2.5 metres (8 feet) patiently continuing to turn up only clean, clear mud – until suddenly human artefacts and implements began to appear once again. As Woolley recalled:

I got into the pit once more, examined the sides, and by the time I had written up my notes was quite convinced of what it all meant; but I wanted to see whether others would come to the same conclusion. So I brought up two of my staff, and after pointing out the facts, asked for their explanation. They did not know what to say. My wife came along and looked and was asked the same question, and she turned away, remarking casually, 'Well, of course, it's the Flood'. That was the right answer ...[1]

As Woolley quickly appreciated, to support the claim that he had found alluvium from Noah's Flood he needed to produce evidence that was rather more impressive than 'a pit a yard square.'[2] So he marked out a 23 metre by 18 metre (75 foot by 60 foot) rectangle and ordered his full team of workers to dig this entire area down to a depth that in the end became 19.5 metres (64 feet).

The occupation layers that thereby became revealed could hardly have been clearer [fig 4]. In the upper part there were eight distinguishable layers, which Woolley labelled A–H, containing mud-brick walls as from dwellings of the Sumerian era and later. Below these there was a 5.5 metre (18 foot) layer of broken pottery amongst which there were found kilns and a potter's wheel, strongly indicative of it having been a potter's workshop. Directly below this was the layer of clean, clear river-borne silt, quite obviously from the nearby Euphrates and deposited all at once. In this particular location the silt lay about 3.5 metres (between 11 and 12 feet) thick, and was disturbed only by graves that had been dug into it at much later periods. Then directly below this there lay a layer of mud-brick, ashes and potsherds that could only date from the 'before the Flood' era. The pottery style was that of the so-called al-'Ubaid people, a culture preceding that of the Sumerians, and dating to around the mid 4th millennium BC. So there could be absolutely no doubt that Ur's ancient inhabitants sometime

Fig 4 The great 'Flood' pit dug by Leonard Woolley's workers at Tell el-Mukayyar in what is today Iraq. In antiquity the town on the site was known as Ur. Woolley found an 11 to 12 foot layer of clean silt, then below this artefacts from an earlier period of occupation, interpreting the silt layer as evidence of the biblical Flood

around the middle of the 4th millennium BC had experienced *a* serious flood. But was it *the* Noah Flood?

Because of the flat, low-lying nature of Mesopotamia's terrain – its elevation drops by only 35 metres (115 feet) throughout the 480 kilometre (300 mile) distance from Baghdad to the Persian Gulf – prolonged periods of unusually heavy rainfall can all too easily cause the meandering rivers Tigris and Euphrates to burst their banks. And when they do so the result is almost inevitably some localised flooding and the depositing of deep layers of the heavy sediment that the rivers typically carry down with them. In fact, besides Ur other ancient sites in southern Iraq, among these Tell Inghara, the ancient Kish near Babylon, and Fara, the ancient Shuruppak, have similarly been found to have Ur-like sedimentary deposits.

For Woolley, important reinforcement of his view that the Ur flood deposit and some of these others were indeed Noah's Flood lay in ancient cuneiform tablets recording the earlier-mentioned lists of Sumer's royal dynasties known as the king lists. These not only referred to a Flood as part of their country's history, they actually distinguished those dynasties of kings who had lived before the Flood from those who lived after. The lists even punctuate the dynasties in question specifically with the words 'The Flood swept thereover'.

However the rather more negative aspect of these Sumerian king lists is that their chronologies relative to the flood period are ones that are utterly impossible to take seriously. They list eight kings who lived before the Flood, then two dynasties that followed this, the time-span of which was purportedly 25,000 years. The kings of this time are represented as impossibly long-lived, even more exaggeratedly so than the 950 years that the authors of Genesis attribute to the biblical Noah (Genesis 9: 28) and 969 to Methuselah (Genesis 5: 27). Many modern scholars now infer therefore that the antediluvian king lists probably derive from an independent tradition of unknown origin that only later became prefixed to the official Sumerian king lists.[3] Certainly (and unlike other parts of the same lists), it is quite impossible to take them at face value.

Sumerian archaeology since Woolley's time has revealed no evidence at sites other than Ur of any really devastating flood that affected the whole country and which might therefore account for a story of the Uta-napishti/Ziusudra variety. For instance, excavations at neighbouring sites such as Abu Shahrein, the biblical Eridu, have failed to reveal a similar silt layer. Even the already-mentioned 'flood deposit' silt layers have been dated by pottery styles and radio-carbon dating to between c.2750 BC, as in the case of Fara, or Sburuppak, and the mid-4th millennium period of Woolley's Tell el-Mukayyar flood. They are not clear evidence of one single, devastating Flood catastrophe.

In the light of such findings it is becoming more and more apparent that Woolley's claim to have found the Flood was in fact a myth of his own making.

Similarly, Woolley is now increasingly widely thought to have erred in his identification of Iraq's Tell el-Mukayyar as Abraham's 'Ur of the Chaldees', there definitely having been more than one ancient 'Ur'. The latest thinking now favours Urfa (ancient name Urrhai) in eastern Turkey,[4] which has never been excavated, as the true Ur of Abraham. Not only does a fierce local tradition directly attest to this identification, with various sites associated with and named after Abraham, but the Turkish Ur is only 48 kilometres (30 miles) from Harran, which is the other main family location biblically associated with Abraham (Genesis 11: 31). Also, when Abraham's son and grandson sought out their wives they reportedly did so in this same region of what is today south-east Turkey (Genesis 24: 10 and 28: 2). Iraq's Tell el-Mukayyar, on the other hand, while it undoubtedly was known as 'Ur' in antiquity, lies over 480 kilometres (300 miles) from Harran, and appears totally unrelated to what biblically would seem to have been Abraham and his family's more logical and true region of origin.

Even Woolley's fellow archaeologists recognised that his penchant for fund-raising publicity could cloud his judgement, particularly when it came to claiming some biblical link. Sir Max Mallowan (1904–78), who was Woolley's assistant at Tell el-Mukayyar, and in 1930 became husband of novelist Agatha Christie, conducted his own subsequent excavations elsewhere in Iraq. He remarked in an otherwise adulatory obituary: 'Woolley was an incomparable showman, a man of knowledge endowed with a vivid imagination which sometimes got the better of him'.[5]

At the University Museum of Pennsylvania, Philadelphia, which partnered and heavily funded Woolley in his excavations (though they are rarely mentioned in his writings), opinions are tending to become blunter. Ninety-two-year-old Near Eastern archaeology veteran Cyrus Gordon, who also worked with Woolley at Tell el-Mukayyar, has recently described him as a master at the 'proving the Bible' game. In Gordon's words, Woolley played this game for all he was worth, because in the circumstances of his time that was the way 'to get money from pious widows who were well-heeled.'[6] The year that Woolley dug his Flood pit, 1929, was also that of the stock market crash, and the subsequent financial circumstances led within four years to the dig's forced closure.[7] Seen in this light, we may fairly and confidently conclude that the Flood evidence that Woolley found at Tell el-Mukayyar, although undeniably real, derived from a localised catastrophe which it was in his interests to promote as the biblical Flood. It had nothing at all to do with the true event that was so powerfully remembered by so many peoples from Greece to the borders of India.

This said, the Iraq-based Flood myth that Woolley created at least commanded scholarly respect and respectability – and on the whole, deservedly so. Whereas the same can hardly be said for another more recent 'Flood myth' – that the original ark of Noah has survived to our own time, and rests to this day high up on Mount Ararat. As rarely realised, this particular myth does have a surprisingly respectable antiquity. To the earlier-mentioned Armenian 'Xisuthros' version of the Flood legend, as recorded by the priest Berossus back in the 4th century BC and relayed by the 9th century AD Byzantine chronicler Syncellus (see Appendix, part 1, document 3), is appended the remark: 'A part of the boat which came to rest in the Gordyaean mountains of Armenia still remains and some people scrape pitch off the boat and use it as charms.'[8]

The 'Gordyaean mountains of Armenia' can only mean the mountain in north-east Turkey that to this day is still mostly referred to as Ararat, though Turkish cartographers prefer to call it Büyük Agri Dagi, which means 'Agri's great mountain'. And if we could believe the Biblical assertion that Noah's Flood covered even the world's highest mountains (Genesis 7: 19), then the Flood really would have been an all-creation destroying catastrophe, since Mount Ararat, a currently dormant volcano, rises to 5,156 metres (almost 17,000 feet) higher than any peak in Europe and more than 600 metres (2,000 feet) higher than the United States' Mount Whitney.

Ascent of Mount Ararat is therefore most definitely not for the faint-hearted. Its slopes are difficult and boulder-strewn, and there is serious danger of avalanche. The local population, many of whom are Kurds, are constantly in strife with the occupying Turks, and even they tend to avoid it – as commented by one guidebook 'either through indifference, or superstition, or both.'[9] The earliest recorded ascent of Ararat, by a Russian, Frederick Parrot, therefore dates only from 1829. In 1876 English aristocrat Lord James Bryce, son of one of England's first geologists, braved the climb at the age of 38. He noted coming across at the 3,900-metre (13,000-foot) level 'a piece of wood about four feet [1.2 metres] long and five inches [13 cm] wide, which had obviously been shaped by means of a tool.'[10] In 1893 the Nestorian Archbishop Nourri reported finding 'dark red beams of very thick wood'. In 1916 an early Russian aviator is supposed to have seen a boat-like shape on the edge of a high-altitude frozen lake. In 1953 an American oil worker claimed to have taken six large, clear photographs which, mysteriously, were nowhere to be found following his death in 1962.[11]

But it was only in 1955 with the publication of French industrialist and amateur mountaineer Fernand Navarra's book *J'ai trouvé l'Arche de Noé* (I found Noah's Ark), that the case for Noah's Ark still existing on Ararat really came to public attention. According to Navarra, on his negotiating a gully on slightly sloping terrain high up on the mountain he saw 'through the thickness of ice, some dark and intermingled outlines. These could only be fragments of the Ark.'[12] Digging his way through the ice, Navarra claimed that he 'touched with numbed fingers a piece of wood, not just something from a tree branch, but wood that had been shaped and squared off.' By way of 'proof' of this, Navarra brought down with him a broken-off spar. Initially, laboratory tests of the cell structure of this spar, as carried out in Paris and Madrid, claimed it to be around five thousand years old, neatly corresponding to the sort of date for the Flood that might have been construed from the Sumerian king lists.

But then radio–carbon dating, as carried out in the United States at the University of Pennsylvania's Radiocarbon Laboratory, and also in Britain at the National Physical Laboratory, Teddington, produced a rather different calculation. According to the report of the Teddington findings, as published in the scientific journal *Radiocarbon*:

Oak wood of uncertain species ... from very large timber
structure under ice at 14,000 ft ASL on NW face of Mount
Ararat, Turkey, Collected between 1950 and 1955 by
Fernand Navarra; submitted by D.H.E. Woodward,
Walker and Woodward Ltd., Birmingham ... Comment:
evidently not the Ark.[13]

The date that Teddington had arrived at was AD 760, and that
by Pennsylvania AD 650. So (assuming a rough average
between the dates) the likeliest explanation is that the wood
derives from some Byzantine hermit's mountain retreat. A
local Armenian tradition certainly attests to some ancient
shrine of this kind. The period given by the carbon dating is
also one when Christian monks all over the 'civilised' world
are known to have gone to sometimes extraordinary lengths
in search of solitude, as in the case of Ireland's St Brendan
who sailed far out into the north Atlantic.[14] Any serious
argument for the Ararat wood structure having belonged to
Noah's Ark was fatally undermined.

Even so, interest in the high altitude wooden structure
did not die out completely. In 1969 Navarra guided an expedition to the same spot that he had found a decade and a half
before. Again this brought down wood, and again this was
found to date to the Byzantine period. In 1971 Americans
began to get in on the act, with expeditions to Ararat
mounted under the auspices of the Institute for Creation
Research, who believe in the Bible's 'to the letter' truth.
Although one such expedition, led by 'arkeologist' John
Morris, claimed several sightings of their supposed ark, they
returned with nothing to show for these. In 1974 there was
another flurry of interest when it was announced that an
orbiting American satellite had photographed an anomaly
that some thought to be a possible candidate for the Ark.
Even former astronaut James Irwin became drawn into the
controversy. Backed by an evangelical group in Colorado
Springs, he led an expedition to Ararat. But instead of this

expedition finding anything of significance, Irwin simply lost three teeth in a serious fall.

Within the last two decades, however, the subject has taken a quite new and unexpected twist thanks to the activities of former merchant marine officer David Fasold, 'biblical archaeologist' Ron Wyatt, Australian 'Dr' Allen Roberts and others. From the two latter have come so many bizarre 'proof of the Bible' claims – marketed with fuzzy videos under the label 'Amazing Truth Publications' – that deep suspicions have been aroused about them, and deservedly so. However with regard to their 'We've found Noah's Ark' claims, at least that the object to which they have called the world's attention is a real one, is reasonably accessible and can therefore be subjected to proper scientific scrutiny.

In 1960 a Turkish army captain named Ilhan Durupinar, in the course of examining aerial photos of the Ararat region that had been taken for NATO's Geodetic Survey of Turkey,[15] happened to notice on these what appeared to be a large boat-like object lying at an altitude of some 1,900 metres (6,300 feet). In 1977 Ron Wyatt, on hearing of Durupinar's observations, flew out to Turkey to investigate. As he discovered, the feature in question, instead of being on Mount Ararat itself, was actually at Akyayla just 19 kilometres (12 miles) to the south-east. Even for the fundamentalist, however, this was of no great moment, since the biblical description of the region where the Ark came to rest refers to this simply as 'on the mountains of Ararat' (Genesis 8:4), and Ararat's peak is clearly visible from the Akyayla site. Convinced by what he saw, Wyatt began trying to attract further interest, and in 1989 published *Discovered: Noah's Ark*,[16] a year that also saw the appearance of a book by Fasold, *The Ark of Noah*,[17] promulgating much the same argument. A year later Australian 'Dr' Allen Roberts visited the site. In collaboration with Wyatt, he then founded an organisation called Ark Search, and like Wyatt and Fasold began widely publicising that the Akyayla boat-shaped feature was the true Noah's ark.

The one indisputable fact is that there certainly is a large boat-shaped feature to be seen at Akyayla. Due to the publicity that Wyatt, Fasold and Roberts generated, tour parties have even been finding their way to it, gamely negotiating the bumpy single-lane track that provides the only road access. Although reported estimates of the dimensions of the 'boat' vary – according to one account it is 170 metres long by 45 metres wide (558 feet by 148 feet),[18] according to another 157 by 42 metres (515 by 138 feet)[19] – neither set of measurements presents any great problem. The dimensions for Noah's ark as given in Genesis 6: 15 are 300 by 50 cubits. The measurement standard for the Jewish cubit varied during ancient times, and some argue for the beams of the Akyayla 'ark' having become splayed outwards, so there is plenty of leeway for number-juggling.

Altogether more contentious, however, are the other claims that have come from Wyatt, Fasold and Roberts. For instance, according to Wyatt he arranged 'chemical analysis' tests of the 'boat' feature that 'positively prove it to be composed of very ancient wood and metal.'[20] The actuality is that the carbon percentages quoted by Wyatt fall within the normal bounds of soil and show no evidence of wood.[21] As for the metal, instead of the 'metal brackets' for ships' fittings, as claimed by Wyatt, the true explanation is that the Akyayla site is rich in naturally occurring manganese nodules that are high in iron.

Fasold, Wyatt and Roberts have also made much of 'subsurface radar surveys' of the Akyayla feature, purportedly showing it to have a ship-like structure in the interior parts to which no one has yet gained access. As reported in the journal *Popular Mechanics*:

He [Fasold] says subsurface radar surveys of the site have yielded good results. The radar imagery at about 82 ft

Fig 5 Part of the boat-shaped feature at Akyayla, in the environs of Mount Ararat, Turkey. 'Arkeologists' such as Ron Wyatt and 'Dr' Allen Roberts have claimed this to be the remains of Noah's Ark.

down from the stern is so clear that Fasold could count the floorboards between the walls. Fasold believes the team has found the fossilised remains of the upper deck and that the original reed substructure has disappeared.[22]

Again the actuality is very different. As reported by Tom Fenner of Geophysical Survey Systems:

In 1987 I performed an extensive GPR [ground-penetrating radar] study in an attempt to characterise any shallow subsurface features in the boat-shaped formation at the site ... A great deal of effort was put into repeating the radar measurements acquired in 1986 by Wyatt and Fasold ... After numerous attempts over a period of one and a half days we were unable to duplicate their radar records in any way ...[23]

Fasold, Wyatt and Roberts have also claimed to find boat ribs, boat rivets, deer antlers and fossilised animal dung.

When they explored the surrounding terrain they also came across huge stones with holes carved in them, which they suggested might have been drogue stones that the ships of ancient times had dragged behind them for stability.

Ian Plimer, Professor of Geology at Australia's Melbourne University, has scornfully repudiated all of this. Plimer took the trouble to visit the Akyayla site with Fasold in 1994. Like Fenner before him, Plimer found it impossible to repeat any of the various radar, seismic, magnetic and electromagnetic tests claimed by Wyatt.[24] During this expedition, apparently Fasold himself came to recognise that what Wyatt had argued to be 'boat ribs' were no longer evident, concluding that these must have been deliberately scraped into the soil to appear as they did in Wyatt's photographs. According to Plimer's professional judgement the Akyayla boat is simply an outcrop of 120 million year old sea floor rocks (ophiolite), around which a more modern (and still moving) mud slide has flowed, this slide even having bits of plastic embedded in it. The 'stone anchors' are blocks of the normal, local volcanic basalt, most likely shaped into cultic stelae by local tribes. Many of these are found tens of miles from the Akyayla site and they bear crosses and inscriptions that have been carved within the last thousand years. In the light of Plimer's findings Fasold, having come to realise that Wyatt and Roberts had behaved deceptively, completely changed his allegiance. In partnership with Plimer he successfully sued Roberts in the Australian Federal Court.[25] And as further related investigations revealed the self-styled 'biblical archaeologist' Ron Wyatt, who died recently, was in fact a Seventh Day Adventist nurse anaesthetist based in Nashville, Tennessee. As for the Florida 'university' quoted as the *alma mater* for 'Dr' Allen Roberts, this has turned out to be a letterbox outside a fundamentalist church from which fake 'doctorates' can be obtained for just a few dollars.

Had the Akyayla 'Ark' been a genuine ancient boat

marooned 1,800 metres (6,000 feet) up in the 'mountains of Ararat', then it might have become necessary to take the fact seriously that some ancient Flood really did occur that was so gigantic it took the world sea-level of the time to at least 1,800 metres (6,000 feet) above its present level. Even Mexico City, had it existed, would barely have escaped such a Flood, and nothing less than a complete revision of all the basic understandings underpinning modern-day geology would have to have been called for. Thankfully, however, no such revision is necessary. The extravagant claims of the Arkeologists may be confidently set aside as modern-day myths with absolutely no serious foundation, and therefore deserving of only oblivion.

But in all this, one fundamental question has continued to niggle. Why, in the story of the biblical Noah, so closely associated as this is with a people who historically have almost fanatically identified themselves with the land of Israel, should the place from which this people's ancestors originated after the Flood have been stated as the Ararat region of north-easternmost Turkey? And why is it that among so many other of the Flood myths that we have iden-tified as belonging to the Noah family should this remote Turkish region be repeatedly indicated? Is it possible that the land that we today call Turkey might have a far closer link to the Flood story than has hitherto been suspected?

As we are about to see, thanks to brilliant theorising and exhaustive researches by two hard-headed American marine biologists whose credentials I have personally checked and found to be in excellent order, that possibility is a very real one indeed.

CHAPTER 4

THE BLACK SEA 'BURST-THROUGH'

The great deep burst through ...
Genesis 7: 11 New Jerusalem Bible translation

The date was October 1961, little more than a year after Turkish army captain Ilhan Durupinar had first noticed the bogus 'ark' on the aerial survey photographs of the Ararat district. Over on the other, far western side of Turkey, the United States survey vessel *Chain*, flagship of the Woods Hole Oceanographic Institution of Cape Cod, Massachusetts, chugged north-westwards. Since having set out from Falmouth, Massachusetts two months before it had crossed the Atlantic and Mediterranean, negotiated the Dardanelles strait and Sea of Marmara, and was now steadily making its way through the narrow Bosporus Strait leading into the Black Sea.

The *Chain* bristled with state-of-the-art echo-sounding equipment. One of the youngest of the technicians on board evaluating the new underwater topographical data being obtained from this was then newly-graduated American oceanographer Bill Ryan, today a Columbia University senior scientist specialising in sea-level and sediments. Eclectic by nature, Ryan was deeply conscious of the historicity of the waterway through which he was passing, with Europe to port and Asia to starboard. Just before entering the Dardanelles strait the *Chain* had passed the site of Homer's Troy. In the strait itself the vessel crossed over the spot where in 480 BC the Persian emperor Xerxes lashed together more than 600 boats to form two bridges via which his army could cross dry-shod into Europe. At the Bosporus there hove into view the domed mosques and soaring minarets of historic Istanbul, formerly Constantinople. Assyrians, Phoenicians, Hittites, Greeks, Romans, Byzantines, Vikings, Crusaders, Arabs, Mongols and not least the now incumbent Turks were just some of the peoples whose ghosts haunted these shores.

But as was explained to Ryan and his companions by the Turkish Navy officers invited on board as observers, the sub-marine hydrography of the narrow, cliff-lined Bosporus waterway through which they were passing was every bit as intriguing as its above-ground history. The strong surface current that was pushing fiercely south-westwards against the *Chain* on its journey northwards was cool run-off gener-ated by the great Black Sea rivers Kuban, Don, Dnieper, Dniester and above all Danube. The combined outputs from these rivers pump a far greater volume of water into the Black Sea than their three equivalents, the Rhône, Po and Nile, pour into the much bigger Mediterranean.

Although this Black Sea-driven run-off down the Bosporus channel was Mediterranean-bound, beneath it lay a significantly warmer counter-current that was pushing equally strongly northwards from the Mediterranean towards the Black Sea. Bosporus fishermen have long known of these two opposing currents, delighting in the trick of lowering rocks in a net to the depth of the deeper of the two. Once reached, the underlying current will propel their boat northwards as if by magic, and against the force of the surface current, without any use of oar, sail or motor. Back in 1680 a 21-year-old Italian Luigi Ferdinando Marsigli, by lowering into the Bosporus a sounding line with white painted corks attached to it, became the first known European to demonstrate the phenomenon scientifically, the sounding line first of all streaming aft of his boat, then after it had reached the appropriate depth, forming an arc to stream in exactly the opposite direction. By taking water samples at varying depths Marsigli also determined that the lower, northward-bound current is significantly more saline than its upper, southbound counterpart.[1]

For oceanographer Ryan the Bosporus' opposing current phenomenon was a new and fascinating one, as was the very marked underwater gorge appearance of the channel's sides at its lower depths, continually recorded by the *Chain*'s echo-sounders. Deep below the surface this gorge was sharply sculpted as if at one time the force of the Bosporus' underlying, northward-pushing current had been far stronger than at present. Indeed, it would have to have been a torrent of quite exceptional violence, though back in 1961 neither Ryan nor anyone else saw any special significance to this.

Before the *Chain*'s assignment was complete the underwater surveying work also took Ryan to the very end of the narrow Bosporus channel and out into the green expanse of the Black Sea itself. On world maps this has the appearance of a kidney-shaped pond, completely land-locked save for the narrow channel of Bosporus. From west to east, however, it is 1,000 kilometres (630 miles) wide, and 560 kilometres (350 miles) from north to south except where Russia's Crimea juts out into it to reduce the crossing to Turkey's northern coast to 230 kilometres (144 miles). Predictably, therefore, the American *Chain* was able to proceed only a little further with its underwater surveying before a tall and highly inquisitive Russian destroyer hove into view. Ryan and his fellow technicians were duly reminded that this was 1961, that the Cold War was a reality, and that except for the Turkish coast the surrounding sides of these Black Sea waters were all under very touchy Soviet control.

Yet despite such Russian shows of deterrence, in the summer of 1969 a United States expedition aboard the vessel *Atlantis II*, also from the Woods Hole Oceanographic Institution, but this time carrying a team of geologists and chemists, managed to do some important further survey work in the Black Sea, almost by accident. Baulked from carrying out their intended programme in the Red Sea due to renewed hostilities between Egypt and Israel, expedition leaders Drs David Ross and Egon Degens decided to try their luck and head for the Black Sea instead. Almost immediately upon their entering the Sea a Soviet four-engined bomber roared over *Atlantis II* at masthead height and 'buzzed' it a dozen times. The Black Sea then threw one of the fierce storms for which it is notorious.

Undaunted Ross and Degens spent two months mapping the entire basin of the Black Sea, carefully surveying all its sediment, structure and biology, including taking a series of core samples from its seabed. On examining these cores they found the top 100 centimetres (40 inches) of each consistently to comprise a dark black jelly-like mud called sapropel, richly gorged with plant and animal remains. Below this there was a light grey clay, the water content of which turned out to be surprisingly fresh.

As the two scientists set out in a subsequent scientific paper,[2] the full significance of which went unnoticed for a long time, sometime since the last Ice Age the Black Sea must have been a freshwater lake. Apart from rainwater, this lake's only replenishment came from the rivers that flow into the Black Sea, which carried with them the light grey clay in milky suspension. Then at some point the Mediterranean Sea broke through the Bosporus land-bridge, which we earlier noted to have formed part of the immediately post-Ice Age world landscape when the sea-levels were lower. As Ross and Degens showed in a graph accompanying their paper this breakthrough of the Bosporus was accompanied by a surprisingly rapid transformation of the former freshwater lake to its present-day saline state. Yet despite this, believing the level of the Black Sea lake and that of the incoming Mediterranean to have been much the same at the time, they assumed that the transformation must have been a relatively gentle affair. They had absolutely no suspicion that it might have been associated with any flood, nor did they have any accurate idea of when the transition might have occurred.

As recently as 1988 another American, Bob Karlin, on a visit to Turkey aboard Woods Hole research vessel, the *Knorr*, made another crucial discovery, yet even then the implications were not put together. Just where the Bosporus joins the Black Sea Karlin discovered evidence of a one-time enormous underwater sedimentary avalanche.[3] As revealed by his echo soundings, the sharp-sided canyon that Ryan had observed deep down in the Bosporus led into an enormous sedimentary apron that fanned out hundreds of kilometres into the Black Sea. It was just as if an immensely powerful torrent of pent-up water from the Mediterranean, after scouring out the Bosporus canyon, had surged northwards to break into the Black Sea at this point. But still it was unclear when and why such a breakthrough might have happened.

Meanwhile Bill Ryan had been working for some decades as a senior scientist at Columbia University's Lamont-Doherty Earth Laboratory, where one of his colleagues was Walter Pitman, a specialist in plate tectonics and developing magnetic profiles of the oceans. Fuelled by Ryan's experience of the Black Sea, the pair had often discussed its oceanography. Neither, however, were expecting the unique combination of circumstances that in 1993 would take them back to it, a very high profile return that was only made possible by the collapse of the Soviet Union little more than months before.

On 19 March 1993 there arrived out of the blue at

Columbia University a fax message addressed to Ryan and Pitman, sent to them from Bulgarian fellow oceanographer Dr Petko Dimitrov based at Varna, Bulgaria. Dimitrov enthusiastically told the pair of research on the seabed of the Black Sea that he had conducted in a small manned submersible during the 1970s. In his words:

> I found an old shoreline about 110 metres [358 feet] under the surface. Then I found evidence of ancient beaches. The old dune formations were extremely well preserved. This proved that they had been covered suddenly by a huge volume of water.[4]

According to Dimitrov, this old shoreline, which would of course have been that of the former freshwater lake, dated back, according to the best calculations he was able to obtain, to c.7750 BC. And because the lake lay so low relative to the post-Ice Age sea-level rise, any inrush into it by the Mediterranean would have meant the displacement of a 'huge volume of water' indeed. Ryan was forcibly reminded of a series of lectures on Ice Age Europe that he had attended more than twenty years before in which the speaker, Jirí Kukla, had shown that conditions of extreme aridity were affecting eastern Europe as recently as 6000 BC. As Ryan realised, such conditions might well have left the Black Sea far less topped up by the great rivers that feed it today. It may have lain like a relatively small puddle in a very weak coffer dam, one breach of which would have unleashed an inrush of quite unimaginably disruptive proportions.

The second out-of-the-blue eventuality for Ryan and Pitman, following hotly upon the first, emanated from an urgent approach for help that the United States had received from authorities in post-Cold War Russia. The Russians were deeply concerned to find out just how badly the river run-off from the recent Chernobyl nuclear power plant disaster might have affected the Black Sea, since any accumulating radioactivity could have disastrous consequences for the Sea's marine life and therefore for the whole food chain. The Russians offered the Americans a share of their world-class expertise in sea-bed core sampling in return for the Americans bringing to the problem their greater expertise and technology in ocean-bottom sonar profiling. The Russians would provide the necessary research vessel, the *Aquanaut*. All that a suitable American team needed to do was get themselves and their equipment to an oceanographic laboratory at Gelendzhik on the eastern shores of the Black Sea that was to be the research project's departure point.

It was just the project that Ryan had been looking for as an opportunity to return to the Black Sea, and unlike Pitman, who was pessimistic about the support systems the Russians were likely to provide, needed no persuading to participate. For Ryan, however, one complication was that he had promised a Connecticut-based undergraduate geology student, Candace Major, that she could spend a six-week research stint at his laboratory during just the period he was being called to go to the Black Sea. When this problem was put to Major she opted for the chance to join the expedition, and set about familiarising herself with the various species of Black Sea mollusc that were likely to be turned up during the seabed sampling.

On Ryan, Pitman and Major's arrival at Gelendzhik there was a delay due to their equipment not having arrived. But when it did Pitman was relieved to see that their main sonar device, CHIRP, a highly sophisticated remote-controlled underwater seismic profiler which he had managed to obtain on loan, had not been damaged during its lengthy and hazardous freighting from Boston. Pitman was further relieved when the Russians lowered the dolphin-shaped CHIRP over the *Aquanaut's* side, and it immediately began sending back excellent images of what it could 'see', through an inevitable accumulation of sediment, of the seabed proper.

In particular, when the *Aquanaut*, only six hours after departing Gelendzhik, approached the Kerch strait at the Black Sea's northern end, the on-board monitor showed up at some considerable distance from the present shore a deeply drowned former coastline. It looked just like what the Bulgarian oceanographer Petko Dimitrov had described of the 'ancient beaches' that he had come across during his underwater researches some two decades before.

Also clearly evident were 4.5-metre (15-foot) high river-banks unmistakably marking the bed of what had once been a very meandering river. As Pitman and Ryan tracked this underwater riverbed northwards they were able to see that at one time this had been an extension of Russia's Don. Today, as for several thousand years into the past, the Don terminates 160 kilometres (100 miles) to the north at the Sea of Azov, this latter being a subsection of the Black Sea just beyond the Kerch Strait. But as CHIRP was revealing, there had obviously been a time when there was no Sea of Azov, and the Don had meandered its way for a further 160 kilometres (100 miles) over what was then a broad flat plain before it discharged at the drowned coastline. All of which could only mean that at this time the level of the Black Sea was a hundred metres or more lower than at the present day, again readily corroborating Dimitrov's earlier submarine insights.

The *Aquanaut*'s next task was to take core samples from the seabed, its coring cylinder being designed to penetrate 3.5 metres (12 feet) into this, unless it encountered any layer of rock or of heavy compacting, such as would be found in an area that had once been dry land. The first core, taken in a mid-shelf area, produced only 1 metre (4 feet) of sediment before being stopped by something solid. And the molluscs that Candace Major found in this core she confidently identified as of the *Mytilus* seawater variety that gastronomes commonly enjoy as *Moules marinière*.

Then the *Aquanaut* moved out into deeper water. The coring team were instructed to pay out their winch at the fastest possible speed in order to obtain maximum penetration of the seabed. Sure enough, they achieved some 0.6 metres (2 feet) greater penetration into the seabed than before, though not without the core meeting resistance. But it was the contents of those last 0.6 metres (2 feet) that were to prove particularly intriguing.

As analysis revealed, the reason for resistance was a layer of gravel at four foot depth. Amongst this gravel there were mollusc shells that were severely fragmented. They were also bleached as from long exposure to sunshine. Yet they were still readily identifiable. And as soon became evident from Candace Major's mollusc analysis, these were no longer of the *Mytilus* sea-water variety, but were *Dreissena rostriformis*, a form which frequents only fresh water. Also amongst this same debris Major identified shells of tiny snails of varieties that frequent rivers, but are never found out in open salt water.

Meanwhile further work with the sonar revealed the contours of some deeply submerged ridges that, with the help of more core sampling, turned out to be sand-dunes. To Ryan and Pitman's astonishment, these dunes still retained the 'pristine' character of their contours, showing scant sign of any of the erosion that wave action would normally bring about in the case of any gradual submergence. Quite obviously what lay below had once been a coastal area of dry land. And in Ryan and Pitman's own words: 'Only a very abrupt drowning could have accounted for [the dunes] remarkable preservation.'[5]

More sampling of molluscs revealed further understanding of this drowned former coastal region. Exactly as had earlier been indicated by Ross and Degens' findings, any marine organisms that were found in the lower part of the cores were always of a freshwater variety. Then above these lay the rich muddy layer of the sapropel, whilst all marine organisms in the upper parts were always of a sea-water variety.

Although Ross and Degens' earlier researches had laid down much of the groundwork, to Ryan and Pitman the deduction was now unmistakable that what we call the Black Sea had once been a low-lying freshwater lake. Conforming to the earlier-discussed model of Ice Age-related low sea-level geography, it was not then joined to the Mediterranean via the Bosporus strait, as it is now. But then something had happened which had caused the salt water of the Mediterranean to burst through, apparently very rapidly in the light of the pristine-contoured dunes. Either the incoming ocean's salinity, or something else, had then rapidly killed off all the freshwater mollusc population. Finally *Mytilus* mussels had apparently been washed into the new Black Sea by the force of the burst-through, to pioneer a new, all salt-water marine population.

But still many questions remained, not least, when this burst-through event might have happened. The crucial indicator had to be radio-carbon dating. The Bulgarian Petko Dimitrov, in his fax of March 1993, had suggested 7750 BC. But was he right? When the work on the Chernobyl run-off was completed, and Ryan, Pitman and Major had returned to the United States, Ryan submitted samples of some of the freshwater molluscs they had collected to a colleague, radio-carbon dating specialist Dr Glenn Jones. Now at the Texas Institute of Oceanography, at that time Jones worked at the National Ocean Sciences Accelerator Mass Spectrometry Facility, part of the Woods Hole Oceanographic Institution. There, the radio-carbon dating unit uses the latest AMS technique of measuring the ratio of stable carbon 12 to whatever amount of unstable (and slightly radioactive) carbon 14 might remain in the sample. It was in mid-February 1994 that Glenn Jones phoned Ryan with the results. As Ryan recalls the phone-call:

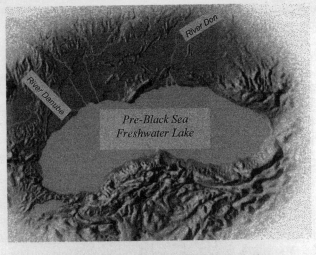

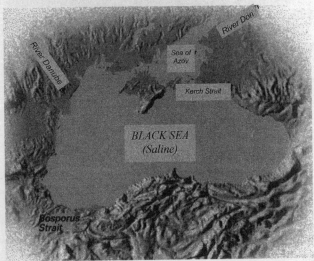

Fig 6 The Black Sea, map of before and after the great burst-through of the Mediterranean, according to the Ryan and Pitman hypothesis

The phone rings. I pick up the phone and it's Glenn Jones on the other end, and he's chuckling. I say 'Glenn, what's the problem?' And he says, 'Have you tricked me?' I say, 'What do you mean, have I tricked you?' He said, 'Have you sent me shells all from the same sample?' I said, 'Of course not! What's the problem?' He said, 'Well the dates are all exactly the same' … Then he gives me the age: 5600 BC.[6] It's not what I was expecting.[7]

Though astonishing to Jones, the news that all the fresh-water molluscs had died at one and the same time was not a surprise to Ryan. Here was positive confirmation that the transition of the Black Sea from freshwater to saline had been very sudden, and very brutal. It is hard to imagine a body of water spanning an area roughly approximating that of the British Isles having its entire shellfish population wiped out at a stroke, but that was the message of Jones' radio-carbon dating.

But the real surprise was that the date should be 5600 BC, when based on Dimitrov's findings, Ryan's expectation was for two millennia earlier. However not only was there a sig-nificant technological difference between east and west before the fall of the Iron Curtain, the whole science of radio-carbon dating had advanced significantly during the two decades since Dimitrov had carried out his Black Sea work.

After much consideration and consultation with other specialists, Ryan and Pitman gradually began to put togeth-er a scenario to account for all the different data that they had now accumulated. As we learned earlier, and was already well established scientifically, world sea-levels in the immediate aftermath of the Ice Age were much lower than they are now. The depression now occupied by the Black Sea had no inlet into it from the Mediterranean to link it with world sea-levels. The narrow Bosporus strait, the length of which Ryan had travelled in the *Chain* back in

1961, simply did not exist, being instead dry land. Aside from post-Ice Age run-off and any contribution made by rainfall, the Black Sea depression was filled solely with the outflows from the Danube, Dnieper, Dniester, Don and Kuban rivers. Since every one of these inputs were of the freshwater variety, the inevitable result was a vast freshwater lake, one of many to be found throughout the immediate post-Ice Age world at that time.

Then with the end of the Younger Dryas mini Ice Age, there occurred a shift in the pattern of post-Ice Age meltwater run-off. Instead of this emptying into the Black Sea lake, as previously, it went westward, to help create the allnew North Sea. Although the Black Sea freshwater-filled depression continued to receive the discharges of its five great supply rivers, with the occurrence of a further very dry spell its overall volume shrank to some two thirds of its present size, that is, to a level approximately 100 metres (350 feet) below that of today. It was at this very time that there lay exposed to the air and the sunshine the now deep underwater coastal beaches that Dimitrov had first noted back in the 1970s, and which in 1993 were confirmed by Pitman's CHIRP soundings on board *Aquanaut*.

Now as we saw earlier, the millennia between 10,500 BC and 5000 BC were notable for a massive rise in world sealevels. So it is important for our understanding of these millennia that we envisage the level of the Mediterranean, linked as this was to world sea-levels by the strait of Gibraltar, to have steadily risen and risen relative to the level of the already seriously low-lying Black Sea lake. In consequence the Bosporus land-bridge (at that time unbroken) would have represented an increasingly fragile dyke holding back the entire Mediterranean, and with it the massive hydraulic force of the entirety of the world's oceans, from bursting into the low-lying Black Sea lake.

It was inevitable, therefore, that sooner or later the dyke

would have to give, and sure enough around c.5600 BC it very clearly did. Possibly it was an earthquake that proved the final straw. NASA satellite views of the Bosporus strait show the split to be very jagged and to this day the entire Anatolian region, which lies at a collision point of several of the great plates forming the earth's crust, is notorious for seismic activity. Whatever the cause, the accumulation of evidence indicated to Ryan and Pitman that the sea-water Mediterranean suddenly burst through the Bosporus dyke and began pouring into the much lower freshwater lake. That this burst-through happened with devastating force was quite apparent from Bob Karlin's earlier-mentioned finding of an underwater avalanche spilling out from the cracked Bosporus and into the Black Sea.

So there can be absolutely no doubt that what Pitman and Ryan had discovered was a veritable Flood of Bible epic proportions. According to their calculations, 'Ten cubic miles of water poured through [the Bosporus] each day, two hundred times what flows over Niagara Falls, enough to cover Manhattan Island each day to a depth of over half a mile.'[8] They estimated that the roar of the rushing water would have been audible at 480 kilometres (300 miles) distance, the speed of the inflow would have been some 80 kilometres (50 miles) per hour, the rise in the level of the Black Sea would have been of the order of 15 centimetres (6 inches) per day, and all around the world the oceans would have been lowered by a foot in order to supply this huge new addition to their capacity. Ryan and Pitman envisaged a period of approximately two years of frantic filling during which some 97,000 kilometres (60,000 miles) of what had formerly been pleasant lakeside dunes and low-lying surrounding grassland became inundated.

Because this inrush was of briny Mediterranean sea water, it could only spell near-instant death for the literally millions of creatures and terrestrial plant-life whose freshwater environment it had invaded, and which had no tolerance for salt-water conditions. Indeed it is now evident that the earlier-mentioned thick rich blanket of sapropel that Ross and Degens so consistently found in their seabed cores can be nothing other than the remains of all these creatures and plants, remarkably preserved for reasons that will become clear in the next chapter.

All of which gives rise to the inevitable question – what do we know about any human settlements that might have existed around the freshwater lake at the time that the great burst-through occurred? Were there many of these, and were they and their inhabitants drowned? Or might some at least have managed to escape, as suggested by the Noah family of Flood legends? Here the Flood's date, c.5600 BC, had to be one of intense interest. For though it was before the age of writing, which came over two millennia later, it was well within the period during which many of the trappings of what we call civilisation were already established. In many parts of the Near East people were not only growing crops and rearing animals, they were also eating and drinking from pottery vessels, living in houses in small townships, and wearing clothes that they created from textiles spun on looms. Furthermore as Ryan and Pitman became increasingly aware, what is now Turkey to the Black Sea's south was far from being behind in such developments. c.6000 BC (immediately before the Flood), Çatal Hüyük, an inland township excavated during the 1960s by the British archaeologist James Mellaart, exhibited more 'trappings of civilisation' than have been found from that early time in either Mesopotamia or Egypt, despite the 'cradle of civilisation' appellation that is commonly given to these latter.

In all logic a freshwater lake, and one that had several rivers flowing into it, situated in a temperate climate zone, could only have been a natural magnet attracting both humans and animals alike. Animals arriving to drink would be available for hunting or capture and crops could be more easily watered. Just as the rivers Nile, Tigris and Euphrates later provided for the later Egyptian and Mesopotamian civilisations, so we would expect people of the 6th millennium BC, particularly if they had been suffering from drought conditions as suggested by Jirí Kila's findings, to have sought out such an ideal location and to have settled in its surrounds.

Yet for anyone who did live in the environs of the former Black Sea freshwater lake, the burst-through into it of the Mediterranean, which we now know to have been a real and datable event, could only have been the cruellest and most devastating of disasters. Had the settlers been nomadic hunter-gatherers as had typified all humanity during the aeons before, they might simply have shrugged their shoulders and moved off to fresh terrain. But for peoples with crops and animal herds, who had expended considerable energy and resources on creating a 'permanent' settlement, no such easy solution would have been available.

They would have needed to do pretty much as described in the biblical Noah story, or the Uta-napishti story, or the Atrahasis story, or the Ziusudra story or the Deucalion story. That is – and always assuming that they had the know-how and wherewithal to build a boat – they would have had to construct a suitable 'people and animals carrying' vessel and load into this all that they needed to perpetuate their lifestyle. Then they would have had to let themselves adrift to make a fresh start somewhere that the floodwaters had not reached.

Given all the indications that we noted earlier suggesting that the Noah family of Flood stories emanated from somewhere between Greece and the borders of India, it might seem to stand to reason that behind these stones lies the real-life event that Ryan and Pitman have now identified. Only those who hold as untenable any possibility that there might be some shred of truth to a 'religious' work such as the Bible, would dismiss such reasoning out of hand.

For when Ryan and Pitman, well-respected senior scientists though they are, began circulating their findings among fellow academics, including archaeologists and specialists in the ancient Flood myths, the response they received varied from the lukewarm to the downright insulting. In late 1996 David Harris, director of the Institute of Archaeology at the University of London, when publicly interviewed on their findings for the purposes of a BBC TV documentary,[9] spoke of them as 'moving into fantasy land'. Assyriologist Dr Stephanie Dalley of the University of Oxford's Oriental Institute, when asked in the same series of interviews whether Ryan and Pitman might have found the Flood as described in the epic of Gilgamesh, sniggered and dismissed it as a suggestion not even worth considering.

Likewise when in 1998 Ryan and Pitman published their findings in a surprisingly modest 'popular' book *Noah's Flood: The New Scientific Discoveries about the Event that Changed History*, the response, both scientific and lay, was muted. And this despite the authors, to their great credit, having scrupulously avoided the sort of sensationalism that is often indulged in by other less scientific-minded authors on Biblical and ancient history topics.

In fairness to the sceptics, what Ryan and Pitman's hypothesis still lacked was any shred of evidence for ancient human habitations having been overwhelmed by this Flood. Without such evidence their impeccable credentials and their well-reasoned scientific arguments could only be considered pure theory. And all the more frustrating was the fact that even should any such evidence exist it would probably lie some 90 to 120 metres (300 to 400 feet) below the level of the present Black Sea – and thereby beyond the range of normal underwater archaeology.

So Ryan and Pitman's theory might have been doomed to remain just that, a tantalising hypothesis that archaeology could not hope to confirm. But waiting in the wings was a resourceful entrepreneur who had already dazzled the world with his re-discovery, 3 kilometres (2 miles) deep in the chilly Atlantic, of the wreck of the *Titanic*. That entrepreneur was one lacking in academic stuffiness, and with no qualms about applying himself and his considerable resources to finding evidence for the biblical Flood. His name: Dr Robert Ballard.

CHAPTER 5

AMAZING FINDS

*This is amazing. It's going to rewrite the history of ancient
civilisations because it shows unequivocally that the Black
Sea Flood took place and that the ancient shores of the
Black Sea were occupied by humans.*[1]

Dr Bill Ryan, on hearing of Robert Ballard's discoveries

The supposed grounding of Noah's Ark on Mount Ararat,
with its relative proximity to the Black Sea, is one of the precious few clues that associate the Noah family of Flood
stories with the Black Sea. Ironically it is also probably the
lack of any popular association of the Flood myth with the
Black Sea that led to the reserve and scepticism with which
Ryan and Pitman's hypothesis was met.

Nonetheless the Mesopotamian Gilgamesh Epic, which
contains the earliest known written version of the Noah
family of Flood stories, strongly suggests that the Black Sea
had a very unsavoury reputation, assuming it is the Black
Sea that it refers to. Before the episode relating Uta-
napishti's recollections of the Flood, Gilgamesh is described
as having to cross a sea to reach Uta-napishti, a sea that is
referred to as the 'Waters of Death': 'Gilgamesh, there never
has been a way across … The crossing is perilous, its way
full of hazard, and midway lie the Waters of Death'.[2]
A cuneiform tablet with a map of the then-known
world shows Uta-napishti's home to the north-west of
Mesopotamia, the Black Sea being the only significant sea in
this direction. And Gilgamesh aside, Roman writers like

Pliny and Ovid, making a play on the Black Sea's Roman name Pontus Euxinus, called it 'Pontus Axenos', or the inhospitable sea[3], while the Turks called it Karadeniz, 'harbinger of death'.

Even today, anyone conducting underwater archaeology in the Black Sea needs to be warned that it offers nothing like the congenial environment that typifies the adjacent Mediterranean. The Black Sea's upper waters, constantly replenished as they are by the river Danube and its partners, have long supported a prolific fish life – abounding in bonito, anchovy, turbot, sprat, whiting and much else – though pollution is today threatening their existence. But towards its central basin the sea floor plummets to over 2,100 metres (7,000 feet), and these and all the Sea's sub-surface waters present a very different environment. At a dangerously fluctuating level sometimes only just over 60 metres (200 feet) below the surface, the Black Sea is not only dead, it is positively lethal. What distinguishes the water at these lower depths is that it lacks dissolved oxygen, and is instead heavily impregnated with hydrogen sulphide, H_2S, one of the world's deadliest gases. Characterised by a 'rotten eggs' smell, just a single lungful of it can be fatal, and since it almost instantly destroys the sense of smell, oil workers are schooled to run at the slightest sniff of it. In fact some minor leaks of H_2S, combined with methane, were noted in some of the core samples that David Ross and Egon Degens took from the Black Sea seabed in 1969.[4]

This environment comprises what some estimate as 90 per cent[5] of the Sea's overall volume, giving it the reputation of the world's largest mass of lifeless water, though similar anoxic properties have been reported in the depths of the Baltic[6] and under some Norwegian fjords. The reason for this has not yet been entirely explained scientifically. Recent radio-carbon dating of the marine organisms in the seabed cores that Ross and Degens took during their 1969 expedition has suggested however that the hydrogen sulphide's formation happened at the same time as the Black Sea Flood.[7] So one possible explanation is that the Sea's freshwater organisms, starved of oxygen by the huge inrush of salt water, turned to the only biochemical process they had left to them, stripping the oxygen from the sea water's sulphate irons, and thereby creating hydrogen sulphide. If this is the correct explanation then the H_2S is in effect the dying freshwater organisms' last breath.[8]

The exploration of so lethal an underwater environment therefore represents a huge challenge. And compounding the difficulty is the fact that the depth of 90 metres (300 feet) or more, which Ryan and Pitman projected for the level at which any 'Before the Flood' people would have been living around the freshwater lake, is well beyond the range of any scuba diver. In the case of underwater archaeological work there are rules governing the amount of time that scuba divers can stay at depths below 10 metres (33 feet), in order to prevent them suffering decompression sickness, or the bends. If the site depth is 15 metres (50 feet) they can stay down for as long as 80 minutes. But if it is 35 metres (115 feet) this reduces sharply to no more than 15 minutes. So any form of scuba diving-based archaeological exploration is simply not an option at depths of 90 metres (300 feet).

However such seemingly insuperable difficulties are ones that the now 58-year-old Dr Robert Ballard is particularly well qualified and equipped to overcome. During the long years that he spent as a director at the Woods Hole Oceanographic Institution, the same organisation responsible for the *Chain* and *Atlantis II* Black Sea surveys, Ballard specialised in developing submersibles capable of going into environments that would otherwise be impossible (or fraught with hazards) for human beings. And following an incident in which he and a fellow crew member nearly died when their submersible became entangled in wreckage deep under water he has increasingly favoured submersibles of the unmanned variety.

Most famous of these has been the *Argo*, which he designed to be remotely controlled, equipped with forward and side-scan sonar devices, a variety of video and still cameras, and tethered to its mother ship by a 6,000-metre (20,000-foot) co-axial cable. On 1 September 1985 Ballard sent the *Argo* down on the now world-famous two-hour, 3-kilometre (1.864-mile) journey into the icy Atlantic from which would come back the first sight of the *Titanic* that any human being had witnessed in 73 years.[9] Four years later, using the same *Argo*, Ballard successfully located the World War II German battleship *Bismarck*, sunk by Allied aircraft and warships on 27 May 1941, hundreds of kilometres off western France in water 5 kilometres (3 miles) deep.[10] Nor has he confined himself to the relatively modern-day. Amongst his recent discoveries have been two ancient Phoenician ships sunk off Israel, the oldest shipwrecks ever found in deep water.

One of Ballard's qualities, that earns him both archaeological and general scientific respect, is that despite seeking out historical remains of enormous popular interest, he does not turn into a treasure hunter upon finding them. In the case of the *Titanic* and *Bismarck* he has insisted on leaving exactly where they lie the many removable artefacts that are clearly to be seen strewn in and around the wrecks. He is equally averse to disturbing surviving remains of any of the hundreds of human beings who perished with these two ill-fated ships.

But daunting as were the problems of exploring at such great depths in the waters of the North Atlantic, the challenge of searching for hard evidence of Ryan and Pitman's Black Sea Flood posed its own individual set of problems, necessitating different approaches and adapted technologies. For such work Ballard, having recently retired from the

Woods Hole Oceanographic Institute, had set up a company
of his own, the Institute for Exploration, based in Mystic,
Connecticut. To help with its funding, Ballard had formed a
working relationship with *National Geographic* magazine. So
in July 1999, little more than a year after Ryan and Pitman
had made their findings public, Ballard was already shipping
his latest array of underwater exploration robots and surface
command systems to the port of Sinop on Turkey's Black Sea
coast. His mission: specifically to conduct a preliminary
reconnaissance in search of evidence to support their claims.

Exactly who founded Sinop, and when, no one can be
exactly sure. But over two thousand years ago the locally-
born Roman geographer Strabo lovingly and accurately
described it as 'beautifully equipped both by nature and by
human foresight, for it is situated on the neck of a peninsula,
and has on either side of the isthmus harbours and road-
steads and wonderful fisheries.'[11] Certainly it provides the
best harbour facilities on Turkey's Black Sea coast.
Throughout the Cold War the Americans used it as a NATO
listening-post for eavesdropping on the Soviet Union, giving
its local Turkish population an unusually close familiarity
with visiting Americans. And the Sinopians were no doubt
particularly gratified when Ballard chartered two local
fishing vessels, the *Guven* and the *Yidiz* as transport for all
his exploration equipment.

So a humble Turkish fishing boat, the *Guven*, found itself
fitted out with equipment light years more sophisticated
than its designers could ever have dreamed of: a high-tech
echo sounder, a satellite-linked high-precision navigation
system to enable pinpoint positioning, and a high-frequency
side-scan sonar fish. Setting out to explore the seabed a few
kilometres north of Sinop, it was not long before the journey
proved worthwhile. From data sent back by the side-scan
sonar fish, those viewing in Ballard's special onboard control
room were able to 'see' at a depth of 170 metres (550 feet)

below them distinctive contours unmistakably denoting an ancient coastline.

This was a coastline very much as Dimitrov had first discovered deep down off Bulgaria's Black Sea coast back in the 1970s, and which Ryan and Pitman had encountered off Russia's Black Sea coast during their 1993 *Aquanaut* expedition. This particular one though had to represent the same former freshwater lake's southern rim. Aided by satellite links providing the very best-available global positioning, Ballard had the *Guven* make repeated sweeps in order to create a suitably detailed map of the exact underwater topography. And again as had been Ryan and Pitman's practice in the northern Black Sea, the composition of the coastline was then electronically evaluated, revealing a classic profile of a one-time sand and shell beach, complete with a flat cobblestone shore area, a ledge leading down to the old water level, mud from what had once been the lake's bottom, and an offshore sandbar. As Ballard described it, it 'looked like any beach anywhere on earth – except it was under 550 feet (168 metres) of water!'[12]

Next it was the turn of the Turkish fishing vessel *Yildiz* to play its part. Over its side went the Woods Hole Oceanographic Institution's Searover Remotely Operated Vehicle (ROV), a descendant of *Argo* that Ballard had chosen for this particular operation. Passing over the same coastline that the *Guven*'s sonar sweeps had disclosed, the ROV visually confirmed the same underwater features. Then, using a scallop dredge that had been converted for geologic sampling work, actual samples were scooped up from the seabed representative of the different underwater coastal features. Amongst the sand, mud and stones that the dredge brought back it also turned up wood, charcoal, bones and a piece of obsidian that, in Ballard's words 'had no business being there'.[13]

At the time of writing little information has yet been

made public concerning any of the insights that may have been gleaned from the wood, bones or (particularly) the obsidian. In the case of the latter its special interest value lies in the fact that it was a hard, brittle volcanic glass that could be chipped like flint and was therefore widely prized in Late Stone Age times for crafting into cutting tools. Its hardness made it the Stone Age equivalent of Sheffield steel. Because in its natural form it is to be found only in the vicinity of volcanoes – indeed it is usually scientifically possible to determine from which volcanic region a particular piece of obsidian has derived – for it to turn up on the bed of the Black Sea certainly suggests human agency. However, without any more meaningful context this proves nothing, since it might at any time simply have been dropped overboard from a passing vessel.

Whatever the obsidian's origin, however, exactly as in the case of Ryan and Pitman's researches, it was a number of molluscs that the ROV's scallop dredge also retrieved from the underwater beach area that proved to be most revelatory. These were sent to the US Academy of Natural Sciences in Philadelphia where taxonomist Gary Rosenberg and his team identified representatives of nine different species. These were then sent to be radio-carbon dated at the Woods Hole Oceanographic Institution's National Ocean Sciences Accelerator Mass Spectrometer, the very same facility that had processed Ryan and Pitman's shell samples. There the shells that were found to be oldest included two varieties of freshwater mussel that ranged in age from c.13,500 BC to c.5500 BC, that is from the time of the retreat of the last major Ice Age to the time that Ryan and Pitman had already identified as that of the Black Sea Flood. These could be regarded as having become extinct since that time, there being no live specimens of these particular varieties anywhere in the Black Sea, their nearest counterparts existing today in the freshwater Caspian Sea.

Conversely every specimen of the seven shell varieties that Woods Hole radio-carbon dated as being younger than the 5500 BC date proved to be all of the salt-water variety. Not only were these shells of varieties that are still to be found alive in the Black Sea, their radio-carbon dates were found to be consistently after 5000 BC, and never earlier. This single further survey by Ballard had therefore richly corroborated Ryan and Pitman's hypothesis. And it had corroborated it on the basis of evidence that had been collected from the opposite ancient shoreline of the Black Sea to that from which they had taken their seabed samples back in 1993.

Though Robert Ballard made the preliminary findings of this 1999 expedition public in October 1999 – findings that the *National Geographic* press announcement bullishly hailed as 'proof of Noah's Flood' – he was conscious that this was everything but a very promising start. He had yet to find the crucial evidence of any actual drowned human habitation that the Ryan and Pitman hypothesis vitally needed in order to be taken seriously. Undaunted, however, in September 2000 Ballard was back in the Black Sea, this time with an expressly avowed commitment to 'searching for man-made structures or other evidence of human habitation along the ancient lakeshore.'[14]

Because a stronger and better equipped support vessel was needed than could be provided by Turkish fishing boats, key members of Ballard's team had earlier arrived in Malta to take temporary charge of a former Hull trawler that had already been converted for research use, the *Northern Horizon*. For Ballard's purposes this was additionally provided with an oceanographic winch and a 4,000-metre (13,000-feet) steel-armoured fibre optic umbilical cable. On to this the team also loaded the containers that housed their command centre with its computers, video screens and other control equipment centre, specially shipped over from

Woods Hole. Likewise winched on board, again after having been specially sent from Woods Hole, were their prized new robotic submersibles *Argus* and *Little Hercules*, both of which were to play a vital role in what was to follow.

Argus, aptly named after Greek mythology's hundred-eyed giant, was a 3.5-metre (11.5-foot) long submersible sled that bristled with lights, and video and still cameras. This was designed to perform in the Black Sea much as the *Argo* had earlier done in sending back images of the *Titanic* from deep beneath the North Atlantic. Likewise *Little Hercules* was designed to perform as a smaller, ancillary 'roving eye' capable of probing at close range, or in tight corners, in ways that would be impossible for its bigger brother. Although *Little Hercules* had to await the later arrival of a key 'pilot', *Argus* was given its maiden dive on 19 August in deep waters off Greece. Then, following much the same route as that taken by the *Chain* back in 1961, the *Northern Horizon* made its way up the Bosporus to Istanbul, where it had earlier been arranged that Ballard and a *National Geographic* film crew would join those already on board. Also taking part was the now long-graduated Candace Major, from Ryan and Pitman's 1993 expedition.

On 2 September 2000, with the Ballard rendezvous having successfully taken place the day before, the *Northern Horizon* began its first proper surveying, of an area off Turkey's northern coast that had already been targeted as a strong possibility for early human settlement. This was the stretch of water between Abana and Turkeli, just to the west of Sinop, which Turkish hydrographic maps suggested might have been the site of a major submerged river delta. In fact, the first survey work with *Argus* showed that the very crudely drawn-up maps were seriously misleading, and that there was no river delta here after all.

However, from a closer look at some of the potential points of interest that the same survey showed up, the Ballard team's interest became focused on a strikingly rectangular feature approximately 12 metres (39 feet) long by 4 metres (13 feet) that could be seen 19 kilometres (12 miles) off the coast at the intersection of two small 'inland' river channels. As Ballard commented in his subsequent report 'I thought it might be a shipwreck but it didn't look quite right'.[15] Then when *Argus* was moved as close as possible consistent with safety, 'logs and timbers' could be seen, except that their sonar profile alone was nothing like that for shipwrecks with which Ballard had long become familiar. Nor was there visible any of the debris that normally accompanies ancient shipwrecks, such as anchors and broken amphorae (jugs). Then much to everyone's frustration *Argus*' sonar system flooded, putting it out of action for three days.

Thankfully by Wednesday 6 September *Argus* was back in action, the video footage that it sent back now revealing some particularly clear pictures. The seabed depth at which the vehicle was operating was quite definitely a hydrogen sulphide environment, since most eerily there was not a vestige of plant or fish life to be seen. But what particularly excited Ballard and his team was that the pictures it was sending back provided the first visual confirmation of something they had quietly long been hoping for. This was that the very anoxic properties of the hydrogen sulphide conditions might actually have served to preserve any remains that had been drowned since *c.*5600 BC, remains that marine organisms would normally have long since destroyed.

On Thursday 7 September *Northern Horizon* was back at Sinop to take on board *Little Hercules*' 'pilot' Martin Bowen, just arrived from the States. Also embarking at this point was the expedition's deputed head archaeologist Dr Fredrik Hiebert, curator of Near Eastern antiquities at the University of Pennsylvania's Museum of Archaeology and Anthropology. By one of life's ironies it was this very same Museum that had co-sponsored Leonard Woolley's 'Flood'-finding excavations

seven decades before. With *Little Hercules* now deployable
and an archaeological expert of Hiebert's standing having
joined the expedition all was now in place for a closer look at
the rectangular building-like feature that had earlier attracted
such interest.

In the event getting *Northern Horizon* back over the exact
site of this feature was not as quick as it should have been
due to a slight navigational error. This had arisen from
faulty positioning of the antenna that provided the link to
the global positioning satellite. However, when this was
corrected the mystery feature was relocated with ease.

At 11.52 am on Saturday 9 September, having been given
its maiden test dive only the day before, *Little Hercules* took
its first close-up look at the feature, descending to a depth of
95 metres (311 feet). And suddenly, on the monitors in the
expedition control room there loomed a notched, unmistakably hewn wooden beam. Dr Fredrik Hiebert frankly admits
that his 'jaw literally dropped'. There could be no question
that this was a beam that had been modified by human
craftsmanship. In his words: 'It was one of the most
astonishing things I've ever seen'.[16]

Further deployment of *Little Hercules* revealed other, similarly hewn beams and also wooden branches. Their disposi-
tion was such that they had clearly acted as supports for the
walls and roof of a building the dimensions of which were
now estimated as 14 metres (45 feet) long by 3.5 metres (12
feet) wide. As Hiebert noted, the type of construction was
quite evidently wattle and daub. This is the same architectural style that is known to have been used by inhabitants of
ancient Turkey at least as far back as the 6th millennium BC, as
at sites such as Çatal Hüyük some 480 kilometres (300 miles) to
the south. But because of the part-mud construction, the walls
had collapsed in situ: 'It's like one of those constructor-kits,
all the pieces are there. It just melted in place', Hiebert
commented to Sicilian archaeologist Francesco Torre.[17]

Fig 7 Some of the first humanly crafted objects revealed by Ballard's underwater cameras

With *Northern Horizon* still over its head, *Little Hercules* continued to be used to great effect, now roving very closely over the building and its immediate surrounds. A near ecstatic Hiebert later reported:

> As we went very carefully – practically inch by inch – over this site we began to see stone tools. These stone tools are pecked stone ... not small blades ... but seemed to be pecked or ground stone. I don't know if they're hammers or chisels. We are not touching anything. We're just photographing them.[18]

Some of these apparent stone tools seemed to be highly polished, and they were carefully drilled with circular holes. There was also a chisel or axe head which Hiebert noted to bear a striking resemblance to one that he had seen in the museum at Sinop.

There were also fragments of ceramics. As Hiebert described these, they:

... were literally exposed on the floor of this structure [the rectangular building]. It was amazing to see this because we imagine that the sediments would have covered them. But here on the ancient coastline sedimentation is so low that the ceramics were exposed. We were able to see that this structure more or less is in the shape of what we would think is an ancient house. It had ceramics. It had these ground stone implements. It had the clear remains of walls made out of mud with sticks and beams as their major [mode of] construction.[19]

As Hiebert was well aware, the fact that there had been a burst-through of the Mediterranean into the Black Sea some seven millennia ago, and that this Late Stone Age-type rectangular building lay at a location 18 kilometres (12 miles) off the Turkish shore and more than 90 metres (300 feet) below the Black Sea's surface could mean only one thing. That there definitely had been human settlement and habitation around the Black Sea freshwater lake prior to the burst-through. Whatever elements of truth may or may not lie behind the Noah family of Flood stories, there had been 6th millennium BC peoples living around what is now the Black Sea who genuinely experienced a Flood that to them would very credibly have seemed an event on an all-world scale.

By any standards the discovery was headline-making, and Ballard lost little time releasing the news to the world, aided by the considerable services of his *National Geographic* sponsors. On 14 September most major newspapers and TV stations around the world carried the story, the TV footage including the first images of the artefacts as filmed by Ballard's underwater robots.

Yet so far, all was just pictures taken remotely more than 90 metres (300 feet) down in the Black Sea. And despite Ballard's commendable reticence with regard to disturbing underwater remains, in this instance, and with no human bodies being visible, hands-on scientific evaluation of some of the artefacts was clearly needed, not least for dating purposes.

So Ballard and Hiebert duly applied to the Turkish government for permission to pick up some sample artefacts from the seabed. And while Turkish bureaucracy is not always noted for its speed, Minister of Culture Istemihan Talay, to his great credit, lost little time in granting this permission.

In fact *Little Hercules* had never been designed with any such sampling work in mind. It had been way beyond Ballard's and Hiebert's expectations that after eight millennia they might find artefacts lying on the seabed just as if they had been abandoned yesterday, hardly even covered by any sediments. However Ballard's ever-ingenious engineers quickly came up with a suitable device, in the form of a simple scoop-type basket that they fixed to the front of the underwater vehicle. This was positioned so that it was readily viewable by its on-board colour camera, and by 21 September it had already retrieved sufficient artefacts to satisfy the expedition's immediate requirements. As Ballard's report noted:

> Using this device we successfully recovered a number of human craft objects from the site, all of which we[re] made of wood.[20]

Laconic as this entry might sound, its implications are considerable. As Hiebert immediately acknowledged, he had incorrectly identified the tools that the TV monitor showed lying around the rectangular building as artefacts made of stone. Historically, most items that have survived to our time from the Late Stone Age era are indeed usually of stone – because any organic materials such as wood will almost invariably have long since perished. So it was stone that Hiebert had understandably expected. Accordingly his awe was all the greater upon finding the tools to be made of wood. Additionally, the same hands-on examination confirmed them to be 'the result of shaping by humans'. In Hiebert's own description: 'They [the tools] have smooth, symmetrical shapes and unmistakable traces of drilling to produce the holes visible on the videos.'[21]

Because of wood's perishability our knowledge of any items crafted from wood from the Late Stone Age era is limited in the extreme. The fact, therefore, that these objects from deep down in the Black Sea were of wood and yet had *not* disintegrated showed that the Sea's anoxic properties had indeed acted as a remarkable preservative, just as the team had quietly hoped.

The real possibility, therefore, was that further exploration might open up a veritable Black Sea bed 'Pompeii' more than five thousand years older than its Roman era counterpart, and promising unprecedented insights into the technologies of an era at the dawn of what we call our civilisation.

The fact that the tools were made of wood has another crucial implication. Stone artefacts, being inorganic, can be dated only from their style, and from the dating of any organic materials found in them. But wood can not only be directly radio-carbon dated, it is also possible, in some instances, to date it very reliably via tree-ring dating. Tiny samples from some of the wooden items retrieved in *Little Hercules'* scoop have indeed been submitted for radiocarbon dating, and we are assured that the results will become available in due course. The only real surprise will be if they are found *not* to be of around the 6th millennium BC period or earlier – though given the clear pattern of dating revealed by two quite separate rounds of dating of the molluscs, any serious discrepancy seems extremely unlikely.

These results, along with stylistic evaluation of the artefacts brought up in the scoop, and any further evaluation of the underwater house, will still only be the tip of the iceberg with regard to what Ballard and others may reveal in the course of future explorations of the Black Sea's 'Before the Flood' coastline.

For what a succession of archaeological studies have been hinting at for a long time, and which the Ballard findings have already strikingly endorsed, is a serious error in the conventional textbook understanding of where and when our so-called civilisation had its origins. In my 1950s school-days, as in most other people's continuing up to the present day, the standard teaching was and continues to be that civilisation began c.3000 BC in the great river valleys of the Nile, the Tigris and Euphrates, in Egypt and Mesopotamia. A disproportionate amount of archaeological effort has been focused on these countries, and on the period from 3000 BC on. It is as if before them there was never anyone or any-thing of significance anywhere else in the world. This has become so ingrained in us that any suggestion that there might have been a considerably older and only little less impressive civilisation – and in Turkey of all places – can seem unthinkable.

But even the meagre Black Sea human artefacts that have so far been discovered suggest that the peoples associated with them had a surprisingly high standard of craftsman-ship for a period nearly three millennia before the building of Egypt's Great Pyramid. Who might these people have been who were living around the Black Sea lake immediately prior to the great burst-through? What sort of civilisation might they have developed, despite the fact that their time was one fraught with rapidly rising sea-levels? As we are about to discover, the 'Before the Flood' peoples have been neglected for far too long.

CHAPTER 6

VERDANT LANDSCAPES

*At the time ... water flowed out of the ground and watered
all the surface of the soil*

Genesis 2: 6

As noted in an earlier chapter, the markedly lower sea-level
of the period immediately after the last Ice Age meant that
for an imprecisely determined time there were significant
localised differences to the present-day continental coastlines. In 1989 – well before Ryan and Pitman launched their
Black Sea Flood hypothesis – the Cambridge University
earth scientist Tjeerd van Andel drew up a map of these
coastline differences as they affected the Mediterranean and
its environs [fig 8]. In an accompanying scientific paper
he described the now long drowned land features that he
envisaged:

Large plains existed off the coast of Tunisia and fringed
most of Italy, southern France, eastern Spain and much of
Greece. Anatolia was connected to Europe by land
bridges across the Bosporus and the Dardanelles, while
most of the Cyclades [a group of some 30 Aegean islands
scattered between the south-western Turkish coast and
the southernmost part of the Greek mainland] were
welded together into a single island... A narrow bridge
joined Italy and Sicily but ... disappeared soon after the

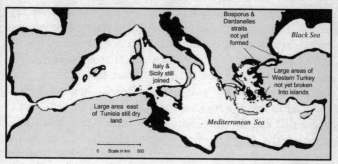

Fig 8 Reconstruction of Mediterranean region coastlines as these would have looked shortly after the end of the Ice Age, showing (in black) large areas not yet claimed by subsequent sea-level rise. After the findings of J. C. Shackleton and T. van Andel

ice melt began. The distances over water between Corsica and Italy, Sicily and Tunisia, or between Crete and the Peloponnese were much reduced.[1]

Notice that Van Andel specifically refers to the Bosporus land-bridge, thus corroborating the land-bridge's existence as part of the post-Ice Age landscape before its demise in 5600 BC.

It is important to try to envisage that as well as the altered coastlines there were other features of this post-Ice Age landscape that both climatically and environmentally were significantly different to present-day conditions. Some of these differences had fundamental implications for where human populations were likely to congregate.

As noted earlier in this book, the ending of the last Ice Age was far from being a regular and orderly affair. The retreating ice-sheets left many dozens of huge lakes scattered across the world. Among these were the appropriately-named Great Lakes between the present-day United States and Canada, but also across in the 'Old World' was the then Baltic lake, the Aral and Caspian Seas, the Black Sea, and many others.

Temporarily the climatic conditions stayed relatively dry, one of the characteristics of this Allerød phase. According to researches by geoarchaeologist Professor C. Vance Haynes Jr[2] of the University of Arizona at Tucson, Arizona, this meant that by c.11,000 BC water tables had fallen to their lowest levels in at least 15,000 years. Streams became reduced to relative trickles compared to the earlier flows of water that had cut the great valleys. During this same period some of the huge mammal species that had been around throughout the last two million years became extinct, amongst these the great mammoths, the giant sloths and the sabre-toothed tigers. While it is by no means clear why these creatures died,[3] with the Allerød dry phase, closely followed by a sudden temporary return to similarly dry and exceptionally cold conditions during the Younger Dryas mini Ice Age, die out they certainly did.

Then sometime between 10,000 and 8000 BC – there are some surprisingly wide variations between scientists' calculations depending upon the date that they give for the Younger Dryas period – the Ice Age finally released its grip. Conditions became substantially warmer and wetter. And with the melting of the ice sheets and the plenitude of rain there occurred not only the marked rise in world sea-levels but also the running of the rivers at full spate, filling up the seriously depleted lakes. Furthermore, the rain fell in some quite different places to ones that we might expect today. In the case of the Sahara, for instance, the off-the-Atlantic east-ward-bound storm track which had previously driven in to the north of North Africa's Atlas Mountains changed its pattern and began driving in to the south, bringing an abundance of rain to the Sahara.

As a result the Sahara, which during the Ice Age had been a little less arid than the conditions with which we associate it today, suddenly abounded in large lakes and rivers. Although most of these no longer exist, geologists can deduce their one-time presence from the blocks of porous limestone called travertine that they left as they dried out. One lake that lay just to the south of Tunis, dubbed Lake Ouargia, was fed from a river which ran northwards all the way from the Tassili highlands, in what is today one of the deepest and driest regions of the Sahara. The track of this river can still be followed. Where today there are just the sandy wastes of southern Algeria and northern Mali there glistened great lakes that geologists have named Taouat, Taoudenni and Azouak. And there were many more that have not been given names. Surrounding these there were grasslands as verdant and supportive of wildlife as those that are today found in South Africa.

Nor was the Sahara by any means alone in this. In what is today Turkey the ending of the Ice Age likewise left some very large lakes, quite aside from the Black Sea freshwater lake (which some scientists have named Lake Novoevskinsky) to its north. Lake Aksehir in the country's west was five times its present size.[4] In the central plateau region the Konya plain featured a vast lake which became seriously shrunk by the Younger Dryas aridity,[5] only to fill up again. To the east of Turkey there lay the Caspian Sea, which in the aftermath of the Ice Age was again much larger than at present.

The now moonscape-like Lake Van area immediately to Turkey's north-east became thickly forested, so that as late as the 8th century BC mighty armies had literally to hack their way through it. Oak, ash, poplar and pistacia trees are known to have flourished in the 7th millennium BC in what is now the arid Halula region of Syria close to the Turkish border.[6] Herds of wild elephant roamed this same region, also in the environs of Lakes Van and Urmia. Throughout much of the Near East there was also a profusion of types of birds, fish, bears and mountain cats that have long since disappeared because the terrain became unable to support them.

Even the Arabian peninsula between the Red Sea and Persian Gulf, another region that today we automatically associate with vast expanses of desert sand, was very much wetter and more verdant. Studies have shown that there were once large lakes in what is today Saudi Arabia's 'Empty Quarter'. Also, during the early 1990s, during the Gulf War, Boston University scientist Farouk El-Baz came across vast numbers of granite and basalt pebbles in and around the tiny state of Kuwait. When he traced the origins of these to Saudi Arabia's Hijaz mountains 1,050 kilometres (650 miles) to the west, he suspected that they had been river-borne all this distance. He was proved right thanks to space shuttle imaging radar echoes, which showed the clear line of an ancient river deep beneath the Arabian sands, which had traversed from the Hijaz Mountains all the way across Saudi Arabia to the Persian Gulf.[7] From the carbon-dating of thick deposits of organically-rich soil found in this same Gulf region,[8] and from analysis of a core soil sample taken from the Arabian Sea not far from Yemen, there is now a general scientific consensus that this region enjoyed a significantly wetter environment from c.7000 to 3000 BC, El-Baz's river thereby almost certainly dating from the same period. Even further east, in what is now the desolate Kara Kum desert region east of the Caspian Sea, the picture of one-time huge lakes is much the same.

Given the existence during the post-Ice Age period of so many lakes and such verdant landscapes accompanying them, often in surprising places, it would be most unlikely that these lakes did not become prime watering holes for large numbers of grazing animals. The congregation of so many edible animals would in turn have attracted groups of human hunters for whom they would have represented a convenient larder. And early though the time was, being well before the invention of narrative writing, there is nonetheless an abundance of human testimony that this was the case.

For one method of human communication that had appeared even before the end of the Ice Age was painting and engraving in caves and rock-shelters, as at Lascaux in south-western France and Altamira in northern Spain. In these the prehistoric painters' subjects were near-exclusively the animals upon which they preyed, and which at the same time they appear to have regarded with a special reverence.

Then with the ending of the Ice Age the prehistoric painters began to include lively, albeit silhouette-like depictions of human beings, again often in the context of the animals which they hunted. Though such rock art is notoriously difficult to date with any precision, it is to be found as far afield as Australia, Brazil and southern Africa, the paintings exhibiting some puzzling similarities to each other for areas so far apart. But one particularly productive and interesting region, because it features a series of different phases that can at least be set in a rough chronological sequence, is the Sahara.

Even as recently as the 1930s, the common supposition had been that throughout the development of humankind the Sahara had been as devoid of any human and animal population as it is today. Then a young French camel-corps officer, Henri Lhote, while working in the Sahara's now remote and desolate Tassili region 1,450 kilometres (900 miles) south of Tunis, came across some rock paintings and engravings that were clearly very ancient.[9] He discovered many of them, scattered over considerable distances which indicated that the region was once populous with human inhabitants. The varieties of animals depicted also confirmed what we have already suggested from the climate studies — that the vegetation was once very different as well. For the animals depicted included African elephant, rhinoceros, hippopotamus, giraffe, gazelle and the extinct North African buffalo, all creatures that daily need plenty of water to drink and plenty of grass to eat.[10]

Fig 9 One of the 'Round Head' period pre-Flood frescoes found during Henri Lhote's expedition to the Tassili region of the Sahara. Note the 'dilly' or gathering bags that some figures wear at their waist

Intrigued, Lhote resolved to mount a major expedition to the Tassili to copy the paintings artistically and otherwise exhaustively to record their particulars and locations. This was essential because the paintings and engravings had often been created on rock-faces, the surfaces of which were far too irregular and weathered for them to show up clearly using any normal photographic means. In the event World War II interrupted these plans and it was not until 1956 that Lhote had the opportunity to carry out his intentions. Because of the Tassili regions remoteness, his expedition was dogged with problems. Some team members were unable to cope with the climatic extremes, and even among the camels which Lhote used to transport supplies up and down the narrow, rock-strewn tracks the attrition rate was so high that at one point the local Tuareg refused to hire any more out to him.

Despite such difficulties Lhote and his team's survivors brought back with them a wealth of images that had been created by hitherto unknown peoples who had inhabited the Sahara in considerable numbers both before the Black Sea Flood and in the millennia immediately after this. There is general agreement that the major phase that Lhote dubbed the 'Round Heads' Period – after the way the heads on the human figures were depicted [fig 9] – corresponds to what we would call the 'Pre-Black Sea Flood' period. Whoever painted these lively Lowry-style figures portrayed them occupied in pursuits such as dancing, swimming, and running with bows and arrows apparently in the course of hunting. Some appear to be naked. Others wear horn-like adornments on their heads, and what appear to be short grass-skirts. Yet others have attached to their waists a distinctively pointed appendage that from equivalent living cultures can be identified as a classic hunter-gatherer collecting bag that indigenous Australians call a dilly bag.

Clearly these were peoples at what anthropologists term a 'hunter-gatherer' phase of their development. And what we are seeing of them in the Sahara may be inferred as pertaining across a very wide geographical area, in view of the vast tracts of new land that had been opened up in the Ice Age's immediate aftermath. For similar figures have been found in Spain, also parts of Africa such as Tanzania well south of the Sahara. Likewise similar rock engravings have been found at Naltepe on Mount Aragats,[11] the twin volcano to Mount Ararat, on the formerly Soviet side of the Turkey/Armenia border. More of the same, again in the form of rock engravings, have been found at Beyuk Dash, Kobystan, on the western side of the Caspian Sea.[12] And yet more at Buqras in Syria, where the rock paintings are notable for their depiction of ostriches.[13] A common theme throughout these widely scattered prehistoric works of art is the use of bows and arrows for hunting. This weapon had clearly been invented no later than the end of the Ice Age. Also common was the depiction of humans moving amongst large grazing animals, particularly deer and bovines, these creatures sometimes appearing enormous compared to the humans surrounding them.

The term 'hunter-gatherer' can conjure up a mental image of 'primitive' people eking out a 'nasty, brutish and short' existence hunting wild animals, spear-fishing in rivers and lakes, and scratching in the dirt to collect edible wild plants. But as South Africa's Laurens van der Post has been at pains to emphasise in his studies of southern Africa's now near-extinct Khoisan bushmen[14] – whom DNA specialists now regard as genetically closest to humankind's common ancestor some 100,000 years ago – 'primitive' is a pejorative and misleading description. It utterly fails to do justice to the high degree of skill and expertise that people living the hunter-gatherer way of life may well have acquired.

For the bushman way of life, in many respects, is far from being primitive, brutish or ignorant. Without any textbooks for guidance, the women who go out daily as gatherers need to have formed an expert botanical knowledge of the fruits, nuts, leaves and roots of wild plants. They need to know which of these may offer safe and palatable nutrition, where and when these may best be found and collected, how to prepare these for consumption, cooked or raw. They need to know which plants may have useful properties as medicines, poisons or hallucinogens, which plants may be serviceable for string or rope, and how best to extract the fibres for this purpose. They need to know how and where to find water when there may be no river or stream nearby. They need to know how to deliver and nurture a baby, also how to treat wounds and fractures. They cannot rely on supermarkets and pharmacies and medical centres as many of us do today.

Likewise men who go out daily as hunters need a similar expertise. To fish they need to have an awareness of when and where fish are most likely to gather and feed, and when to expect the associated high and low tides. They need to know how and from what to construct temporary shelters. Also, without using metal of any kind, for these are still Stone Age people, they need to know how and from what to manufacture serviceable weapons such as spears, knives, bows and arrows. During a hunt they need to have a zoologists' knowledge of the habits of the particular animal they are stalking, its distinctive tracks and what these can convey of its sex, build, and so on. They need a meteorological appreciation of wind direction so that they can get close to the animal without its scenting them, and a ballistic knowledge of the right type of arrow or spear to use, an anatomical knowledge of where to aim to kill the creature most expeditiously and thereafter how to butcher it. They need a keen sense of direction and distance to find their way back to where their particular group last made their camp. They need to have mastered how to rotate a stick in order to kindle a fire for cooking purposes, also in the case of large game animals how to portion and dry the animal's left-over meat for long-term storage. Male and female hunter-gatherers alike also need to know how to skin an animal and make this and any other of its body parts serviceable for clothing and decoration purposes, for waterproof shelters or for portable containers.

If you live such a way of life it is axiomatic that you will move from one place to another, taking your cue from the animal herds upon which you prey and moving on when one pasture has been exhausted or a water hole dried up. For childbearing women, breast-feeding may need to be sustained until the child reaches the age of five or even six. As anthropologists have determined,[15] because of the relatively low calorific value of the hunter-gatherer diet, much of a mother's food intake will go to the child during this time, so that she will not ovulate. Because of this principle hunter-gatherer populations tend naturally to stay at subsistence-level lows, as also seems to have been the case in prehistoric times.

Yet such a way of life does not necessarily mean the lack of any cultural side. As Laurens van der Post has pointed out, while today's last surviving bushmen no longer create rock-shelter paintings, they are insistent that their ancestors did, the evidence for this being found in rock paintings all over Africa. The very fact that painting, including hand prints, had so early become widely developed as an art form is in itself one indication of the truth of this. Music is another cultural form enjoyed by living hunter-gatherer peoples, and which undoubtedly had its origins well before the end of the Ice Age (flutes have been found dating back to Neanderthal times), even though there is relatively little evidence of it in the paintings.

Religion is another cultural activity evident in the lives of present-day hunter-gatherer peoples. They exhibit reverence for the natural world around them, and the process by which life comes into being, as reflected in the elaborate religious ceremonies they conduct. The repertoire of rock paintings by hunter-gatherer peoples, ancient and modern, as found throughout the world, also includes hand prints, which appear to have been created during special ceremonies and to have some magical or religious significance.

That such practices and attitudes hark back to a very distant past is readily indicated by 'fertility goddess' statuettes which have been found dating from as early as 20,000 BC. While facial details are often absent, these positively flaunt the greatly exaggerated breasts and hips that Khoisan bushmen admire to this day. Likewise the very name that the Khoisan give themselves, Qhwai-xkhwe, reflects their pride in the fact that from earliest infancy their males sport naturally semi-erect penises, a condition that they retain throughout their lives.[16]

Something similar to this hunter-gatherer way of life would undoubtedly have been being pursued by people throughout the world during the last millennia of the Ice Age, and the first millennia of its aftermath. In all sorts of ways it was in harmony with the post-Ice Age geographical changes – the constantly rising sea-levels, the coastlines disappearing beneath the waves, the unprecedented high rainfall punctuated by the intermittent periods of aridity. No one owned any one particular patch of land, nor had anyone yet devised the permanent type of house that you might erect on such land. So if the task of satisfying your food and water-supply needs became too difficult in any one locality you simply moved on to another. Ice Age or no Ice Age, that was the way that people had survived for countless millennia.

But then, and very particularly all around those Black Sea environs, a most profound and far-reaching change in lifestyle began to happen.

CHAPTER 7

THE FIRST GENETICISTS

There can be little doubt that the principal plant domesti-
cates and some of the animals too came ... from Turkey.[1]
Colin Renfrew, Professor of Archaeology,
University of Cambridge

Among the rock engravings that have been found carved by ancient hands into the limestone at Kobystan, in former Soviet Armenia on the western side of the Caspian Sea, is a scene that at first sight may seem nothing special. Male figures are depicted driving cattle and goats (or possibly sheep with a goat-like appearance) into what looks to be either a net, or some sort of fenced enclosure [fig 10].[2] This scene is in fact representative of a profound revolution. For no longer are the people depicted as hunting the animals

Fig 10 When man turned from hunting to animal husbandry? One of the earliest known depictions of cattle and goats being netted or herded into a pen. Rock engraving from Beyuk Dash near Kobystan on the Caspian Sea

upon which they had long preyed. Instead they are apparently corralling them in order to exploit them on a more long-term basis.

This is not to suggest that this particular Kobystan engraving is necessarily the earliest known evidence for this kind of activity. Prehistoric works of art are notoriously difficult to date with any precision, even to the nearest millennium, and this one is no exception. It would have been created at some point after the end of the Ice Age and before the Black Sea Flood. But it is certainly representative of what prehistorians have come to call the Late Stone Age Revolution.

Not long after the end of the Ice Age and some while before the onset of the Black Sea Flood, there occurred in certain localities an unprecedented scaling-down of the old hunter-gatherer ways. Instead of the former hunters roaming around hunting animals that they regarded as good meat-providers, wherever these might happen to congregate, some decided to capture a number of these animals and confine them to chosen locations. They would then milk them where appropriate, and purposefully breed from them, culling some of the progeny for food, while retaining others for ongoing selective breeding.

Likewise, in the case of the plants, the former gatherers rather than collecting these wherever they might happen to grow wild, began to collect the seeds of those plant varieties that they had selected as most useful for their purposes. They would then scatter or dig the seeds into the ground in chosen locations in order to purposefully grow the plants.

These fundamental changes in behaviour patterns had a number of knock-on consequences. For instance, if the products of, say, cereal growing, meant that particularly large amounts of this crop needed to be gathered in, then purpose-built cutting implements, such as sickles, needed to be invented and fashioned for this purpose, still at this stage using Stone Age, that is non-metal materials. Likewise, these changes meant that the people looking after the plants and animals had to remain in the same place over long periods of time, so dwellings of a more permanent type than had ever been used before were now required. These dwellings there-fore needed to be designed and built using more long-lasting materials.

Such is the broad picture, and although many of the details are far from clear, science has recently developed some fascinating ways of retrieving data that might have been supposed lost for ever. For instance, in only the last few decades archaeologists and palaeoethnobotanists have devised a now well-tested method of determining the vari-eties of crops that were being grown by communities many millennia ago. Called 'flotation', this is based on the principle that if soil taken from a dated level at an archaeological site is immersed in water, the lower specific gravity of its potential-ly interesting organic residues – seeds, plant remains, and so on – will cause these to stay afloat. Stones and other unwant-ed debris, with a heavier specific gravity will sink to the bottom.[3] Seeds that have been carbonised through a fire have been found to survive particularly well. After the flotation process, the seeds are sieved, dried, and examined under a microscope, so that palaeoethnobotanical experts can often quite easily identify the particular plant variety from which they have derived. The same expertise can even distinguish wild plant varieties from domesticated ones.

Much the same principle can be applied to the evaluation of animal remains that are found at archaeological sites, experts again being able to distinguish the different species represented. If a particular species is present in very high proportions, this may be a powerful indicator that they were being kept in managed herds rather than hunted out in the wild. Lower leg bones may show signs of tethering over long periods. And in some instances it is also possible to distinguish human-bred, or domesticated species, from their wild counterparts.

Plant domestication may actually have happened by accident when, with the ending of the Ice Age, there was a prolific growth and spread of edible wild grasses – the ancestors of our cereals – due to the abundance of lakes on the land in the wake of the ice sheets' withdrawal. Peoples settled in the vicinity of these rich and readily storable food sources, which also attracted herds of grazing animals. They developed tools for harvesting and preparing these – sickles, mortars, pestles – and found that they did not need to move around as much as they had of old.

This was the phase that archaeologists have labelled the Natufian culture, a typical site of this being Tell Abu Hureyra in the Euphrates valley where this flows through northern Syria, not far from Turkey's south eastern border. Excavations that were carried out here during the early 1970s by archaeologist Andrew Moore of Oxford's Pitt Rivers Museum,[4] between c.11,000 BC and 9500 BC – that is between the end of the main Ice Age and the onset of the Younger Dryas mini Ice Age – determined that a pioneer group of humans built themselves some simple reed huts. Their intention was clearly to harvest the stands of wheat and rye that grew naturally in this region, using sickles fashioned from deer antler that they then studded with flakes of flint. Experiments have shown that even with so 'primitive' an instrument a family group could in three weeks easily provide themselves with enough grain to last a year.[5] With herds of gazelle also grazing in the vicinity, no doubt sometimes availing themselves of the same grasses, the Tell Abu Hureyra folk also appear to have mounted hunting raids to net these creatures and bring them back to the settlement for meat.

The work of detailed analysis of Tell Abu Hureyra's plant and animal remains fell principally to Moore's co-worker Gordon Hillman. From Hillman's finding of a high proportion of young male gazelles represented among the animal bones he inferred that these had been specially chosen in order to optimise the breeding potential of the rest of the herd – the beginnings of animal husbandry. Further, similar analyses revealed that the early Tell Abu Hureyra folk had fished and gathered mussels in the nearby Euphrates, and collected wild lentils, hackberries, caper berries and a variety of nuts similar to pistachio.[6]

But this seemingly near-idyllic way of existence came to a harsh end with the onset of the Younger Dryas mini Ice Age, and widespread desiccation. Both in Tell Abu Hureyra's middle Euphrates region, and also at other Natufian sites such as Jericho, Beidha and Mureybet in what are now Israel and Jordan, the food supply became so seriously depleted by the new markedly drier and colder conditions that the settlers' only recourse was abandonment. Almost all the Natufian-phase archaeological sites exhibit much the same evidence of this. By inference, those inhabitants who did not starve to death were forced to return to the ancestral nomadic hunter-gatherer ways. Or they temporarily went somewhere else to regroup. Perhaps this was to coastal sites that today have been lost to archaeology because of sea-level rise, or perhaps it was to the environs of the Black Sea freshwater lake. We simply do not know.

Then with the ending of the Younger Dryas, toward the end of the 9th millennium BC, Tell Abu Hureyra and many of the other former Natufian sites definitely became re-settled, and this time far more populously than before. This new generation, whether comprising complete newcomers or descendants of the old, had not yet invented pottery, but the developments that they brought with them from wherever they had come, were significant ones. These included new rectangular house-building styles, clever use of reeds for basketry, and a new penchant for burying their dead beneath the floors of their houses.

We will devote more attention to these lifestyle changes a little later. Firstly, however, one of the most fascinating innovations that this post-Younger Dryas generation brought with them – and it has to have been from somewhere other than Tell Abu Hureyra – was an understanding of genetics. They knew how to create genetically as proper domesticated cereals the grasses that their Natufian predecessors had previously harvested wild. For there would now manifest, at sites spread far and wide around the Near East, the earliest known domesticated wheat, known as einkorn, or to give it its scientific name *Triticum monococcum* subspecies *monococcum*.

Among scholars there is considerable debate as to whether this genetic modification occurred from the outset through someone's deliberate intention, or whether it was through circumstances that human enterprise, as a result of observation, caused to repeat. This debate revolves around the fundamental difference between wild wheat and domesticated wheat, specifically concerning how strongly the nutritious seed may or may not be attached to the rachis, or upper part of the plant stem.

In wild wheat it is in the plant's interest for the seeds' attachment to be weak. This will enable them more easily to break away and scatter, and thereby propagate the plants next generation. The cultivator, on the other hand, wants the seeds' attachment to be strong, so that the seeds will not spill on to the ground and be wasted the moment the plant is cut down, but instead remain with it until all the harvest has been brought together for threshing. Given the considerable impact that Stone Age sickles would have made upon the einkorn's stems, those plants with the toughest rachis would inevitably be the ones that were gathered in. The seeds retained from these for the new sowing would then automatically have possessed the stronger rachis properties that they could then pass on to the next generation, and the next, and so on. But whether by accident or design, ulti-mately human observation must have become involved – not least with regard to the crucial act of holding back and planting seeds – for what we may now term 'agricultural choices' have to have been made. These advances are similar then to those that the Natufian hunters made with regard to the beginnings of animal husbandry.

All too often scholars writing on these topics assume that it must have been the men in prehistoric societies who took the crucial decisions whereby their society changed from that of roaming hunter-gatherers to settling as cultivators and herds-people. However this may reflect current rather than past male-mindedness. Since traditionally women were prehistoric society's prime gatherers, arguably it is they who would have made most of the valuable day-to-day observations of plants' and captive animals' sexual behaviour upon which the life-changing decisions were based. It is they who would then have been the repository of what today we would term scientific wisdom, although in their time this would have come more into the category of religion, mystery and magic. It may therefore be no accident that the surviving religious statuettes from the Late Stone Age period are almost all of fertility goddesses, not gods.

But whatever the answer, there is one further hard fact that can positively be retrieved from this phase of prehistoric past, in this instance thanks to the development of the modern-day science of DNA fingerprinting. This is determin-ing the likeliest location of the first switching of einkorn wheat from its wild form to its domesticated one. In the mid 1990s a consortium of European scientists, Manfred Heun from the University of Norway, Ralf Schäfer-Pregl and Francesco Salamini from Cologne's Max Planck Institute, and others, assembled specimens of ancient einkorn that had been collected from a number of post-Younger Dryas archae-ological sites in an arc stretching from Iran to the Balkans.

The sites that they sampled included Tell Abu Hureyra and Mureybit. They also assembled specimens of einkorn that still grow wild to this day. From extensive DNA profiling of all the assembled specimens the team's clear finding was that the earliest domestication of einkorn had happened not at Syria's Tell Abu Hureyra, nor in Israel, Iraq or Iran. Instead it was in the environs of a volcanic mountain called Karacadag amongst the Taurus mountains in eastern Turkey.[7] The closest match the team found to the earliest domesticated einkorn was a wild strain *Triticum monococum* subspecies *boeoticum*, which today still grows in this same mountain region. So was it Turkey that at this point of time was acting as a cradle for humankind's most innovative developments?

Because it is still so difficult for people to accept Turkey, rather than Egypt or Mesopotamia, as any kind of early cradle of civilisation, Heun and his colleagues' findings were greeted more with scepticism[8] than any enthusiastic acceptance, just as were those of Ryan and Pitman. Yet these findings are readily corroborated by other studies which similarly indicate that the cultivated varieties of a number of other plants originated very broadly from these same environs of the Black Sea area. Decades before the Heun team's findings, the plant specialist M. Hopf produced a most intriguing agricultural map. This showed that besides einkorn, other cultivators' staples such as barley, lentils and chick peas, rye and broad beans all originated in the environs of Turkey and upper Mesopotamia before then diffusing across Europe and into North Africa. Indeed, it was effectively from this same western Asian region that there originated virtually all Europe's subsequent plant cultivation knowledge. The spread of this can be traced slowly but steadily, making its way westwards over a period of some four thousand years, a rate that has been calculated as an average of one kilometre (half a mile) a year as the crow flies.[9]

Another plant that originates in western Asia and appears on Hopf's map, to be used in this instance not for food, but for woven clothing, is *Linum usitatissimum*, or flax. The decision to cultivate this was another major developmental milestone. For as we have earlier inferred, in the immediate aftermath of the Ice Age any clothing, such as is known to have been worn at all, was mostly made from animal skin, or from grass, or from string. Indeed, in the case of women, a string skirt would seem to have been in vogue from at least as far back as 20,000 BC and for many millennia after. This was featured in the Tassili frescoes,[10] its skimpiness seemingly suggesting that it was designed more for titillation than for warmth.

But again sometime around the 8th millennium BC a momentous innovative leap forward took place. The process of soaking the flax plant to produce thread that could be gathered on a spindle for making string had already long been developed, in all likelihood way back in the Ice Age. Now someone decided to affix the linen threads vertically at close intervals on a rectangular frame, then to pass other threads horizontally across these at similarly close intervals. While initially this may have originated accidentally, as a mere variant of the dextrous plaiting of palm leaves at which Melanesians (for one) are so adept to this day, the result was revolutionary. Suddenly here was a type of covering surprisingly strong, yet very light and supple, that overnight was born and would become the textile industry.

And where was the world's earliest known scrap of textile found? At Çayönü in south-eastern Turkey, an ancient site that is located in the upper reaches of the Tigris river, and is part of the very same Taurus foothills region that, to the best of our present-day knowledge, also saw einkorn's first domestication. The textile scrap in question was found in the early 1990s during excavations by archaeologists from the University of Chicago and Istanbul

University. It appears to have ended its useful life rather ignominiously, serving as a rag to enable someone to get a better grip on a handle. But the important fact, as the University of Chicago team have stressed, is that radio–carbon dating has showed it to date to *c*.7000 BC, thereby giving it a currently firm place in the record books as the world's oldest known piece of textile. Furthermore, as the archaeologists pointed out, when they had found flax seed at Çayönü, they had supposed that this was used only for the production of linseed oil. However, in the light of the find of the textile scrap they had to revise their opinion, to con-clude that the seeds were sown and flax was cultivated and processed into linen threads, and the cloth woven from these, all at the same Çayönü site.

Of course this is not to say that the first ever cultivation of flax for textile use occurred at Çayönü. The survival of tex-tiles from the ancient past is so much a matter of chance that such a deduction would be rash indeed. But undeniably the region in which there originated a major step on the road to 'civilisation' again seems to have been Turkey and (very broadly) the environs of the Black Sea.

Even before the finds at Çayönü, the plant geneticist Dr Hans Helbaek of Copenhagen had specifically suggested that linen textiles and agriculture both originated from much the same Anatolian (Turkish) region. He based this on his studies of *linum bienne*, which grows wild in Turkey, and which he interprets as the direct ancestor of 'domesticated' flax (*linum usitatissimum*). However there can be no certain-ty, since there are indirect indications of textiles, though no specific textile fragments, also from around the 7000 BC period, that have been found at Jarmo in north-eastern Iraq in the form of the impressions of woven fabrics found on lumps of clay.[11]

In the case of animal domestication it was again in the environs of Turkey and the regions immediately to its east

that there roamed wild the varieties of sheep and goats that
were the earliest to be domesticated, those who domesticated them thereby arguably hailing from these same regions.
Sheep have been domesticated for so long that it is easy to
think of them as a pushover for any hunter. However this is
to forget that their ancestor was the mouflon, a mountain
animal still to be found in the Sahara, where it is highly
respected as an agile beast, full of courage, with a very acute
sense of smell, around which has developed a rich folklore.[12]
To this day amongst the Tuareg a mouflon hunter, who traditionally hunts with a spear, commands far more esteem
than a gazelle hunter.

The archaeology of Turkey and the Near East shows that
it was specifically in the post-Ice Age pre-Flood period that
the discovered animal remains reveal clear indications of a
major transition from their being hunted to their being kept
as livestock.

At Zawi Chemi, a site just south of Turkey's south-eastern
border with Iraq, prehistoric animal bones of wild sheep,
wild goat and red deer, suddenly give way in the uppermost
level, datable c.8000 BC, to a very high ratio of young
animals. For archaeologists this represents a strong indication that sheep herding had become the prevailing
occupation.[13]

At 'Ain Ghazal in Jordan, settled around the end of the
8th millennium BC, while the archaeologists found the animal
remains to include more than 45 wild species (not all
necessarily hunted – they included tortoise), around half the
settlement's overall meat consumption was represented by
domesticated goats. The fact that these goats were fully
under human control was clearly indicated by bony growths
to their ankle joints, showing that they had been kept tethered for long periods of time, and on soft farmland instead of
the stony terrain that they prefer.[14] It is impossible to determine with any precision exactly where animals were first

domesticated – it is extremely difficult to draw a line between the keeping captive of certain wild animals, and the embarking upon full domestication pasturage and breeding programmes for them. However, a recent study led by Melinda Zeder of Washington's American Museum of Natural History has shown that in the Zagros mountain region of what is today Iran and Iraq to Turkey's east, the goat had already become domesticated as early as 8000 BC.[15] And back in the early part of the last century the Australian archaeologist Vere Gordon Childe certainly established that Europe's oldest domesticated sheep is descended from an Asiatic species, *Ovis vignei*, native to Turkestan and Afghanistan.[16]

Cattle seem to have been domesticated a millennium or so later than sheep or goats, arguably because some of the prehistoric wild varieties were large and fearsome creatures such as the now-extinct aurochs. The evidence for this will be reviewed in a later chapter, but suffice it to note that when cattle domestication does occur, it is again in the Turkey/Anatolia environs that this appears to have happened, at least from the best available evidence.

As the eminent Cambridge University archaeology professor Colin Renfrew summed up the matter even back in the late 1980s, before the Taurus mountains einkorn and textile findings: 'There can be little doubt that the principal plant domesticates and some of the animals too came ... from Anatolia [Turkey]'.[17]

We are then faced with the fact that during the post-Ice Age, pre-Black Sea Flood period, when sea-levels were rising, and the land suffered some savage shifts from drought to heavy rainfall, the environs of the Black Sea was peopled with some surprisingly innovative individuals. So does this give us any more insights into the owners of the 6th millennium BC houses that Robert Ballard has begun to find beneath the Black Sea? First we need to look to the other evidence of how far this society had developed at a time five millennia before Egypt had built its first pyramid.

CHAPTER 8

THE FIRST ACCOUNTING

About 8000 BC ... an entirely new system of clay tokens was created to keep track of goods ... Since these counters seem to stand for quantities of cereals and units of animal count, this suggests that grain and flocks played a predominant rôle in the first accounting.[1]

Denise Schmandt-Besserat

Today we take so much for granted that it is often difficult to appreciate that for virtually every aspect of our everyday lives there has been one particular time and place in our human development when it was introduced. Already we have seen this in the case of the cultivation of the first true cereals and the weaving of the first true textiles around the 8th and 7th millennia BC. And we have also found, perhaps to our surprise, that instead of such developments happening in those traditional cradles, Egypt or Mesopotamia, they actually surfaced in Turkey, where we might have expected to find hardly any civilisation at all at so early a period.

But what about something as basic as the invention of the first rectangular room? As we noted of the earliest, Natufian phase at Tell Abu Hureyra, the pre-Younger Dryas people lived in simple reed huts, the basic floor plan of which was round. This shape of floor has in fact never completely died out, persisting in North Africa into Roman times in the form of traditional thatched huts called *mapalia*, with some cultures, such as Zulus with their *kraals*, perpetuating it to this day. The similarly traditional 'yurt' is a design still chosen today for some Australian homes.

But when Tell Abu Hureyra became re-settled after its Younger Dryas mini Ice Age evacuation, c.9000 BC, among the several startling and seemingly unprecedented innovations that its new inhabitants brought back with them was a rectangular architectural design plan. This they used for the floors and walls of both their rooms and what we can now call houses as distinct from huts. Another concomitant major and very long-lasting innovation was that they began using significantly more permanent construction materials, such as stone, wood and mud-brick, for these houses. Also making its debut at this time was the use of lime plaster as a smooth coating for the house walls, to complement their rectangularity by giving them a clean, regular surface.

Elsewhere the dwellings that were built at several other post-Younger Dryas sites – most notably Asikli in central Turkey, Çayönü in eastern Turkey, Tell Halula and Mureybet in north Syria and Beidha in Jordan – likewise began to feature some if not all of these same revolutionary new features. Frustratingly, the vagaries of radio-carbon dating make it as yet impossible to determine exactly who amongst these was the first with any one such idea. A further complication is that certainly at sites like Çayönü and Tell Abu Hureyra some archaeologists have freely admitted they are stumped to explain where the settlers could have been during the Younger Dryas that they came back (or arrived new), with so many fundamental innovations.[2]

The Asikli site, a 15-metre (50-foot) high mound which stands on the western side of present-day Turkey's Konya plain, to the south-east of the town of Aksaray, is particularly interesting from this point of view. Even today the Konya region has the reputation for being well watered and serving as the 'breadbasket' of Turkey. But back in the early post-Younger Dryas period, when the rains had resumed in earnest, its environs were even more watery. The Asikli settlement stood on the western shores of the then vast Konya lake, of which the present Lake Tuz may be a remnant, and it had a most spectacular backdrop of the 10,673-foot high Hasan Dag volcano's twin peaks, an important source for the obsidian so highly prized for cutting implements during this period.

As revealed by excavations carried out by University of Istanbul archaeologists in 1989 and 1990,[3] Asikli is formed from at least ten different building levels. The earliest of these, although inaccessible because of the Konya plain's high water table, would seem to date from shortly after the end of the Younger Dryas arid period, that is c.9000 BC. Some 400 of its houses have been excavated. These were built from mud-bricks and meticulously-shaped blocks of the local volcanic stone, and were laid out with courtyards and roadways in a rigorously orthogonal street plan suggestive of proper town planning, another near if not actual world first for Turkey.

Entry and exit to the dwellings was via holes in the roof, openings that served also as chimney-type ventilation for the hearths. The floors were plastered, and then protected with mats woven from reeds and grain stalks, some of which left clear imprints of themselves on the plaster. The dead were buried beneath the rooms' floors, and laid to rest complete with their jewellery, one woman being found adorned with necklaces of beads, semi-precious stones and copper, one of the very earliest known examples of the use of metallurgy.[4] The surrounding fields were tilled for growing cereals, the Konya plain then, as today, no doubt producing abundant crops. And there were also in the environs open-air shops whose owners apparently worked and traded in the obsidian derived from the volcano.

But just when life might have seemed positively humming, Asikli was to have its own individual taste of disaster. Around 8000 BC the Hasan Dag volcano erupted. And although the inhabitants appear to have been able to make their escape, the settlement and its surrounding fields were buried beneath a blanket of volcanic ash.

It is important to bear in mind that Asikli was simply representative of a number of settlements, not only in Turkey, but also further east, in Northern Syria and Iraq, and in Palestine, many of which exhibit similar developmental advances. We cannot therefore point a finger at any one region where these advances might primarily have been coming from. Nowhere at this early time do we see anything of the concentration and centralisation of wealth and power into the hands of one autocratic individual, such as a king or a queen, which would later characterise Egypt and Mesopotamia. Indeed this is one of the reasons why it is so difficult to convey just how civilised these early societies had become.

Black Sea Flood or no Black Sea Flood therefore, this is not to suggest that these early Turkey and northern Mesopotamia based societies were under some master-potentate's control whose headquarters have yet not been found. Rather, what is exciting about them is that the innovations appearing amongst relatively small, autonomous communities were made possible because of the greater ease by which, thanks to the developments of agriculture and animal husbandry, they could now obtain their food. This at least allowed certain individuals amongst them the time and leisure to specialise experimenting in new technology and new materials, the birth of the first trades.

Thus, although the occasional human figure had been carved in bone from as long ago as the Ice Age, it was again during the 8th millennium BC that there appeared the earliest known example of one modelled in clay. A nude female figurine found at the early site of Mureybet in northern Syria has been called the first clay sculpture. From such modelling with clay it could only be a matter of time before the technique would be adapted to create liquid-carrying vessels, thereby bringing into being the western world's first pottery.[5] And indeed this happened within a millennium.

While again because of the vagaries of radio-carbon dating it is impossible to be exactly sure where the very first true pottery artefacts were made, in keeping with the trend for Turkey to have been a major source of innovation, Beldibi in south west Turkey is certainly one of the leading contenders.[6] However Ganjdareh 1,370 kilometres (850 miles) to the east in the Kermanshah region of western Iran also produced some very early pottery. With the further complication of such a wide geographical difference clearly it is impossible for anyone to be sure which came first.

Archaeologists tend to make a great fuss of pottery, because the varying fashions in it from one period to another provide an important means of sequencing and dating levels of occupation. In fact, it is just one of the more durable and visible of the Late Stone Age period's technological innovations. From the very manner in which pottery often appears comparatively late in the occupation levels of the earliest settlements it is clear that back in the 'Before the Flood' era peoples may well have prioritised all sorts of other developments. However, direct evidence of these does not always survive.

Woodworking and basketry, for instance, were almost certainly produced to a high level of craftsmanship, although all too often these can only be merely glimpsed at, as in the case of the impressions made by the rush mats as used at Asikli. At several sites, such as 'Ain Ghazal in Jordan, also dating from this same c.8000 BC period, the finding of burin-type flint chisels strongly suggests that these had been developed to work on the plant materials used in basketry, as well as for shaping wood and bone. However because, unlike pottery, such organic materials will almost invariably have perished after ten millennia, we can merely guess at the period's woodworking and basketry accomplishments.

Advanced as we are finding the 'Before the Flood' epoch to be, there is of course one development that we would certainly not expect to find until several millennia into the future: writing. This is because all textbooks about ancient history dictate that hieroglyphs and cuneiform were first used for writing purposes sometime in the 3rd millennium BC, and in Egypt and Mesopotamia.

The use of symbols or tokens to denote an object or commodities is one of the fundamental principles from which the invention of writing sprang. Recent findings suggest that even in this there were some important developments which took place during the 'Before the Flood' era.

For in 1969 the Radcliffe Institute[7] based at Cambridge, Massachusetts, gave American graduate scholar Denise Schmandt-Besserat the task of studying how clay was first used in the Near East before this region had developed pottery. With characteristic diligence Schmandt-Besserat sifted patiently through innumerable museums' dusty collections of clay objects that archaeologists had turned up at 'Before the Flood' sites in Turkey, Iraq, Iran, Syria and Israel. In collection after collection she came across strange miniature clay cones, spheres, disks, and so on.

From the care with which these objects had been shaped, and the special hardening by fire to which they had been subjected – they may well have been the first clay objects to receive such treatment – it was self-evident that some considerable importance had been attached to them. Yet when Schmandt-Besserat questioned the archaeologists in whose excavations these objects had turned up, they all expressed bafflement concerning what function or purpose they might have served. Some archaeologists had even omitted to mention the objects in their archaeological reports, while others had simply catalogued them as 'of uncertain purpose'.

In fact, the key to understanding these mystery objects has been around for decades, in the form of a peculiar egg-shaped hollow tablet of the 2nd millennium BC that was found as far back as the late 1920s at Nuzi, north of Babylon. This was inscribed in cuneiform:

> Counters representing small cattle
> 21 ewes that lamb
> 6 female lambs
> 8 full grown male sheep
> 4 male lambs
> 6 she-goats that kid
> 1 he-goat
> 3 female kids
> The seal of Ziqarru the shepherd[8]

When Nuzi's excavators opened up the hollow tablet they found it to contain 49 counters, exactly corresponding to the number of animals listed on its outside. However so little attention was paid to the shapes of the actual counters – these were described simply as 'pebbles' in the original site report – that they were not recorded properly and in subsequent years disappeared. Other ancient texts, such as one referring to the remainder of 'the account' being 'held in the leather pouch' were not understood as referring to accounting tokens.[9]

It took years of research and all Schmandt-Besserat's powers of detective-work and deduction eventually to recognise that here, specifically from the 'Before the Flood' period, lay a surprisingly sophisticated accounting system, as such undoubtedly the very oldest in the world. Different shapes of counter were used to denote different livestock and commodities [fig 11]. At the last count Schmandt-Besserat had identified some 80 intact and unopened

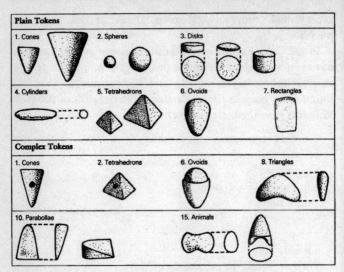

Fig 11 Token accounting system, dating back to *c*.8000 BC, i.e. before the Flood, as discovered by Denise Schmandt-Besserat. Each shape of token denotes a different variety of animal or commodity

'accounts', and had also found that in another form of the system the counters had holes drilled through them so that they could be kept on a string, as a prehistoric form of tally.

According to Schmandt-Besserat the earliest of the tokens can be dated to *c*.8000 BC, no less than five thousand years before the first Egyptian hieroglyphs and Mesopotamian cuneiform. Yet when they appeared they did so in a surprisingly advanced form, the oldest known collection, for instance, consisting of 6 cones, 101 spheres, 5 disks, 73 cylinders, 1 tetrahedron, 4 ovoids, 1 rectangle, 1 triangle and 1 animal head. This example happens to have been found at Tepe Asiab in the Zagros Mountains in the Kermansha area of Iran. Here the comparatively primitive inhabitants had only recently turned from hunter-gathering to growing cereals, and appear to have turned to the token system to keep track of their new grain-based economy.

So the question arises – did these rather remote Iranians invent a system that then became surprisingly international, or did they simply borrow it from someone else who had invented it yet earlier? As Schmandt-Besserat has been at pains to stress, the answer to this is far from clear. The inhabitants of 'Ain Ghazal in Jordan, who specialised in goat-keeping, also had the tokens at a very early period.[10] And Beldibi in south-west Turkey was also using them before the end of the 8th millennium BC. So it is quite possible that the system, which became very widespread, originated at an eastern Turkish site which has yet to be found, though at the present stage of the evidence, this remains but one possibility. In Schmandt-Besserat's own words:

> northern Mesopotamia [which includes eastern Turkey adjoining the south-eastern corner of the Black Sea] cannot be dismissed as a possible cradle since the absence of early 8th millennium tokens in the region probably reflects only a lack of excavations.[11]

The Late Stone Age Revolution of c.8000 BC meant the production of quantities of cereals and animals. Some method of keeping track of these units was required, and once a whole new, and surprisingly international, accounting system had been invented, then controlling numbers quite clearly became a matter of serious concern.

There is also another notable new feature of so many of the the post-Younger Dryas, Pre-Flood settlements. This is that although they were small villages by our modern standards, by the earlier prehistoric norm they were very large indeed, far larger than the groups of old who had lived by hunter-gathering. As indicated by the number of houses in any one settlement, from what had been dozens the community numbers quickly and unprecedentedly rose to hundreds and even the low thousands.

One intriguing explanation that anthropologists have offered for this population increase is the fact that cereals provide a very much more calorie-rich diet than the day-to-day products of hunter-gathering.[12] We noted earlier that present-day Khoisan hunter-gatherer mothers commonly breast-feed their babies to the age of five, causing a serious drain on their own calorie-intake. A human female needs to be above a certain level of body fat in order to ovulate, so when hunter-gatherer mothers continue to breast-feed for five years or more, they will become pregnant far fewer times than would otherwise have been the case. In cereal-growing societies, by contrast, the high nutrition value in cereal grains cancels out the calorie drain. Providing the supply of grain is reasonably constant it keeps the females comfortably above the critical minimum, enabling them to produce babies considerably more often.

So there is a reasonable case for the post-Younger Dryas rapid population rise of c.9000 BC having been due to the elimination of this natural birth-rate regulator. Whatever the reason, the population rise did occur and from communities that only relatively recently consisted of small wandering groups, there now sprang up significant-size townships. And the inhabitants of these townships came to possess a great many more accoutrements than anyone had ever had before, such as agricultural implements, herds of livestock, and so on.

This immediately raises the issue of what might happen to these large communities and all their assemblage of livestock, goods and chattels, should circumstances change for the worse. Hunter-gatherers, if faced by some threat to their survival such as a flood or a drought, have relatively few encumbrances to hinder them from relocating in a new terrain that might have the resources to sustain them for a while longer. But for those who have grown accustomed to cereal growing and to animal husbandry the sudden non-viability or loss of the terrain on which they had previously carried out these pursuits is a very different matter. Their livelihood depends on their maintaining the number of animals that they have bred, preserving the resources and know-how that they have assembled to grow grain, and finding land to which they can transport their herds, seeds, agricultural implements, and so on to start again. Any such relocation has to be a major and traumatic affair. And if they need to cross water, they may even need to devise or procure some means of transport for this – just as the biblical Noah and his counterparts are described as having done when they were confronted with their Flood.

For, if one artefact stands out above all others in the Noah family of Flood stories, it has to be the boat, or ark. In order to transport across open water the eight humans and large numbers of livestock that is inferred from any sensible reading of the biblical story, the vessel can hardly have been built just from some hollowed out log. It would have to have been a vessel of substantial size. So what do we know of the 'Before the Flood' society's capabilities to produce such a vessel, and when and where did the invention of boats occur?

Even during the Ice Age, and tens of millennia before the first horse and cart, people were moving around the world in boats. For instance, according to the latest radio-carbon datings, those who moved into Australia from south-east Asia did so around 60,000 BC. To make the crossing they had to negotiate at least 170 kilometres (105 miles) of open sea, because even when the sea-levels were much lower than now there was always a major ocean channel separating Australia from Asia. So they had to have had boats even back then.[13]

Likewise, boats were certainly traversing substantial

distances across the Mediterranean during the early post-
Younger Dryas/pre-Black Sea Flood period. This is evident,
even without the discovery of any actual boats surviving
from this period, from the far-reaching trade in the prized
cutting stone obsidian that was being carried out during this
time. One feature of obsidian is that each piece carries a
characteristic structural signature that enables its place of
origin to be scientifically traced.

For instance, in the case of an intensively-studied cave at
Franchthi, Greece, which was inhabited from the 8th millennium BC onwards,[14] scientists have determined that the
obsidian found amongst the debris of its early occupation
levels was brought to it from the island of Melos. This lies
120 kilometres (75 miles) across the sea to the south-east. In
this part of the Mediterranean any lower sea-levels at that
time would have made little difference to the sea journey.
And while it is possible that a longer, more indirect route
could have been taken, going partly overland, even this
would have involved several hops from one island to
another.

Much the same can be inferred from recent discoveries
concerning the earliest human colonisation of the
Mediterranean island Cyprus, just south of Turkey. As
Cyprus' geological record shows, the island, at present 70
kilometres (43 miles) from the coast of Turkey, was never
much closer to it, let alone joined to it. It is also known that
up to the 10th millennium BC its only native animal species
were dwarf elephant, pygmy hippopotamus, two species of
mouse and one of a shrew. And when the Younger Dryas
mini Ice Age occurred and the elephant and hippopotamus
population was wiped out, this left Cyprus just to the mice
and shrews.

Then in c.7000 BC the first human colonists arrived. They
were quite a maverick group, who settled in some 30 different sites, the most well-known of which is Khirokitia. And

they constructed some rather old-fashioned style round-houses for their dwellings, utilising the excellent local stone for this purpose.[15]

But, for our purposes, the most interesting aspect to the colonists is that they introduced to Cyprus plants and animals that the island had never seen before. Suddenly there appeared on the island sheep, goat and pig, plus wild deer. As evident from bone counts, the wild deer, of the fallow variety *Dama mesopotamica*, actually constituted between 20 and 50 per cent of the islanders' total meat intake, a pattern not seen elsewhere. Although wild deer cannot be domesticated in the manner of farm animals, they can be hand-fed and kept tame in confined areas of grazing land, then culled when the next meal of venison is required, which seems to have been the pioneer Cypriotes' policy.

All of which leads to the fundamental deduction, that sometime around 7000 BC one or more vessels – carrying a migrant human population, breeding populations of their livestock, and plant and seed varieties for cultivation pur-poses – must have set off from the Turkish mainland for Cyprus. Even before the Black Sea Flood, there took place a major relocation by herds-people and agriculturalists very much in the manner of Noah in his ark.

Of the mode of construction of such vessels Genesis 6: 14 mentions reeds having been used for Noah's ark. Likewise the Gilgamesh version of the Noah family of Flood stories describes Uta-napishti, the Akkadian 'Noah', as being instructed to demolish a 'reed fence', in order to provide materials for his Flood-beating boat. This is corroborated by the earliest surviving depictions of prehistoric boats. The Tassili rock paintings, and ancient Egyptian petroglyphs feature boats that appear to have been made from bundles of dried reeds. And unlikely as it may sound, the bundling of reeds provides a most serviceable material. Naturally buoyant, when lashed together to form a floating platform, reeds are more than capable of coping with the open sea, particularly if the prow and stern are raised by further lashing. As commented by the Norwegian navigator Thor Heyerdahl, of 'Kon Tiki' fame, whose ocean-going 'Ra' was constructed in precisely this way:

> A reed boat of the classic type ... is beyond any doubt the safest type of watercraft ever invented by maritime experts. Compact as a hard rubber ball and buoyant as a cork, it will ride the crest of the waves like a seabird and survive any hurricane, because it has no hull to fill. The bundle-body of the reed boat permits it to enter surf and shallows without need of bailing or fear of springing a leak. In stability and carrying capacity it exceeds any wooden hull of the same size.[16]

For archaeologists, the reed boat's one great disadvantage is that its components are so environmentally friendly. This has to mean that the chances of any such vessel surviving in any recognisable form across nine thousand years are minute. But even without the archaeological discovery of a single cargo boat from this early period, the evidence from Cyprus and elsewhere for such boats' existence – and built to a substantial size – is irrefutable. Which makes one of the most crucial components of the Noah family of stories, the existence, as early as the 6th millennium BC, of an ark capable of carrying a substantial number of humans, totally possible.

So far then, we have seen the pre-Flood period to be a perhaps-surprisingly advanced one, involving the invention of several of the elements that we most take for granted in our 'civilised' life. We have also seen how settled communities increased greatly in numbers compared to those of their hunter-gather forbears. Even so, however, in most places the numbers remained relatively small. Khirokitia's pre-Flood inhabitants, for instance, probably never numbered more than 300 to 600.[17] Asikli's may have mustered around a thousand, likewise pre-Flood Jericho.

But was there anywhere larger? From all that we have seen of it, the pre-Flood era appears to have been before the custom for autocrats to rule their empires from large capitals. Despite this was there a New York, Manchester, or Sydney of the time? Was there a pre-Flood metropolis?

As we are about to see, there most certainly was. Even though it was discovered four decades ago, it has so far remained little known outside archaeological journals. And it too was in what is now Turkey. Its name? Çatal Hüyük, the mound (*hüyük*) at the road-fork.

CHAPTER 9

A STONE AGE METROPOLIS

Neolithic civilisation revealed at Çatal Hüyük shines like a supernova among the rather dim galaxy of contemporary peasant cultures.

James Mellaart

It was just before nightfall on a chilly day in November 1958, and literally in the teeth of hostility from local sheep-dogs, that the then Ankara-based British archaeologist James Mellaart, with two companions, made the first visit to Çatal Hüyük which fired him to excavate the mound. The site covers 32 acres and is at an elevation of 910 metres (3000 feet) – very safe from any Black Sea Flood. It stands on Turkey's well-watered Konya plain some 210 kilometres (130 miles) south of Ankara. As Mellaart later recalled of his first inspection of it:

> Much ... was covered by turf and ruin-weed (*peganum harmala*) but where the prevailing south-westerly winds had scoured its surface bare there were unmistakable traces of mud-brick buildings, burned red in a conflagra-tion contrasting with patches of grey ash, broken bones, potsherds and obsidian tools and weapons. To our sur-prise these were found not only at the bottom of the mound, but they continued right up to the top, some 15 metres [50 feet] above the level of the plain.[1]

To Mellaart even these cursory observations indicated that

the mound was late Stone Age, and that a substantial-size
town of this period had long flourished on the site, only to be
abandoned, thereby saving it from any disturbance by later
cultures building on top of it. Accordingly in 1961 he began
full-scale excavations, concentrating on opening up whole
structures rather than using the theoretically more scientific
grid system of excavation[2] then advocated by fellow-archae-
ologist Kathleen Kenyon under whom he had worked as a
young field-hand at Jericho. Just as the Turkish archaeologists of three decades later would find at Asikli – which
before its volcanic demise faced Çatal Hüyük on opposite
shores of the then huge Konya Lake – the swampy nature of
the ground prevented any reaching down to virgin soil
underneath the site. It was therefore impossible to determine
exactly when the site had first been occupied. Even so
Mellaart was able to reveal 14 building levels one on top of
the other, suggesting perhaps a thousand years of settlement.

The area on which Mellaart principally concentrated his
dig was a small sector of the south-western part of the site,
an area that would prove remarkably productive. Again
exactly as the Turkish excavators would later find at Asikli,
the Çatal Hüyük houses were designed to be rectangular in
shape and therefore much more 'modern' than either the
reed huts of the relatively recent past, or the circular houses
at Khirokitia in Cyprus. As at Asikli the houses lacked external doors, entry being via ladder from holes in the roof.
Although these wooden access ladders had long perished,
their existence could be readily inferred from the clear
marks that some had left where they had rested against plastered walls. Some rooms had ovens and hearths fitted in
them, the positioning of these being standard between one
house and another. And the houses were built in such a way
that only those on the edge of the town had external walls.
So the only natural light came from above, as each dwelling
had a roof level different from those of its neighbours, with

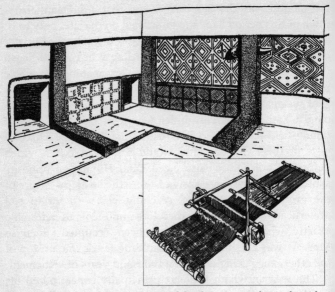

Fig 12 *Kilim* patterns decorating one of the shrines at Çatal Hüyük, with (inset) the most basic loom used for weaving *kilim*, as still used by modern-day nomads

an opening in the uppermost part. Internally there were door-less portholes to enable access between one room and another.

One way in which Çatal Hüyük was different to Asikli, though arguably because of differing availability of materials, was with regard to other construction methods. Whereas at Asikli the builders made good use of the local volcanic stone in combination with mud-brick, at Çatal Hüyük, certainly in its earlier levels, the preferred method was timber-frame. That is, first constructing a skeleton of hardwood that could stand by itself, then cladding this with non-load-bearing walls as required, much as houses used to be built in mediaeval and Tudor England. Hardwoods such

Fig 13 The world's earliest-known landscape painting as found at Çatal Hüyük, depicting a town with a volcano erupting in the background. From a copy of the original painting as made by James Mellaart

as oak and juniper were chosen for this, needing to be specially brought down from forests in the hills set some distance away, probably by floating them down-river. They were then carefully squared using specialist carpentry before being fixed into position as posts and roof beams. The walls were then built up in mud-brick, using rectangular bricks that had been carefully formed to consistent sizes in a wooden mould squared with an adze.[3]

Çatal Hüyük ranks therefore as one of the world's earliest known examples of the use of properly squared-off bricks (albeit unfired) for house building. Its construction methods are also important, particularly the squaring of the hardwoods used for the timber framing. These appear to bear some significant resemblances to those reported for the dwellings that Ballard found out in the Black Sea nearly 480 kilometres (300 miles) to the north (see p.72). Although any such interpretation can only be provisional, since substantially more details are awaited concerning the Black Sea buildings, there is nonetheless a significant inference that both belonged to much the same culture.

Mellaart conducted his excavations at Çatal Hüyük between 1961 and 1965, concentrating his attention on just the easternmost of what are in fact two mounds at the site, the western one, as he determined from superficial surveys, dating from a later period. Overall, even from his opening up of a mere thirtieth of this eastern mound, he brought to light some 150 building units. Extrapolated over the whole mound this means that in Çatal Hüyük's heyday, the 8th and 7th millennia BC, it is likely to have supported a population of between five and seven thousand, larger than anywhere else known from this early time. In common with most other settlements of this relatively peaceful epoch, it was without any kind of defence walls, and by modern-day urban standards would have appeared very rustic. Set on the shores of the then vast but now long dried-out Konya Lake, the first impression that any 8th millennium BC visitor is likely to have gained would be of a thriving farming community. Cattle and sheep would be grazing and extensive crops of wheat and a surprising variety of vegetables would be growing in the surrounding fields. Yet in many respects this pre-Flood metropolis – dating from a time five thousand years before the building of Egypt's Pyramids – was quite extraordinarily advanced and very much an equivalent of, say, a Chicago or Geneva in our own time.

For instance, besides evidence, as at Asikli, of some of the world's earliest known town planning, the general standard of housekeeping in Çatal Hüyük would seem to have been excellent. They kept their rooms clean and tidy, the finding of bones from meal left-overs being rare. They gave the walls a fresh coat of plaster virtually annually. For good sanitation, they even operated an unusually well-ordered refuse system, rubbish being deposited in private courtyards between houses, then regularly burnt.

Everywhere the timber frameworks were painted red, as if this was some kind of 'team' or 'national flag' colour for the town.[4] It also served to emphasise the timber-frame method of house construction, though as noted by Mellaart, the later buildings used less of this and more load-bearing mud-brick. At all periods the mud-brick walls, floors and ceiling were carefully plastered with a fine, locally obtained white clay, then decorated with lively murals and sculptures. And it is particularly the murals – arguably the earliest-known true 'house decorations'[5] – that give us some tantalising glimpses of just how technically and culturally advanced Çatal Hüyük's people had become by the 8th and 7th millennia BC.

Some of the white-plastered walls bear abstract designs which as noted by Mellaart, are complex textile patterns that subsequently became used for Turkish *kilim*, traditional Turkish rugs that are woven on looms. Furthermore since Mellaart insists that the wall-paintings were definitely copied from woven *kilims* rather than the other way round[6] the making of these rugs and the lore associated with them (each design element is said to tell a story), has now to be reckoned to date back an astonishing nine thousand years. To this day *kilims* are often found as colourful wall and floor accessories in Turkish households, in certain communities the more traditional of these being created with the aid of a basic but still technically impressive horizontal ground loom device.[7] We may therefore infer that 'Before the Flood' weavers at Çatal Hüyük had developed at least similar technology, and as such – failing at least any other known predecessor – another world first.

Mellaart also found an important landscape painting on one of the Çatal Hüyük walls. Necessarily dating back some nine thousand years, this of course constitutes a further world first [fig 13]. But what makes this particular landscape so extraordinary is that besides its featuring in its foreground the world's first ever depiction of a town (or at the very least a cluster of town houses), clearly visible in its background is an erupting volcano. As Mellaart has described this:

A clearer picture of a volcano in eruption could hardly have been painted: the fire coming out of the top, lava streams from vents at its base, clouds of smoke and glowing ash hanging over its peak and raining down on and beyond the slopes of the volcano are all combined in this painting.[8]

Because the 7th millennium BC artist depicted the volcano as one with twin peaks, Mellaart and others have confidently identified it as Hasan Dag. Readily visible across the other side of the Konya lake to Çatal Hüyük, Hasan Dag is the only Central Anatolian volcano with this distinctive feature.[9] It was an eruption of Hasan Dag that caused the demise of Asikli, as a result of which one scholar[10] even has suggested that the wall-painting may be a memory of this same eruption. However, the Çatal Hüyük painting dates around a thousand years after the Asikli event. Hasan Dag remained active to the 2nd millennium BC, so the more likely explanation is that the artist simply painted what he (or she), had personally witnessed from Çatal Hüyük.

Other scenes in the Çatal Hüyük wall-paintings provide some striking glimpses of the pre-Flood township's inhabitants and their lifestyle. Men, some wearing leopardskins, are depicted dancing and hunting, a few with dilly bags at their waists, in scenes that bear a striking resemblance to those from the 'Roundhead' phase of the Tassili frescoes. Some depictions show them clad in what appear to be loom-woven loincloths, with their skin being conveyed in red. Sometimes the men's quarry is red deer (*cervus elaphus*), which they are depicted hunting with bow and arrow. In other wall-paintings we find them surrounding, though notably not killing, huge bovines that are identifiable as aurochs (*bos primogenius*), an enormous and now extinct variety of wild cattle.[11] In the opinion of Mellaart's consultant zoologists, Dexter Perkins and Pierre Ducos, the Konya region's abundance of water made it particularly favourable for producing the maximum sizes in such species.[12]

That the rearing of impressive cattle was a pursuit of the greatest importance to Çatal Hüyük's citizens is in fact apparent from a completely different aspect of the archaeological findings, analysis of their food remains. These have showed that some 90 per cent of the town's meat supply derived from cattle, with the creatures also being used as draft animals. Expert study of the bones has also revealed that these animals were already domesticated even from the town's earliest levels. So whatever else we may or may not know about Çatal Hüyük, nine thousand years ago it could certainly be described as a Cattle Town, cattle breeding and raising clearly having been mastered following the earlier domestication of goats and sheep that had been achieved a couple of millennia before.

The successful keeping of domesticated cattle – whether or not these were first domesticated at Çatal Hüyük is impossible to say – was by no means the Çatal Hüyük people's only notable attribute. Some of the best encyclopaedias accredit the ancient Egyptians with being the inventors of the earliest proper bread-making. Yet five millennia before the Egyptians' earliest dynasty, the Çatal Hüyük citizens can be seen to have sufficiently developed the culinary usage of their wheat and barley crops that they were already producing bread. This is surely the only explanation for the fact that Mellaart found baking ovens, as distinct from cooking hearths, in each domestic dwelling, a feature that caused him specifically to remark 'one is given the impression that each family baked its own bread'.[13] Furthermore at two of the site's 7th millennium BC levels[14] two huge brick-built bread ovens were found in a courtyard, directly interpreted by Mellaart as suggesting a full-scale bakery.[15]

Other food commodities that have been identified as common fare for the Çatal Hüyük people include peas, oil from mustard seed, edible acorns, capers, crab apples, hack-berries, grapes, junipers, walnuts, pistachio nuts, birds' eggs, fish and game birds. These pre-Flood citizens enjoyed an impressively varied fare that would scarcely be put to shame by any equivalent town of the present day.

In an earlier chapter we noted that the world's earliest scrap of cloth had been found at Çayönü, which lies some 400 kilometres (250 miles) east of Çatal Hüyük. Wall-paintings make it clear that weaving of clothes was well-established early on at Çatal Hüyük. Besides the earlier-mentioned loincloths worn by men, the women are seen to wear gaudily coloured and patterned dresses that were clearly made of some kind of woven fabric. In one baked clay statuette the rather buxom female subject is clad in a daringly brief mini-skirt decorated with a fringe, and topped by a leopard-skin blouse held up by shoulder-straps,[16] a fashion that would not have looked out of place in the 1960s. By way of actual physical evidence of textiles, Mellaart found carbonised textile fragments sufficiently well preserved to indicate the use of plain and other weaves.

With regard to how the Çatal Hüyük fashion designers might have created patterns on the dresses, Mellaart found a number of baked clay seals, some round, others oval-shaped, and yet others flower-shaped, but always with a flat lower surface bearing spiral and other patterns. These he interpreted as having been used for printing the dress patterns[17] though others have suggested they were used for creating patterns on the skin, some statuettes suggesting that body-painting may well have been practised at Çatal Hüyük. But whatever the answer the seals surely represent one of the very earliest forms of printing technology, dating eight thousand years before Gutenberg invented his printing press.

As we noted in an earlier chapter, evidence of woodwork-ing all too rarely survives the ravages of time, but Çatal

Fig 14 Examples of the world's earliest-known high quality woodworking (above), and printing devices (inset) as found at Çatal Hüyük

Hüyük happens to be a notable exception to this, as Mellaart's findings included woodworking crafted to an exceptionally high standard [fig 14]. For instance, despite the nearest source of fir being the Taurus Mountains to Çatal Hüyük's south-west, the town's wood-carvers, using merely stone tools, used fir to carve oval bowls and meat dishes shaped so expertly, complete with decorative handles, that their designs still look modern today. With much the same skill and good taste they also fashioned wooden boxes fitted with handles and snugly fitting lids. Mellaart even found a perfectly-shaped wooden egg-cup, maybe yet another world first for so specialised a vessel.

Besides woodworking, the abundance of reeds in the local

marshes suggests that basketry would have been similarly well developed, and again Mellaart managed to find either imprints or carbonised remains of basketry items at virtually all Çatal Hüyük's occupation levels. Basketry was used for all manner of containers – food storage, grain bins, mirror holders, even children's coffins. Along with woodcrafting it seems to have been practised in preference to pottery by the local craftspeople. For although pottery was found even at Çatal Hüyük's very earliest accessible levels, together with the kilns that were used to fire it, it is clear that the then more traditional products were the ones preferred. This much is evident from the fact that Çatal Hüyük's pottery was not given the colourful decoration frequently accorded to other surfaces, and that it was often made in the semblance of some other form of container, such as a wooden box or leather bag, rather than as an art form in its own right. Even so, Çatal Hüyük's pottery still ranks among the western world's oldest, and could indeed be the very oldest if it is found at levels below those reached so far.

No less proficiency was exhibited by the workmanship in bone and stone. Accompanying the skeleton of one of the male citizens Mellaart found a ceremonial flint dagger, its blade superbly shaped and serrated for maximum sharpness. This had then been fitted with a bone handle most stylishly carved in the shape of a snake, the creature's body painstakingly dotted with tiny pinpoints to simulate its scales. Lime mixed with resin is thought to have been used to fasten the handle to the blade, the firmest possible hold being achieved by using fine twine wound tightly round the lower part of the handle. Both the design elegance and the quality of craftsmanship would be difficult to improve upon even today.

Everywhere that Mellaart dug at Çatal Hüyük he found evidence of a technological specialisation that staggered him. How, he asked, 'did they polish a mirror of obsidian, a hard volcanic glass, without scratching it, and how did they drill holes through stone beads (including obsidian), holes so small that no fine modern steel needle can penetrate?'.[18]

This immediately reminds us of the drill holes that Robert Ballard's archaeologist Fredrik Hiebert observed in the pre-Flood tools that he retrieved from the bed of the Black Sea. Furthermore, this same technology was almost certainly used for the earliest known example of dentistry recently discovered at Mehrgarh in what is now Pakistan. Among the burials at a village near-contemporary with Çatal Hüyük, and similarly growing crops and crafting sophisticated jewellery, University of Missouri archaeologists have discovered a skull, one of the teeth of which had been expertly drilled with a tiny, perfectly rounded hole. Electron microscopy – unavailable to Mellaart back in the 1960s – revealed a pattern of concentric grooves 'almost certainly formed by the circular motion of a drill with a stone bit.'[19]

The people of Çatal Hüyük were also proficient in metallurgy. At one of the lower, and therefore older levels,[20] probably dating around the beginning of the 7th millennium BC, Mellaart found copper and lead that had been used for beads, pendants and other trinkets, as well as in tube form for a woman's string skirt. Although these mostly needed only the hammering of copper lumps, in one of the upper levels[21] Mellaart found slag, indicating extraction of copper from ore by smelting, and therefore true metallurgy. As he acknowledged 'it would not be surprising if gold and silver were also known, even though they have not yet been found or recognised.'[22] So when and where could these people have learnt to smelt metals?

Leaving this particular mystery still dangling, we must ask questions as to who exactly these people were. Undoubtedly they trod the soil of Turkey long before any Turk, Mongol, Arab, Roman, Greek or Hittite had arrived. So what do we know of their race or language? This is important, since the answer to this could also help us to understand more of the identity of those who owned the pre-Flood timber-frame houses that Robert Ballard found so deeply drowned off Sinop.

As found by Mellaart, it was the Çatal Hüyük custom, as also at Asikli, for at least some of the citizens, particularly the women and children, to be buried beneath the floors of the houses, therefore readily enabling a study of the bones found at these locations. Unfortunately, however, the 1960s, when Mellaart conducted his excavations, was before the introduction of DNA analysis to archaeological work, the then prevailing fashion being for anthropological analysis of skull-types. As reported by Mellaart's principal anthropological consultant, Denise Ferembach of the French Institut de Paléontologie Humaine, some 59 per cent of the Çatal Hüyük people were long-skulled so-called Eurafricans, 17 per cent were lighter-built Mediterranean peoples similarly with long skulls, and 24 per cent were short-skulled individuals associated with Alpine environments.[23] Although such modes of classification are today regarded as of little worth, it is at least evident that Çatal Hüyük's population was already quite a mixed one rather than belonging to one single distinctive racial type. And the peoples' stature, arguably aided by the good diet, was little different from that of modern-day, the men averaging between 178 centimetres (5 foot 10 inches) and 163 centimetres (5 foot 4 inches), and the women between 163 centimetres (5 foot 4 inches) and 152 centimetres (5 foot).[24] Yet none of this gets us much closer to determining the human group that they may have belonged to, or the family of languages from which their particular language may have come.

This said, what we are comparatively well informed about is their religion. It seemed quite possible to Mellaart that the sector of Çatal Hüyük which he uncovered had been a religious quarter, since every fourth house seems to have been a shrine. These shrines contained some of the earlier-mentioned wall-paintings as well as a wealth of information concerning the Çatal Hüyük people's remarkable and distinctive religious practices.

First and foremost the town's main deity would appear to have been a very powerful woman. Because we do not know the language that the Çatal Hüyük people spoke, we cannot know her name. However, from the various ways that she was represented there can be little doubt that she was a Great Mother Goddess who was deeply revered. She was

Fig 15 Two of the many shrines found at Çatal Hüyük indicative of a bull cult, as reconstructed by James Mellaart

responsible for the sexuality and fertility of humans, for animals, both domesticated and wild, for plants domesticated and wild, for insects, for the rites of passage from birth to death, and much else.[25]

Closely associated with this Great Mother Goddess was the bull. Among the most striking elements found in Çatal Hüyük's shrines were bulls' heads mounted on the altar wall [fig 15], much as 19th-century hunters mounted on the walls of their drawing rooms trophy heads of stags and tigers that they had gunned down. Sometimes the Çatal Hüyük bulls' heads appear singly, and sometimes in threes. Sometimes they are topped with high relief sculptures of the Great Mother Goddess in a 'doing the splits' pose that seems to convey childbirth, or in this instance, bull-birth, since in some examples a bull's head can be seen emerging from her vulva. Scholars suggest that the bull's head was thought of as representing masculinity, with the goddess apparently exhibiting her supremacy over this. Some of the trophy bulls' heads were made in clay, others in plaster, and yet others were the real thing. Common amongst the same shrines were low pillars fitted with real bull's horns, an element which when found in later cultures is often referred to as horns of consecration. Where bulls are depicted in the Çatal Hüyük shrines' wall decorations they are always represented facing the Taurus or Bull Mountains,[26] which as Mellaart has dryly noted, is 'perhaps not a coincidence'.

However the Çatal Hüyük people's pantheon was not totally female, Mellaart also having found statuettes of a young male god represented seated. In otherwise similar statuettes found elsewhere the figure sometimes has an erect penis, at least one of the Çatal Hüyük examples showing signs of this having been broken off.[27]

Other recurring elements that Mellaart found in the shrines indicate that the Çatal Hüyük folk already had an advanced theology and mythology. There seems to have been something special pertaining to twins for two goddess sculptures had, in some shrines, been created side-by-side on a shrine wall. Also found in a shrine was a group of statuettes created in blue and brown limestone, which, though broken in an apparent attempt to decommission its magical properties, depicted two goddesses with a young child, perhaps a Trinity. This same sculptural group also included a leopard, an animal that appears to have had a sacred royal significance for the people of Çatal Hüyük, since in one of the shrines a pair were sculpted in high relief heraldically facing each other.

The very fact that the Çatal Hüyük folk buried their dead beneath the floors of houses – or more accurately, beneath the platforms which the living used as beds – suggest that they believed in an afterlife. Indeed, this same practice indicates a belief in the ability of the dead to communicate with them via dreams, as many tribal peoples continue to hold to this day.

But unlike the later ancient Egyptians they do not appear to have regarded it as necessary to try to preserve the dead person's flesh, rather the opposite. In some Çatal Hüyük shrines great vultures, some with human legs as if they are the Goddess in bird guise, are depicted pecking at dead bodies. The bodies appear to have been specially laid out in the open for the birds to do so, much as is still practised amongst those Tibetans of today who manage somehow to perpetuate their traditional religion. There can be no doubt that the bird depicted in the Çatal Hüyük shrine is the griffon vulture (*gyps fulvus*), an impressive creature with a 275-centimetre (9-foot) wingspan that can be seen to this day soaring over the Konya plain, every so often making a swoop to feed on carrion. As remarked by Mellaart of these, their beaks 'leave no marks on the bones, they only tear off the flesh, and the brain inside the skull is not disturbed'.[28] Arguably the Çatal Hüyük people regarded the vultures as embodiments of the Goddess transporting the deceased's soul aloft into the afterlife, after which process they could bring their defleshed bones back to the homestead to stay on with the living family. One curiosity Mellaart noted of the Çatal Hüyük burials is that most were of women and children, as if men might not have been so privileged.

Whilst the Çatal Hüyük Goddess was one of death, she was also one of copulation. A relief of a copulating couple that Mellaart found in one of the shrines is the earliest known depiction of a theme to recur in later cultures as that of the so-called Sacred Marriage. The Goddess was also very definitely a patroness of the fruits of such a union, childbirth. One of the shrines that Mellaart found at Çatal Hüyük he dubbed the Red Room because throughout his excavations it was the only one he came across in which even the lime-plastered floor had been coloured red, along with the rest of the furniture and fittings. On one wall was a painting of figures in the childbirth position, and Mellaart's interpretation was that this room functioned as Çatal Hüyük's mid-wifery unit or maternity suite – as such surely yet another world first.

However perhaps most indicative of this childbirth attribute of the Goddess was a statuette that Mellaart found in a grain bin close to Çatal Hüyük's uppermost level, thereby dating immediately before the town's demise [fig 16]. This mere 13-centimetre (5-inch) high statuette depicts her as 'royally' enthroned between two leopards, the earliest known depiction of a goddess in this mode, though as we will discover, very far from the last. But while she was represented with much the same massive breasts and hips as the more ancient 'Fertility Goddess' figures, the distinctive feature of this particular statuette is that clearly visible between her thighs is a child in the process of being born.

There can be no doubt that this figurine was regarded as of magical significance, because again its head had been

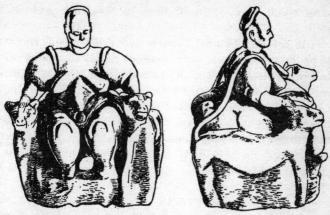

Fig 16 Front and side views of a clay statuette of the Great Mother Goddess giving birth, enthroned between two leopards. The goddess's head, found deliberately broken off, has been restored

broken off in order to destroy its potency, so that no one else could use it after it had been discarded.

The really interesting question is: what could have been the circumstances that prompted it to have been desanctified and discarded in this way? There can be little doubt, because of the finding of this particular statuette so close to the Çatal Hüyük mound's surface, that the circumstances were most likely the same as caused the demise and abandonment of Çatal Hüyük itself.

What, in turn, could have caused *this* to happen? Something very powerful indeed had to have affected the Çatal Hüyük community in its last hours. As Mellaart's findings showed, after the community had lived peaceably at this prime, well-watered site for upward of a thousand years, suddenly they uprooted from the site lock-stock-and-barrel. They gathered what belongings that they could carry with them (the Great Mother Goddess figurine being one of their discards), and to all appearances vanished into thin air. So what could have possessed them to take such a drastic step?

The date of this abandonment can be determined with some certainty. It was on or about 6000 BC, just four centuries before the Black Sea Flood. And one important clue, of which Mellaart was well aware even back in the 1960s, was that the Çatal Hüyük people were far from alone amongst communities of the time in having suddenly fled their long-time place of settlement. As we are about to find, the 6th millennium BC period seems to have been fraught with not just one, but two major catastrophes.

CHAPTER 10

DOUBLE CATASTROPHE

*This flume already bore two hundred times the volume of
water that today flows over Niagara Falls, enough to raise
the Black Sea by six inches a day ...*

William Ryan and Walter Pitman

When an archaeologist finds an ancient settlement of which
even the uppermost, and therefore most recent, layers date
from the late Stone Age – as Mellaart observed during his
very first inspection of Çatal Hüyük – then the only reasonable inference is that the human occupation must have
ceased at that same very early point. Such a cessation may
be considered certain in the case of Çatal Hüyük's eastern
mound, as so strongly featured in the last chapter.

Mellaart's system of notating Çatal Hüyük East's occupation levels recorded the oldest as X and the final, or most
recent, ones as Levels 0 and I. Three other levels were
recorded as subdivisions within his system. Because these
levels were uppermost, some allowances have to be made for
any effects upon them of weather erosion during all the millennia since. But from all the signs available to him Mellaart
formed the opinion from the outset that the formerly thriving and precociously advanced town had 'died' uncannily
peacefully.

Innumerable cities of the ancient world underwent sack
by invaders, and the archaeological evidence of such events
is almost always obvious in the form of smashed monuments,

vandalised shrines and bodies found lying in open streets having been left unburied where they fell. Although Mellaart found evidence of some houses having suffered fires, these were due to mere localised accidents, such as when rubbish-burning had got out of control, not the work of hostile outsiders.

Likewise Mellaart found no evidence of any devastating epidemic. In these circumstances the norm is for bodies to be found left either unburied, or tossed in heaps into mass graves. But whatever happened at Çatal Hüyük, its seven thousand or so citizens seem 'simply' to have gathered up their portable belongings, and in good order quietly left the township that had been their ancestral home throughout perhaps a millennium or more,[1] their reason for leaving, and their onward destination unrecorded and unknown.

In the 1960s when Mellaart was working, radio-carbon dating was still a relatively new science. From wood and grain samples that he took from Çatal Hüyük's most recent layers the radio-carbon dating calculations made at the time were that the abandonment had taken place sometime around 5600 BC.[2] Since then there have been changes to the fundamental assumptions upon which carbon-dating is based, as a result of which this date has been adjusted backwards by up to six centuries. However given radio-carbon dating's ongoing imprecision, for working purposes 6000 BC may be regarded as the likeliest date within a margin of error of a couple of centuries or so.

One of the few clues to any stress that Çatal Hüyük's inhabitants may have been under just prior to their departure derives from the fact that whereas hardwood timber-frame had been the favoured mode of construction during the town's earlier periods, in the later, more recent levels such wood became used considerably less. From around Level V and later the builders certainly began to put significantly greater reliance on using mud-brick for load-bearing

walls, and by Level II they were using mud-brick buttress-
ing on its own.[3] This may simply have been due to improve-
ments in brickmaking and all-brick house designs, but
alternatively it may have been because wood was in shorter
supply, or was becoming more difficult to transport to Çatal
Hüyük, perhaps through climatic changes.

One quite definite factor, however, is that Çatal Hüyük
was far from alone in its having been mysteriously abandoned sometime around 6000 BC. Shortly before starting
work on the mound, Mellaart had excavated a similarly late
Stone Age site at Hacilar, a village that was likewise located
on Turkey's broad central plateau, though some 190 kilometres (120 miles) west of Çatal Hüyük, and roughly due north
of the Mediterranean port of Antalya. Where Hacilar's levels
were directly contemporary with those of east Çatal Hüyük
Mellaart found it to have had some similar features, such as
rectangular buildings. However it had not achieved quite
the same level of development, its range of agricultural
products, for instance, being much simpler, and no pottery
of any kind being used. Yet it too became abandoned at
much the same time.

And this abandonment pattern was extraordinarily
widespread. An earlier chapter referred to the settlements in
Cyprus that had been founded when a number of domesticated animals and cultivated plants had been brought to the
island from the mainland. The people of these settlements
had also developed a flourishing and apparently established
culture. They opted for making stoneware from the local
andesitic stone rather than developing pottery, even though
they began with the latter. Exactly as at Çatal Hüyük the
archaeologists found absolutely no signs of these Late Stone
Age Cypriots having been overcome by any incoming
human invaders. Yet suddenly, despite all their apparently
successful earlier efforts at introducing crop cultivation and
farm animals to Cyprus, they abandoned their well-

established settlements and disappeared into the unknown, necessarily doing so, just as they had arrived, by sea-going boat.[4]

In Palestine and also in the Syrian steppe, the pattern was exactly the same. Beidha, the earlier-mentioned site south of the Dead Sea near Petra, which had become reoccupied after abandonment by Natufian settlers during the earlier Younger Dryas drought, then exhibits unbroken occupation throughout what archaeologists call the PPNB, or Pre-Pottery Neolithic [Stone Age] B period. While the inhabitants still pursued some hunting in its rocky surrounds, their diet was as dominated by the meat of domesticated goats as was that of the Çatal Hüyük by cattle, and at much the same time. The Beidhans also cultivated wheat and barley, and consumed an apparent abundance of pistachio nuts, together with field peas and wild lentils.[5] The cutting tools that they used included obsidian traceable to central Turkey, indicating that they maintained peaceful trading connections over several hundred kilometres, and further attesting to widespread international harmony. All the signs, therefore, are that they enjoyed a well-established, unthreatened existence, exactly as had been enjoyed at Çatal Hüyük. Yet suddenly they abandoned the site, for it never to be occupied again. The same fate befell the similarly PPNB Jordanian sites Wadi Fellaah and the terrace of al-Khiam.[6]

As noted earlier, Mellaart as a fledgling archaeologist had worked alongside Kathleen Kenyon at Jericho. This site, notable for a spring that to this day produces 76 litres (17 gallons) of water per second, lies 250 metres (820 feet) below even the present-day sea-level. Certainly the world's lowest city, it is also still claimed by some to be the world's oldest, despite Çatal Hüyük having been three times larger and quite possibly equally as old (if its earliest occupation levels were reached). As at Beidha, Jericho's PPNB culture thrived on a mix of agriculture and hunting, the latter pursuit, together with the normally prolific spring, arguably capable then of sustaining a population in the event of an agricultural failure on its own. Jericho, like Beidha, obtained its obsidian from Turkey, so it too seems to have had good trade connections. Yet some time around 6000 BC it too became abandoned, just as mysteriously as the rest. It was as if some calamity had so devastatingly befallen the Near East that the entire area became all but deserted.

Clearly suspicion has to fall on some climatic change having been responsible, and even back in the 1970s the first indications of this were beginning to come to light, particularly from studies made by botanists. From core samples taken from the Sea of Galilee and from Lake Huleh, which also lies in the Galilee region, the volume of tree pollen could be seen to exhibit a marked decrease culminating c.6000 BC, just as if the trees were under severe stress at this period.[7] Agriculturalists studying the early history of the Mesopotamian steppe found much the same, as in a contemporary phase at Alikosh in the Zagros Mountains foothills, today a border region between Iran and Iraq.[8]

In Africa the Sahara, noted earlier to have been a prolifically lake-filled and populous region during the immediate post-Ice Age period, suffered a particularly severe drying-out that can only be regarded as the preliminary to the onset of its present desert status.[9] The formerly vast Lake Chad, on the borders of what are today Niger, Chad and Nigeria, shrank dramatically.[10] The lake at Agorass n'essoui, Adrar Bous, dried up,[11] with the people of Adrar Bous forced to abandon it and find their livelihood elsewhere. Undoubtedly much the same happened to the other former great Saharan lakes even though no direct studies are necessarily available for these. Even Lake Victoria, far to the south on the equator, suffered a huge drop in its water-level.[12] So there can be little doubt also that Turkey's great lakes, including

Çatal Hüyük's Lake Konya, must have been similarly drastically affected, even though the scientific studies to tell us this directly have so far been lacking.

Given our focus on such predominantly temperate and warm climes it may seem incredible that the best source for telling us exactly what happened to all these places eight thousand years ago should be the icy wastes of Greenland, yet this is precisely the case. Greenland's great advantage for preserving a chronicle of the world's climate derives from the fact that the Ice Age has essentially never left it throughout the last hundred thousand years. Each year's fall of snow in Greenland freezes to form a distinctive layer, encapsulating with it any atmospheric peculiarities that may have pertained to that year. So when the northern hemisphere's overall climate has been warm and moist the proportion of methane that becomes trapped in Greenland's ice will always be significantly higher than when it has been cold and dry. Drill down through the ice-cap's layers and you can then sample different years and read off their climatic history much as you can detect more recent changes by examining the varying thicknesses of a tree's tree-rings.

This said, getting really good continuous cores from Greenland is by no means an easy task. The full 100,000-year-old ice-cap is 3 kilometres (2 miles) thick, and an ideal core is 20 centimetres (8 inches) in diameter. To obtain any core there is no alternative but to lumber some very heavy drilling equipment to a suitably remote and intensely freezing part of Greenland. You then have to have some means of keeping the huge lengths of ice deep-frozen all the way back to civilisation, and thereafter. However in 1992 a European team with 150 tonnes of equipment managed to do just that.[13] In a mountainous part of Greenland they set up a camp at an elevation of more than 3,050 metres (10,000 feet) and the following year they were joined by an American team who drilled a second core alongside them.[14] These expeditions clearly revealed the earlier Younger Dryas mini Ice Age at its appropriate period around 9000 BC. So the layering of the ice cap means that dating readings from it can now be regarded as very much more precise, virtually down to the exact year. This is far more accurate than is possible by radio-carbon dating.

Having determined this, they also came across the crucial evidence to explain all the evacuations. The low methane levels that they found locked in one thick sector of the ice cores indicated unmistakably that even after the Younger Dryas mini Ice Age that followed the main Ice Age there had been a further mini Ice Age again marked by very cold and dry conditions. This had begun c.6200 BC and had lasted to c.5800 BC.[15] Since this was so near synchronous with the dates that had already been determined by radio-carbon dating, it was quite obvious that this savage climate deterioration had been responsible for the widespread abandonment of so many former agricultural towns and settlements, including Çatal Hüyük.

Today it is only farmers who may be able properly to appreciate just how devastating a return to near-Ice Age conditions would have been to the Late Stone Age peoples. These were, after all, peoples who had long been living by plant cultivation and animal husbandry, and who although they still practised some recreational hunting, had no doubt forgotten many of their ancestors' hunter-gatherer arts.

For the Çatal Hüyük people and others, the first sign of a problem would have been a marked diminution of the warmth and the abundance of rainfall to which they had become accustomed, and upon which they had come to depend to provide a good harvest and good grazing for their livestock. And while to live 900 metres (3,000 feet) up on the great Turkish plateau would have been agreeable and sensible when the conditions at lower attitudes were overly humid because of a general abundance of warmth and moisture, once such warm temperature and high rainfall were removed it would have been a different matter. They would have had insufficient grazing for their animals. Their harvests would have failed. There would be a disagreeable chill in the air, definitely demanding some rather warmer covering than mere loincloths and mini-skirts. They would have found themselves confronted by the very real danger of starvation.

Now while the hunter-gatherers of the earlier millennia would have needed little more than to take up their dilly bags to follow animal herds to where these would seek out fresh water-holes and suitable accompanying vegetation, for the newly-fledged agriculturalists of the late Stone Age it would have been a different matter. Even had they been disposed to return to the old hunter-gatherer ways they had become far too populous for this, since only small, readily mobile groups are viable for hunter-gathering. So they would have had to make some life-and-death decisions on behalf of their animals and plants, and to take the best of these and all their more portable accoutrements, journeying with them to wherever it might be possible to continue their agricultural way of life.

So where might they have gone? Since the two priorities uppermost in their minds would have been finding warmth and fresh water, descent from Turkey's now arid and chilly plateau region would have been the first logical step. And between the two alternatives of going south or north, the latter, with its large Black Sea freshwater lake would certainly have seemed the more sensible. For archaeologists of just a generation ago one of ancient Turkey's great mysteries was the apparent paucity of any evidence of Late Stone Age human settlement in the northern part of the country. The 1971 *Fodor Guide to Turkey* blandly remarks of the country's Black Sea coast: 'There is little of historical or archaeological interest in these parts.'[16] And when in 1980 Ian Todd of the

University of Birmingham published his doctoral thesis on Turkey's prehistory in the late Stone Age period he specifically remarked on this:

> The more northerly half [of the great plateau on which so much of Turkey rests] is sadly lacking in any recognizable trace of Neolithic [Stone Age] material. At present the writer can offer no plausible reason for this.[17]

Of course what Todd had no way of knowing at that time – and would very likely have ridiculed even had it been suggested to him – was that the place to look for any Stone Age settlements was not along the northern coastline as this exists at the present day. Instead the true old coastline was 19 kilometres (12 miles) out into the Black Sea, and 90 metres (300 feet) down. And still today, until Robert Ballard's explorations are considerably expanded – a process that in all logic must take many years – we can only guess at the extent of any already extant Stone Age settlements that may have stretched all the way along that long-drowned coastline. The sparse known facts are that the Black Sea's predecessor of that time was freshwater, and that its then surrounds were grasslands and steppe, both of which would have provided most welcome grazing for refugee farmers' parched livestock.[18]

There could well have been a substantial accumulation of settlements along the then lakeside Black Sea coast even before the c.6000 BC mini Ice Age desiccation. However, their numbers would certainly have been swelled considerably once entire town populations from the southern plateau country began arriving with all their flocks and herds. Even so, whatever strains the streams of refugees from inland imposed on their compatriots must as yet remain conjectural, just as we have no idea of the movements of those uprooted elsewhere, on Cyprus, in northern Syria and in northern Africa.

What is certain, at least based on the evidence from the Greenland ice-cap, is that the very cold snap lasted some four hundred years – the amount of time that separates England's Queen Elizabeth I from Queen Elizabeth II – before the climate became warmer and moister again. Furthermore when nature has exhibited one extreme, such as a drought, it tends to lurch to the other extreme of flood. So, as argued by Ryan and Pitman, the years 5800 to 5600 BC are likely to have been both warmer and much wetter ones.

In their scenario, pouring rain and renewed ice-melts now raised world sea-levels to unprecedented new heights. And since the Black Sea freshwater lake, not least because of all the earlier desiccation, lay 150 metres (500 feet) below the then world sea-level,[19] this would have meant that the Bosporus land-bridge holding back the Mediterranean from breaking into it became subjected to the most intense strain.

For those living close to the Bosporus land-bridge, the visually-evident disparity between the level of the Mediterranean, lapping close to the top of the land-bridge, and that of the low-lying land behind with its pleasant lake may well have become a matter of concern. Some may even have gone to the trouble of building a special evacuation vessel in the event of the seawall becoming breached, since some kind of forewarning is certainly the implication behind the Noah family of Flood stories. But whatever premonitions any neighbouring human populations may have had, just two hundred years after the end of the devastating mini Ice Age, disaster certainly struck again. Its impact this time was much more overt and immediate.

Whether it was through sheer weight of the outside sea-water, or through some seismic shift to which the region is prone, suddenly the Bosporus' natural dam became breached. The Mediterranean began gushing hundreds of tons of its brine through into the Black Sea freshwater lake with tremendous force, according to Ryan and Pitman's best estimates: 'Ten cubic miles ... Each day, two hundred times what flows over Niagara Falls, enough to cover Manhattan Island each day to a depth of over half a mile.'[20]

Oceanographers and marine biologists are not often accredited with vivid imaginations. However William Ryan and Walter Pitman in the opening pages of their book *Noah's Flood*, certainly did their best to envisage how the Flood would have impacted on those whom only now we *know* to have been living around the Black Sea lake, some of them arguably descendants of the refugee Çatal Hüyük people. While those living closest to the Bosporus would have become immediately affected by, and perhaps swept away by, the devastating in-rush of water, for those further along the shores towards the east the first sign was most likely a distant roar, accompanied by an ominous vibration.

Then would have begun the steady rise of the lake-water. At first this may well have been seen as beneficial, ensuring that the next harvest would be a good one. But as the roar became louder and more incessant, as unusual amounts of flotsam began to appear in the lake-water – amongst this no doubt whole trees, and animal and human carcasses – also as the lake-level rose inexorably, concern must quickly have escalated to alarm. With a lake-level rise that Ryan and Pitman estimate to have been at least 15 centimetres (6 inches) a day, whole settlements would all too swiftly have become inundated, with even the most orderly evacuation turned into rout. Within a year, everything that had former-ly been at the level of the old Black Sea freshwater lake lay 54 metres (180 feet) beneath the new, salt-water Black Sea, and with the water level still rising.[21] Even from what little is yet known of the fate of the settlements now submerged 90 metres (300 feet) beneath the Black Sea, the fact that Ballard's expedition discovered tools that had been left lying out in the open tells its own story – one of a frantic escape by those mobile enough to do so.

The survival of the Noah family of Flood stories, consistent in their description of world-scale annihilation, bespeaks that many – probably many thousands – perished along with their precious animals and plants. Yet as the same stories also convey, there have to have been some who were sufficiently resourceful, perhaps by building a makeshift boat, to escape with these same.

Even so, more questions are raised than are answered. Where did those who escaped principally congregate? Why is it that much the same Noah-type Flood story is remembered from Greece to India? Does this mean that just one group came out of their ark and then quickly scattered to those countries? Or did they at first stay relatively close to their roots in what is now Turkey, and only later spread further afield, perhaps in the wake of later, quite different crises? The pioneering Ryan and Pitman have tried to come up with answers to at least some of these questions. But were they the right answers?

CHAPTER 11

WHITHER THE DIASPORA?

Except for refugees wishing to risk a voyage at sea, it is likely that those on the northern and western edge of the flooding Black Sea lake escaped into Europe and the Ukraine, and those on the southerly side fled into Anatolia and points beyond.

William Ryan and Walter Pitman

When Pitman and Ryan wrote *Noah's Flood*, it was principally the eclectic-minded Bill Ryan who addressed the issue of where those who survived the Black Sea Flood might have fled in the wake of the catastrophe. In a chapter entitled 'The Diaspora' he included two authoritative-looking maps showing a number of post-Flood migration routes that he hypothesised spreading out westwards as far as Paris, and eastwards as far as the borders of China [fig 17]. The unmistakable impression made by these maps, and indeed by the accompanying text, is that those who escaped were minded to get as far away from the Black Sea as possible.

Amongst reviewers, particularly the ones with archaeological knowledge, it was this 'diaspora' aspect of the Black Sea Flood hypothesis which provoked the most outright scepticism. Partly this was because Ryan, understandably in the course of such a far-reaching book, tended merely to suggest the possible migration paths that he envisaged, rather than to elaborate a fully developed argument for any one of them. Partly it was because too often he neglected sufficiently to show how a particular culture which mysteriously appeared, say, in Yugoslavia, shortly after 5600 BC

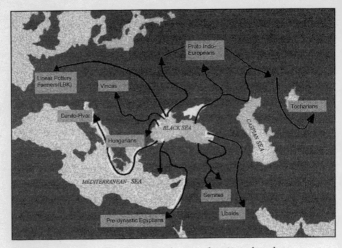

Fig 17 A conflation of William Ryan's maps showing where he hypothesised refugee populations having fled to in the wake of the Black Sea Flood

might have had its origins in the environs of the Black Sea. And partly it was because, in the case for instance of the European-looking Tocharians, he insufficiently accounted for where these people might have been between their hypothesised flight from the Black Sea *c.*5600 BC and their appearance in the Tarim Basin on China's borders *c.*2000 BC.

One culture that Ryan was bound to look to for some link to the Black Sea Flood was that of the Sumerians, since as we saw earlier, it was from them that the earliest versions of the 'Epic of Gilgamesh' with its Flood story had emanated. The Sumerians' Flood hero Ziusudra, the equivalent of the Babylonian and Assyrian Flood stories' Atrahasis and Uta-napishti, effectively represented the oldest-recorded counterpart to the biblical Noah, even though their Flood story was obviously untraceable in written form earlier than when narrative writing itself was invented in around 3000 BC.

Furthermore Ryan was particularly intrigued by how the Gilgamesh Epic's tablet immediately preceding the Flood story, despite its hailing a long way from the Black Sea, exhibits evidence of someone, at some point in the story's origination, having some impressive local knowledge of the Bosporus strait as this had been created by the Black Sea Flood 'burst-through'. Earlier in this book we mentioned how the Epic described Gilgamesh, on his route to visit Uta-napishti, having to traverse the 'Waters of Death', which we suggested to have been one and the same as the Black Sea. According to the Epic, Gilgamesh so distrusted these waters' fearsome reputation that on his arrival at the difficult passage where he was to be ferried across, he became immediately suspicious of 'things of stone' that were apparently the boat's means of propulsion. Greatly angered, he destroyed these, whereupon he was told by the ferryman:

> The stones, O Gilgamesh, enabled my crossing …
> In your fury you have smashed them
> The stones were with me to take me across.[2]

Lacking the stones, Gilgamesh was apparently obliged to rely on a number of much less effective punt poles in order to propel himself across.

This episode is utterly meaningless except in the context of just one place in the world – the Bosporus strait leading into the Black Sea – where as we learned earlier in this book (p.45), stones lowered by rope to the underlying counter-current can indeed help to propel a boat across it. The inclusion of this passage in a story, the earliest known form of which was Sumerian, and which goes on to a Flood narra-tive, therefore strongly indicates some close link between the Sumerians and the Black Sea Flood event.

Except, as Ryan rightly recognised, since the Sumerians arrived in Mesopotamia only in the 4th millennium BC, very likely the story did not come directly even from them. It was more likely to have been the Ubaid people who preceded them, and whose arrival – from an as yet undetermined location – was sometime vaguely around 5000 BC, and therefore just credibly post-Flood. Hence it was not the Sumerians but the Ubaidans whom Ryan marked on his map as having made the original post-Flood migration from the eastern side of the Black Sea to Ubaid in what is today Iraq.

And in favour of it having been the Ubaidans who passed the Flood story on to the Sumerians, it was the former who left a significant literary and linguistic legacy to the latter. One example of this was the number of non-Sumerian words for specialist occupations, tools and such-like that became introduced into the Sumerian language. Though arguably these were originally Ubaidan words, they appear to have been adopted by the incoming Sumerians because the Ubaidans had already developed these occupations and artefacts, whereas the Sumerians had not. As noted by the great American Sumerologist, the rather aptly named Samuel Noah Kramer:

> Among these words were those for farmer (*engar*), herdsman (*udul*) and fisherman (*shuhudak*), plow (*apin*) and furrow (*apsin*), palm (*nimbar*) and date (*sulumb*), metalworker (*tibira*) and smith (*simug*), carpenter (*nangar*) and basketmaker (*addub*), weaver (*ishbar*) and leatherworker (*ashgab*), potter (*pahar*), mason (*shidim*) and perhaps even merchant (*damgar*).[3]

If we reflect back to the earlier chapter on Çatal Hüyük, the professions on this list represent virtually a roll-call of the specialist occupations that were to be found at pre-Flood Çatal Hüyük. Furthermore, some of these, such as the metalworking, were to be found at virtually no other known location at this early post-Flood time. Accordingly, if Ryan is right that the Ubaidans came from the Black Sea, then in these otherwise unknown Ubaidan words we could be glimpsing something of the original pre-Flood language that would have been spoken by at least some of those who had been living around the Black Sea c.5600 BC. Since Kramer noted of *damgar* that this 'has almost universally been taken to be a Semitic hallmark',[4] there has also to be a hint that at least some among the pre-Flood people spoke a proto-Semitic language, though this must as yet remain tentative.

Whatever name the Ubaidans may have called themselves is unknown. This modern appellation derives from a mound called Tell el-Ubaid, 6.5 kilometres (4 miles) to the north of Leonard Woolley's Ur, where the British Museum's Dr H.R. Hall first identified them as a distinctive culture in 1919. Subsequently they were also found to have occupied other sites in the region, including Ur itself. Indeed because Leonard Woolley found their remains below his so-called Ur 'Flood' deposit, he identified them as an immediately pre-Flood culture, whereas we would call them a post Black Sea Flood one.

Supporting Ryan's view that the Ubaidans had come from the Black Sea, they were certainly what Kramer called 'enterprising agriculturalists'. Somewhere, possibly while trying to survive the 6200–5800 mini Ice Age on the shores of the former Black Sea lake, they had learnt some skills in irrigation. Also, wherever they had come from, they obtained their obsidian from Turkey, and they painted or tattooed their bodies rather like the Çatal Hüyük people.

Now while we cannot of course be sure that Çatal Hüyük was representative of those who settled directly on the Black Sea lake's shores immediately prior to 5600 BC, surviving Ubaidan art bears scant resemblance to the distinctive style that Mellaart found at Çatal Hüyük. As a whole the Ubaid culture exhibits little of the remarkable precocity of the Çatal Hüyük people. In Mellaart's view Ubaidan pottery 'is native north Mesopotamia, a poor descendant of Halaf wares',[5] the Halaf being a farming and livestock-keeping people who again appeared in the south-east Turkey/north Mesopotamian region around the 6th millennium BC, and whose pottery is notable for its rather beautiful geometric designs. And in fact certain Samara painted pottery that has been found some distance to the north, and which dates nearer to the time of the Flood, is rather closer to Çatal Hüyük, particularly in respect of depictions of women with their long hair streaming behind them.[6] It should not be ruled out therefore that the craft-type words which the Sumerians acquired into their language derived from their contact with perhaps Halaf or with some other people, rather than the Ubaidans.

Another culture that Ryan marked on his map as having fled from the Black Sea in the wake of the Flood was that of the Vinca. Their migration route he projected as having been overland westwards, following the route of the river Danube where this acts as a border to what are today Bulgaria and Romania, all the way to the environs of Belgrade in Yugoslavia. It was in 1908 that a local archaeologist Miloje Vasic came across distinctive ancient remains at a site called Vinca high up on the banks of the Danube just 16 kilometres (10 miles) from Belgrade. This led him to name the newly discovered culture after the site. Unlike the Ubaidans, the Vinca culture was so advanced that Vasic and others initially supposed it to date from as late as the 1st millennium BC. However, with the invention of radio-carbon dating, this was pushed back to an astounding c.5300 BC, and therefore to as near immediately after the Black Sea Deluge as the parameters of radio-carbon dating accuracy will allow.

While there is no certain information where the Vinca originated, like the Çatal Hüyük people they lived in towns, their houses of wattle and daub construction having in fact developed to feature proper streets. Like the Çatal Hüyük people, the Vinca had shrines that they decorated with bulls' heads, these even being attached to a wall-beam in much the same manner. These shrines also had the horns of consecration [fig 18]. And again like Çatal Hüyük people, the Vinca deeply revered a Great Mother Goddess as indicated by the discovery of many hundreds of female figurines of this deity.

However perhaps the greatest evidence of Vinca precocity, in this instance exceeding even anything known from Çatal Hüyük, turned up in 1961 when the Romanian archaeologist Dr N. Vlassa was excavating a prehistoric site at Tartaria near Turda in western Romania. At the site's lowest layer, which he knew specifically to belong to the Vinca culture, he came across a pit containing an adult skeleton, 26 burnt clay figurines; two alabaster figurines, a spondylus shell bracelet and three clay tablets.[7]

And it was two of these tablets that were the cause for Vlassa's astonishment. For although the apparent date of the Vinca burial was between 4500 and 4000 BC, these tablets bore proper pictographic writing, as distinct from the Schmandt-Besserat accountancy symbols [fig 19 left]. The world's first recognised true writing, on pictographic tablets found at Uruk in what is today Iraq is understood to have been developed by the Sumerians [fig 19 right]. Yet the

Fig 18 So-called 'horns of consecration' as found (left) at c.6000 BC Çatal Hüyük and (right) at 5th millennium BC Vinca sites

writing on these tablets from Tartaria seem to date from as
much as a thousand years before. Equally astonishing was
that despite the substantial geographical and chronological
differences between the Vinca and the Sumerian cultures,
Uruk lies some 2,400 kilometres (1,500 miles) – including
directly across the Black Sea – to Tartaria's south-east, the
pictographic signs were so similar to those found at Uruk
that even the most orthodox scholars felt bound to acknowledge that there had to be some relationship between them.
As noted by the highly respected British archaeologist
Sinclair Hood:

> The signs on the Tartaria tablets, especially those on the
> roundel no. 2, are so comparable with those on the early
> tablets from Uruk ... as to make it virtually certain that
> they are somehow connected with them. Several of the
> signs appear to be derived from Mesopotamian signs for

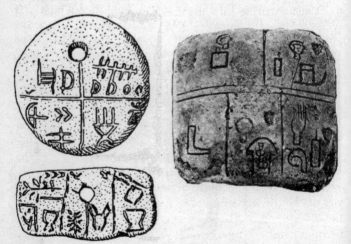

Fig 19 (Left) Two of the so-called Tartaria tablets of the Vinca culture,
dating from c.4500 BC, with (right) one of the earliest-known Sumerian
examples of pictographic writing, dating c.3500 BC

numerals ... In addition the shapes of the tablets and the system of dividing groups of signs by means of incised lines recur in Mesopotamia.[8]

Hood went on to remark that the signs on the Tartaria tablets also bore some striking similarities to pictographic writing that would appear several hundred years later still in Minoan Crete. And the Minoan examples, like the Tartaria ones, also exhibit string-holes (a feature that the Mesopotamian ones lack), thereby apparently perpetuating an early feature of the Schmandt-Besserat accounting tokens.

Whatever the explanation of the Tartaria tablets, at least there can be no doubt of their genuineness. Once the writing had been recognised as such, other examples came to light, including some on pottery fragments that had been first discovered back in the 1870s. Until Ryan and Pitman's Black Sea discoveries, however, it was quite impossible for anyone to fit such writing into any fresh hypothesis for how and where writing might have developed earlier than the 3rd millennium BC, and in some place other than Egypt or Mesopotamia. It is only now that a very tentative possibility arises, particularly given that the Schmandt-Besserat accounting system was long established by the time of the Flood. That possibility is that the Vinca, Sumerian and Minoan writing systems might all have had their origins in an ancestral one which had already been developed somewhere prior to any of them, arguably in the environs of the Black Sea, and around the time of the Black Sea Flood.

Another migration route that Ryan included on his map was one all the way south to Egypt, on the basis that some of the Black Sea Flood survivors may have wandered south to found the ancient Egyptian civilisation. Despite the further demands that this made on many sceptics' credulity, Ryan undeniably has a point that it was only in the wake of the

Flood that pottery-making became introduced into Egypt, also 'domesticated cereals and animals with direct genetic affinity to Asia.'[9] Furthermore archaeologists have long recognised that the earliest significant phase of Egyptian art, the 4th millennium BC's Gerzean phase, is the one period in which there appear some striking affinities with Mesopotamian art. Such similarities are to be found at no later stage, when in all logic one would have expected them, given the greater trade links between the two cultures.

For instance a Gerzean flint knife found at Gebel el-Arak in Upper Egypt, features on one side of its superbly crafted ivory handle a bearded Gilgamesh hero between two lions.[10] Not least because of the beard, this could easily be taken for Mesopotamian were it not for its provenance in Egypt, and also a traditionally Egyptian water battle scene carved on its reverse side. Although the Gerzean era was well over a thousand years after the Black Sea Flood, it was also a thousand or so years before the building of the Pyramids. So was this perhaps a period in which the still embryonic Egyptian and Mesopotamian civilisations were both under the influence of communities descended from talented Flood refugees who had taught them all they knew?

Whatever the validity of this, the Ryan Diaspora hypothesis has a huge difficulty to overcome. It is this. Why, between the Flood in 5600 BC and the flowering proper of the Egyptian and Mesopotamian civilisations c.3000 BC, should there be no culture outside Turkey which quite unmistakably shows all the hallmarks of having inherited the precocities of a pre-Flood Çatal Hüyük?

Yet paradoxically, a few thousand years later – and without any obvious clues as to what has gone on in the interval – certain surprisingly far-flung cultures *do* display remarkable signs of some distinctively Çatal Hüyük-type traits. It is just as if somewhere, somehow much of the pre-Flood Black Sea environs' culture and expertise had been perpetuated. Except that as yet we cannot quite see where this occurred, or how.

One culture certainly to exhibit Çatal Hüyük-type traits is that of the Minoan civilisation of Crete, which entered its heyday c.2000 BC, well over three millennia after the Flood. Just as Çatal Hüyük had been a cattle town, so too the Minoans of Crete were cattle people. Minoan art, just like that of Çatal Hüyük, was full of superbly crafted bulls' heads [fig 20] and lively depictions of unarmed humans cavorting with bulls, as in the case of the famous 'bull-leaping' fresco found at Knossos. The Minoans too had horns of consecration as a repeatedly recurring motif in their shrines [fig 20, top right]. The Minoans too reverenced a Great Mother Goddess, whom they depicted in their shrines in the company of animals. Exactly as in the art of the Çatal Hüyük, the Minoans exhibited an extraordinary reverence and fascination for the animal world in all its forms, virtually to the exclusion of all other themes. After the Çatal Hüyük people, the Minoans were virtually the first known people to produce wall paintings featuring landscapes. Architecturally, the Minoans made their rooms and build-ings rectangular, and they painted their plastered walls with frescoes, just as at Çatal Hüyük. There are also some striking affinities between the Minoan palace complex as excavated at Knossos and the complex of shrines excavated at Çatal Hüyük, as if both were designed as dwellings in which the living and the dead could live together.

Çatal Hüyük's excavator James Mellaart, for one, has long recognised such parallels between the Minoans and the much earlier Çatal Hüyük people. He strongly suspects that what-ever the language which was spoken at pre-Flood Çatal Hüyük, that of the Minoans of Crete was descended from it.[11] This obviously has some profound implications for some of the mysteries pertaining to the Minoan culture as a whole, the origins of this, and the language they spoke, being far from

Fig 20 Above: The bull cult on
Crete. Bull's head drinking vessel
found at a 2nd millennium BC
Minoan palace at Knossos

Top right: Minoan horns of
consecration also from Knossos,
and (right) the same motif as found
at pre-Flood Çatal Hüyük

clear. Yet, as we must repeat, the Minoans only began to flour-
ish four thousand years after the 6000 BC abandonment of Çatal
Hüyük. And unlike the inland Çatal Hüyük people, they were
very much a maritime people. So in the interim how and
where could Çatal Hüyük's pre-Flood culture have gone
underground so invisibly, and for so long?

Another post-Flood culture which exhibits some rather different aspects of pre-Flood Çatal Hüyük influence, and which
dates from substantially closer in time to it, is that of the people
who built the great megalithic shrines on Malta and Gozo. It is
only by visiting these islands that it is possible properly to

appreciate just what an extraordinary phenomenon is represented by these superbly crafted edifices.

Malta has the earliest and most interesting complex of megalithic temples in the world, of which one of the most splendid examples is that of the Hypogeum of Hal Saflieni. Built on several levels hollowed out below ground level, its superbly engineered interior gives the same labyrinth-like impression as the Çatal Hüyük shrines and the palace of Knossos. First discovered in 1902, it was sadly rather badly damaged shortly afterwards, and then very badly excavated. Despite the bones of some seven thousand people having been found buried in it, frustratingly we know very little about them except that the bones were disarticulated, suggesting the same sort of excavation practice as at Çatal Hüyük. Although little is visible now, the walls were once covered with paintings of animals, including bulls and fish. On the stone ceiling there was traced in red ochre a spiral motif, like a rolling wave, which recurs again and again, often in sculpted relief form, throughout other megalithic sites, as well as on Minoan Crete, and in coastal post-Flood Turkey. Another motif that appeared for the first time in Malta, but would also do so later in Crete and elsewhere, is a Tree of Life which a Maltese sculptor created on a pillar altar found at the temple of Hagar Qim.

In all, Malta and its near neighbour Gozo have some thirty megalithic temples, their now impenetrable names – such as Hal Saflieni, Hal Tarxien, Hagar Qim, Mnajdra, Ggantija – seeming to derive from the unknown language of those who built them. All were superbly crafted from colossal blocks of stone, an incredible oeuvre for what can never have been a large island population. And they were once much higher, having been covered with roofs made of blocks of stone that were arranged in a corbel style in the manner of Çatal Hüyük. Further, some of these were painted red inside, recalling the red painted beams and all-red midwifery unit or maternity suite at Çatal Hüyük.

To the best of anyone's determination Malta's earliest human inhabitants arrived on the island, probably from nearby Sicily, c.5000 BC, within just a few centuries of the Flood. A further wave, this time of temple builders, followed in around 3500 BC. Neither group had weapons, so the second wave seems to have been more like an arrival of close relatives than an invasion. And exactly as in the case of the Vinca people, it was a great shock in archaeological circles when radio-carbon dating determined the Malta megalithic shrines to date so early. The fact had to be faced that instead of these shrines being built later than the pyramids, as had confidently been supposed, this handful of people on a tiny, far-flung island had actually preceded the Egyptians in displaying such extraordinary feats. So whoever built these Maltese structures, where had they *first* originated, that they possessed such engineering skills so long before Egypt and Mesopotamia had developed theirs? Surely not Sicily, their recognised stepping stone before arriving in Malta? It is a question to which scholars have still not come up with entirely satisfactory answers.

At first sight, the fact that the prime Maltese building material is stone, and such huge blocks of it, might seem a million miles removed from the wattle and daub that we saw at Çatal Hüyük. And although some volcanic stone had been used at Asikli, this was as nothing compared to the Cyclopean blocks deployed on Malta.

But the horned facades on the approaches to the Maltese temples immediately recall the Çatal Hüyük-like horns of consecration that were so prevalent in the bull shrines. And most pertinent of all are the goddess figures found on Malta, which exhibit all the same steatopygous, or grossly fat, exuberance of buttocks and breasts as those of the Great Mother Goddess of Çatal Hüyük. A particularly fine 4th millennium BC example was found in the Hypogeum of Hal Saflieni in the form of a figurine featuring a massive buttocked woman

Fig 21 (left) Figurine of seated goddess c.3000 BC as found in Hagar Qin temple, Malta, and (right) near-identical figurine c.6000 BC, found at Çatal Hüyük

wearing a bell-shaped skirt. Depicted asleep, as if she is 'receiving' communications from the dead in her dreams, this is exactly as we have inferred of the practices of the Çatal Hüyük people.

However, the female figurine of particular interest is one found in the Hagar Qin temple, seated on the ground with massive limbs and tiny hands and feet, and minus her original head [fig 21 left]. In one of the Çatal Hüyük shrines Mellaart found an almost identical example, with exactly the same corpulence and tiny hands and feet, except that she still had cross patterns painted all over her body [fig 21 right]. And she too was headless, clearly having suffered exactly the same deliberate decapitation to decommission her as a magical idol that we earlier noted to have been practised at Çatal Hüyük. Yet these figurines are separated in time by some three thousand years and in distance by 1,600 kilometres (1,000 miles) of land and sea.

So should we dismiss such parallels as mere coincidence? Or conceivably do we have an important clue that Pitman was absolutely right that there was a widespread post-Flood diaspora? May he simply have erred in not looking seawards and sufficiently far to the west for some of his hypothesised migration routes?

The phenomenon of the building of megalithic monuments right across Europe, of which Malta was one of the earliest examples, is of course a major mystery in its own right. And it is one that has already attracted far too many weird and wonderful theories, to which I have no inclination to add. But what is particularly notable about the appearance of these megalithic monuments – and until Ryan and Pitman came up with their theory no one had even had a chance to consider this – is that it only began *after* the Black Sea Flood. It then spread steadily westwards across the Mediterranean touching Tunisian north Africa, Malta, other western Mediterranean islands and the Spanish coast, before travelling through the straits of Gibraltar and up the Spanish and French coasts to the British Isles as far as Ireland and the Orkneys.

So it was always coastal, strongly suggesting that its transmission was by people who had arrived in boats to settle, had practised agriculture, and had then built great shrines for their dead. The dead who, as in the instance of Isbister in the Orkneys, were laid out to have their bones picked clean by sea eagles, exactly as the Çatal Hüyük people had had theirs picked at by the vultures of the Konya plain, three thousand years before. And dead for whom extraordinary houses were built. Houses which required huge blocks of stone to be quarried, shaped and manipulated, and which no conceivable natural catastrophe could destroy, not even a biblical-scale Flood.

The builders of these megaliths would have to have been as technically proficient as those at Çatal Hüyük had been, even if they had not necessarily practised such skills back in their original homeland. So is it possible that the great megaliths of Europe were built by descendants of survivors of the Black Sea Flood, their doing so having been perhaps a reaction to that event? As yet this must be considered but an intriguing thought, but it is one that we will return to.

For if these Black Sea Flood refugees arrived by sea, then not least of the issues to be considered is whether, at this still very early time, the post-Flood inhabitants of Turkey would have had boats capable of venturing as far as Malta, North Africa and beyond. And as we are about to see, the answer is that indeed they did.

CHAPTER 12

WHO HAD THE SHIPS?

Certainly the earliest detailed representation of ocean-going ships yet known outside Egypt
James Mellaart, of ships engraved on an
ancient north-west Turkish sword-blade

When considering the Black Sea Flood it is important not to overlook that its root cause had been a marked post-Ice Age rise in the Mediterranean's sea-level. As we noted in an earlier chapter, scientists have determined that this rose quite dramatically, together with that of the world's oceans to which it was linked. And very likely this happened in spurts, while the last Ice Age went through its dying paroxysms.

So quite aside from the now well-established trauma that affected Turkey's Black Sea coast c.5600 BC, there must have been a number of other coastlines all around the Mediterranean that at different and as yet undetermined times suffered their own more localised Flood disasters.

Referring back to the general post-Ice Age sea-level rise for the Mediterranean area as plotted by the scientists Shackleton and van Andel (see map p.79),[1] we may recall that among the more significant happenings were that Sicily separated from Italy (thereby also creating Malta), and that a large portion of land east of present-day Tunisia became submerged. Directly affecting the shorelines around Turkey itself, a large chunk of what had been the south-western part of the island of Rhodes disappeared into the sea. Numerous sections of what had been Turkey's western, or Mediterranean coast became off-shore islands. And to Turkey's north-west a large area of plain in the region of north-east Greece, later to be known as Thrace, disappeared beneath the sea, one section of higher land remaining above water to form the island of Samothrace.

It is quite definite that these events happened sometime between the end of the Ice Age and the advent of surviving written records. Unlike in the case of the 5600 BC Black Sea Flood, what no one has yet determined is exactly when any of them occurred within those parameters, or how local peoples were affected. However, given that the period was one when the Mediterranean undoubtedly had human settlements scattered all around it, it is not unreasonable to expect that some related folk-memories might have survived among the region's later coastal and island populations – perhaps at least up to the Roman era.

And indeed we find this to be so. Thus in the case of Sicily, there comes from the writings of the Alexandria-based scholar Philo Judaeus, who lived around the turn of the Christian era:

> Consider how many districts of the mainland, not only such as were near the coast, but even such as were completely inland, have been swallowed up by the waters; and consider how great a proportion of land has become sea and is now sailed by innumerable ships. Who is ignorant of that most sacred Sicilian strait, which in old times joined Sicily to the continent of Italy? And where vast seas on each side being excited by violent storms met together, coming from opposite directions, the land between them was overwhelmed and broken away ... in consequence of which Sicily, which had previously formed a part of the mainland, was now compelled to be an island.[2]

Our interest, however, primarily concerns the Mediterranean's eastern region. And for this a particularly useful authority happens to have been a 1st century BC Sicilian, Diodorus Siculus. Diodorus' *magnum opus* was a Universal History, much of the research for which he carried out at the famous Royal Library of Alexandria in Egypt.[3] This library was destroyed by fire in 48 BC, only shortly after Diodorus had worked there.[4] In many instances, therefore, Diodorus drew upon and uniquely recorded, earlier writers' collections of ancient peoples' histories and folk-memories which otherwise would have been lost to us.

As might be expected of anyone trying to write a history of the world from such materials, Diodorus Siculus' critical judgment of these is at times faulty, for which he has rightly been castigated by modern scholars. This said, back in the 19th century even some of the writings of the highly respected 5th century BC Greek historian Herodotus, such as his descriptions of the customs of the Scythians, were widely disbelieved, only for recent archaeological findings in Scythian tombs to have proved him right.[5]

And in Diodorus Siculus' defence, what he has to say regarding eastern Mediterranean sea-level rise, like Philo's information, has received some striking modern-day scientific confirmation, as in the case of his remarks concerning the island of Rhodes:

> The island which is called Rhodes was first inhabited by the people who were known as Telchines; these were children of Thalatta [the Sea] ... At a later time ... the Telchines, perceiving in advance the Flood that was going to come, forsook the island and were scattered ... And when the Flood came the rest of the inhabitants perished – and since the waters, because of the abundant rains, overflowed the island, its level parts were turned into stagnant pools. But a few fled for refuge to the upper regions of the island and were saved ...[6]

If we turn to Shackleton and van Andel's map it will be seen that, just as we mentioned earlier, part of what had been the island of Rhodes indeed became submerged as a result of the post-Ice Age sea-level changes. So from a Rhodian folk-memory preserved in the library of Alexandria back in the 1st century BC Diodorus has apparently relayed on to us a faithful memory of the post-Ice Age sea-level rise as this affected people who lived on Rhodes perhaps more than five thousand years before his time. Diodorus even got right (at least, assuming that the van Andel and Shackleton reconstruction is accurate) that Rhodes had always been an island rather than, like Sicily, having once been joined to the mainland.

As Diodorus further related, the Rhodians 'introduced many new practices in seamanship', suggesting that they were proficient mariners. Diodorus even ventured that one of their number, Aetis – a name that we will find later to be associated with a ruler on the Black Sea's south-eastern coast – went off to Egypt to found the city of Heliopolis known by the Egyptians as On, near modern-day Cairo. This founding would subsequently be forgotten, except by the Egyptians. Could this be a far memory of the post-Flood migration from the Black Sea to Egypt that Pitman suggested, only to be met with scepticism?

In this instance the issue is of no immediate consequence. For rather more important is that Diodorus' account of the sea-level rise as this affected Rhodes formed part of his more general account of the early history of other Mediterranean islands. And what he had to say concerning a similarly Flood-related folk-memory from Samothrace is nothing short of astounding. The island stands directly at the entrance to the Dardanelles strait (known in antiquity as the Hellespont), which via the Sea of Marmara leads into the Bosporus. In Diodorus' own words:

The Samothracians have a story that, before the floods which befell other peoples, a great one took place among them, *in the course of which the outlet at the Cyanaean Rocks was first rent asunder and then the Hellespont* [italics mine].[7]

Now the Cyanaean rocks were two islets which in Diodorus' time stood at the eastern end of the Bosporus strait where this joins the Black Sea. The very highly regarded Roman geographer Strabo, who was born in what is now Turkey, referred to them,[8] and they appear to have existed up to the 16th century. So the spectacular part of Diodorus' information is that he was clearly referring to the Samothracians remembering that the former Bosporus land-bridge had been 'rent asunder' by a burst-through of water. Making this completely unequivocal is the fact that in the very next sentence Diodorus went on to make the equally astounding statement that the Black Sea had formerly been a lake:

For the Pontus [the ancient name for the Black Sea] *which had at that time the form of a lake* [italics mine], was so swollen by the rivers that flow into it, that, because of the great flood which had poured into it, the waters burst forth violently into the Hellespont ...[9]

In all the writings that survive from antiquity this is the only one to recall what we now know to be a fact, that the Black Sea was indeed a lake before 5600 BC. And although before the Ryan, Pitman and Ballard findings scholars would have dismissed this information from Diodorus as just another piece of fancy, it is now quite clear that in this information at least he deserves considerable respect. The only significant point on which he or his Samothracian informants erred pertains to which side of the Bosporus the burst-through might have come from. For Diodorus it was the Black Sea which burst through into the Mediterranean, breaching first the Bosporus then the Dardanelles (or Hellespont) former land-bridges in the course of this. For Ryan and Pitman, on the other hand, it was the Mediterranean which burst through into the Black Sea, thereby having breached the Dardanelles first, followed by the Bosporus. However, given the undoubted confusion that would have prevailed back in 5600 BC, and the fact that to this day the Bosporus currents make it appear that it is the Black Sea, swollen by the Russian rivers, which flows into the Mediterranean, such a discrepancy is surely but a trifle.

Diodorus went on to provide further accurate information as to how the island of Samothrace became broken off from the Thracian mainland by a sea-level rise, just as we have already learned from Shackleton and van Andel:

> [The rising waters] flooded a large part of the coast of Asia [i.e. Asia Minor, or modern-day Turkey] and made no small amount of the level part of the land of Samothrace into a sea ...[10]

In fact Samothrace became an island specifically as a result of the sea-level rise. Albeit indirectly, Diodorus further explained how the tradition could have been handed down through five and a half thousand years:

> The inhabitants who had been caught by the flood ... ran up to the higher regions of the island; and when the sea kept rising higher and higher, they prayed to the native gods. And since their lives were spared, to commemorate their rescue they set up boundary stones about the entire circuit of the island and dedicated altars *upon which they offer sacrifices even to the present day* [italics mine]. For these reasons it is patent that they inhabited Samothrace before the flood ...[11]

Even down to Diodorus' own time, therefore, five and a half millennia after the Black Sea Flood, descendants of the original Samothracians had been continuing to commemorate their salvation from the sea-level rise. Just as punctiliously as Jews, in their Passover celebrations, have continued to commemorate their salvation from slavery in Egypt throughout well over three millennia. Further notable is Diodorus' information that the form of the early Samothracians' commemoration of their experience, besides their offering sacrifices (just as Noah, Uta-napishti and the others had done), was to erect stone monuments. This corroborates therefore our earlier tentative suggestion that the Flood and subsequent proliferation of megaliths might in some way have been linked.

Furthermore, even at the present day in the northernmost part of the island of Samothrace, looking towards the mainland, there stands what is called 'The Sanctuary of the Great Gods'. The Sanctuary's main surviving monuments date from the classical period, when initiation into Samothrace's ancient mystery religion was reputed to bring divine protection from shipwreck,[12] making it a Lourdes for sailors. Nonetheless there is general agreement that it rests on a far more ancient, pre-Greek shrine that was devoted to a fertility cult presided over by the Great Mother Goddess of prehistoric Turkish origin, later to be known as Cybele. Other lesser pre-Greek deities who were associated with this same shrine and cult were a male fertility god with erect penis called Kadmilos, whom the later Greeks identified with their Hermes. Also venerated were twins called Cabeiroi, believed to be protectors of sailors, but who were otherwise regarded by ancient writers with great fear and ignorance.[13] All these deities were regarded as having been from before the time of the Greeks.

The ancient Samothrace Sanctuary's pantheon of a Great Mother Goddess, an inferior male god and mysterious twins exhibits some striking similarities to the cult that Mellaart found in the shrines of pre-Flood Çatal Hüyük. Corroborating this, Cabeiroi is a non-Greek word, indicating that those who had lived on Samothrace since the time of the great sea-level rise were non-Greeks and spoke an as yet unidentified pre-Greek language. Indeed Diodorus specifically noted that the Samothracians used 'an ancient language which was peculiar to them and of which many words are preserved to this day in the ritual of their sacrifices.' Independently we know that *Samos* is another non-Greek word, apparently meaning 'high' in Phoenician. So if the original post-Flood inhabitants of Samothrace were indeed of much the same stock as the pre-Flood people of Çatal Hüyük and Stone Age Turkey, then this at least sustains the still tenuous possibility that their common pre-Flood language may have been an early form of Semitic, the Phoenicians having been both Semites of uncertain origin, and renowned seafarers.

But what of the Samothracians and seafaring? If you ascend the 1,600-metre (5,249-foot) high Mount Saos on Samothrace, you are provided with a most stunning watery panorama. This includes to the south-east the approaches to the Dardanelles strait through which the Flood waters had to have rushed before reaching the Bosporus. And a few kilometres to the south-west you can look out towards what is now the island of Lemnos. Although now Greek, this was joined to the Turkish mainland before the post-Ice Age, sea-level rise, and apparently had much the same cult as that on Samothrace, including the Great Mother Goddess and Cabeiroi. Excavations that Italian archaeologist Alessandro della Seta carried out on Lemnos during the early 1930s revealed at the ancient site of Poliochni two late Stone Age settlements that have been described as 'the most advanced Neolithic civilization in the Aegean'.[14] Arranged in streets with crossroads at right-angles, the large roomy houses were even equipped with stone baths in the later of the two settlements. As late as classical times the Lemnians maintained a reputation for their women being the more dominant of the two sexes.[15] And exactly as on Samothrace, they spoke an

ancient language far too different from that of the Greeks for
the latter to comprehend.

However also viewable from Samothrace's Mount Saos,
on the Turkish side of the mouth of the Dardanelles strait is
the mound called Hissarlik, the site of Homer's Troy, which
the German archaeologist Heinrich Schliemann famously
excavated during the 1870s. According to Greek mythology
the god Poseidon watched the Trojan War from Mount Saos,
millennia before this, indeed shortly after the Flood. But also
recorded in mythology, is the tale of Dardanus who travelled from Samothrace by boat across the mouth of the
Dardanelles to found an as yet unlocated city on much the
same stretch of coast on which Troy would later be built.[16]
As Diodorus Siculus told the story:

> Dardanus ... was a man who entertained great designs
> and was the first to make his way across to Asia in a
> makeshift boat, founded at the outset a city called
> Dardanus, organized the kingdom which lay about the
> city which was called Troy at a later time, and called the
> people Dardanians after himself. They say that he ruled
> over many nations throughout Asia and that the Dardani
> who dwell beyond Thrace were colonists sent forth by
> him.[17]

Bearing in mind that Dardanus is a mythological figure from
a seemingly impenetrable prehistoric past – could this
north-eastern corner of the Mediterranean, at a very early
time have been a point from which boats went out to found
colonies, using it as a base for some kind of maritime
empire?

One difficulty here is that today's Turks were comparatively late immigrants into the country that now bears their
name, and traditionally they have had scant interest in their
more ancient predecessors. This has given rise to one of the
great problems with the archaeology of Turkey, as distinct

from that of Egypt or Mesopotamia, that there has simply not been enough of it in relation to the enormity of the country's ancient past. Furthermore, while looting and vandalism have beset most countries with ancient remains, in Turkey this has long been a multi-million dollar industry, with government controls near-non-existent until quite recently. While Turkish traders have been able to make a good living supplying looted antiquities to accomplice dealers in the United States, Germany and elsewhere, all too often the context and provenance of antiquities of real importance has become lost, the antiquities themselves likewise disappearing into private hands.

Such problems particularly pertain to what may well have been one of the most spectacular archaeological finds ever to be made in Turkey. Were it not for the fact that its documentation and original artefacts have been similarly lost to scholarly scrutiny.

Several years before James Mellaart began his 1960s work opening up Çatal Hüyük he was invited to a wealthy private home in Izmir. There a woman who insisted on great secrecy showed him a collection of very ancient artefacts, the degree of culture of which amazed him as much as their antiquity. This collection, he was given to understand, had been found during the early 1920s – the time of the war between Greece and Turkey. Just over a hundred kilometres east of Troy, on the southern shore of Lake Apolyont, near the modern town of Bursa and just a little inland from the Sea of Marmara, had been excavated an ancient cemetery on a hill slope. The collection, known as the Dorak hoard after the nearby village of Dorak, consisted of grave goods, which had been taken from the tombs of three individuals of apparent royal status. Mellaart was well aware that the collection was unique in all western Turkey, but to his intense frustration he was not permitted to photograph any of the artefacts. He was however allowed to make careful drawings of them, in which regard we are fortunate that he is an accomplished artist. He was also shown notes, drawings and photographs made at the time of the original excavation.[18]

From such data it was evident that the find had consisted of two main tombs, both of these apparently lined with huge stonework that had been carefully cut square in the manner of advanced cultures who valued rectangular architecture. The first of these tombs contained a single male skeleton, apparently that of a king, who upon its opening up could be seen to be lying on a woven rug. Sadly this rug began to disintegrate literally before the excavators' eyes, so that their only recourse was to make a coloured drawing − which Mellaart duly copied. But clear from this is that the rug was a *kilim* in the same tradition as those known from the designs found at Çatal Hüyük. The strong inference, therefore, was that this Dorak culture, in Turkey's north-western sector, had some significant continuity with that at Çatal Hüyük.

Yet this *kilim* was but a trifle compared to other spectacular objects among the tomb's contents. Under, beside and behind the king's body there were no less than eleven elaborately crafted swords and daggers. From the point of view of early north-west Turkish seafaring, one of these in particular was revelatory. This specimen was the only one in the collection bearing a silver blade, and on it was engraved a fleet of seventeen ships each propelled by anything up to 30 oarsmen [fig 22].[19] Clearly evident is that these were substantial vessels with beak-like prows as later used by Greek triremes (galleys). They had high stern-castles from which they could be steered in the ancient fashion with the aid of a side-slung steering oar. And five of the ships had their power supplemented by a large square sail. These were unmistakably vessels capable of coping with open seas.

So at what date did there live this north-west Turkish king who apparently had command of, or access to, so

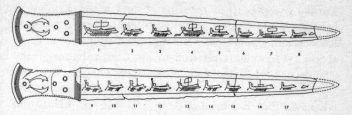

Fig 22 Early 3rd millennium BC silver sword blade as found in one of the early Dorak tombs, depicting seventeen ocean-going ships, all oar-powered, and five of these with the extra assistance of a sail. This is one of the earliest-known detailed depictions of ocean-going vessels found outside Egypt

impressive a fleet? The quite staggering aspect of the whole Dorak hoard is its extremely early date. Despite the two tombs' contents having been wrenched from their context, at least the collection had been kept together. And by great good fortune one object that was found in the second tomb, which contained a male and female skeleton (thought to have been a king and queen), provided the necessary means of dating. This object – the only item thought to have been of foreign manufacture – was a wooden throne of which little remained but its gold ornament. But one piece of this gold ornament was embossed in Egyptian hieroglyphs with the name and titles of the second king of Old Kingdom Egypt's 5th Dynasty, Sahure, who reigned about the middle of the 3rd millennium BC. And since this date is consistent with the designs of some of the other artefacts – which are similar to so-called Yortan artefacts found in this part of Turkey – the two tombs can be attributed to much this same period. This makes them as early as anything of similar quality found in Egypt and Mesopotamia.

Similarly, the representations of ocean-going ships rank among the very earliest known that have been found any-where in the world. Much later the Greek historian Herodotus hints at some such very early sea-power off

Turkey's west coast in speaking of the Carians, a people in
his time occupying Turkey's south-west corner adjacent to
Rhodes, and whom Homer had described as 'men of uncouth
speech'.[20] Herodotus referred to the Carians as 'originally
islanders' who 'when they inhabited the islands ... were
known as Leleges' and crewed the ships of Minoan Crete
whenever they had need of them.[21] So it is possible than in
the vessels depicted, we may well be seeing both descendants of the fleet of the world's first great maritime sea-
power in the wake of the Black Sea Flood and also
precursors of the sea-power that would later be called
Phoenician.

Yet even this by no means exhausts the interest value of
the Dorak hoard. For among the weapons that were found in
the first tomb was also a sword, the hilt of which was
superbly crafted in black obsidian in the shape of two leopards. As we may recall from Çatal Hüyük, two leopards were
used as if heraldically in the shrines. They also featured as
supports to the throne of the Great Mother Goddess in the
statuette found in the grain bin. This sword's most astonishing feature, however, was not its hilt but again its blade.
Instead of this being made of the bronze as used for most of
the other weapons in the tomb – and indeed for most
weapons made during the 3rd and 2nd millennia BC – it was
made of iron. While this might seem nothing special to us, in
fact, because of smelting difficulties, iron was still extremely
rare. This was true even as late as the time of pharaoh
Tutankhamun (14th century BC), whose tomb provided one
of the only other examples of iron-bladed weapons earlier
than the beginning of the Iron Age proper, c.1000 BC.[22] And
from the design of the Tutankhamun specimen, it too is
thought to have been made, not in Egypt, but somewhere in
ancient Turkey.

So the question arises, just who were these people from
this north-western Turkish culture who had so precociously

developed metallurgical skills that it would take the
Egyptians and Mesopotamians another 15 centuries to
master? As we have already seen, they appear to have had a
fleet of ocean-going vessels. Other objects in the two tombs,
indicating that they had formed some impressive trading
links, corroborate this. The amber, for instance, as used for
part of the decoration of the iron sword's hilt had most
likely been brought all the way from the Baltic, since there
is no known source for it anywhere in the Near East. The
ivory used for a comb of otherwise local craftsmanship had
most likely come from Africa. They had quite definitely
made some seafaring contact with Egypt, hence the gilded
throne, which was arguably a royal gift from the king of
Egypt to his north-west Turkish counterpart. And that they
had lived in a style easily equivalent to their Mesopotamian
and Egyptian contemporaries is evident from the elegant
styling of the gold, silver and electrum cups and jugs that
were deposited with them for their afterlife. Equally evident
is that they did not slavishly copy these from Egyptian and
Mesopotamian equivalents, since similar objects found at
Troy and dating many centuries later, show that they had
been crafted to a local Dardanian or Trojan styling that had
arguably already been long-established since well before
c.2500 BC.

We have scant evidence as to the appearance of the men
whose skeletons were found in the tombs, except that the
kings apparently carried globe-headed sceptres or maces as
emblems of their authority, and they sported an impressive
armoury of swords and daggers, together with axes and
spears. The 'king' in the double tomb had laid at his feet his
dog, which had even, as a homely touch, been provided
with a stone feeding bowl.

Body ornaments were found on the queen's skeleton but
sadly the textiles that were seen around and below the
skeleton when the tomb was opened did not survive

exposure to the air. The queen also had an impressively modern-style interest in cosmetics and toiletries, as demonstrated by her toilet set. This consisted of a spatula, toilet spoon and tweezers, all in silver, together with three small silver tubes that are thought to have contained rouge, kohl (the ancient mascara) and green eye-shadow. The drawing that the 1920s excavator made of her skeleton shows a single circlet around her head exactly like the head-dressing of the Çatal Hüyük Great Mother Goddess.

But what did provide a most fascinating glimpse of what these early north-west Turkish women wore were five exquisitely crafted female figurines, each about 15 centimetres (6 inches) high, in bronze, silver and electrum, also found in the queen's tomb. The two in bronze represented women who may have been priestesses. These were depicted wearing stylish ankle-length skirts which, though crafted in silver, were patterned as if woven or dyed using colourful materials. Equally stylish were their short-sleeve bodices, fastened just below the bust, but then opening out to expose the navel.

These women were the modest ones, however, for the two crafted entirely in silver, thought to have been attendants, were represented nude except for gold tiaras, armlets, anklets, necklaces, belt and in the case of one, tiny briefs. This latter was also carrying a tambourine-like musical instrument. And most interesting of all was the third, crafted in electrum, an alloy of silver and gold, and similarly scantily clad [fig 23]. From her Dervish-like high head-dress, ear-rings and more elaborate armlets and anklets, Mellaart identified her as a goddess – except that as he noted, her objects of jewellery were exactly the same as those worn by the queen in the double tomb. She can also be seen to be wearing a string skirt just like the one noted at Çatal Hüyük, also the 'White Lady' in the Saharan Tassili frescoes, and the fertility goddesses of old. So did the Dorak queen perhaps

go to her death attired as the Great Mother Goddess —
because in life she was regarded as her earthly representative? Among the clues to this, the comb in her hair had a
centre roundel depicting two finely carved wild-goats or
ibexes and two dolphins, both among the creatures who, as
evident from later cultures, were regarded as sacred to this
same goddess.

Whatever the answers, clearly in the environs of
Turkey's western coast, and its neighbouring islands there
survived from the Stone Age into the Bronze Age some fascinating vestiges of the culture that arguably had originated
in this same region before the Flood. We can be quite sure
they were not Greeks, since as we learned earlier from
Diodorus Siculus, the Greeks quite definitely saw them as

Fig 23 Electrum figurine from the Dorak queen's tomb, thought to be of
the Goddess, or of the queen herself

foreigners in terms of both language and religious customs. Likewise they were certainly not ancestors of the present-day Turks who arrived comparatively late in what is now Turkey. So what might we be able to learn about them from similar remnant peoples perhaps surviving elsewhere in and around the land today called Turkey – including, perhaps, whoever they obtained their iron from at so early a period?

CHAPTER 13

WHO STAYED AT HOME?

Noah ... was the first to plant the vine

Genesis 9: 20

Many modern interpreters of wine history suggest that Georgia has yielded the earliest evidence of winemaking in the world.

McGovern et al, *The Origins and Ancient History of Wine Making*

Mention ancient Egyptians and most of us, even from a minimal acquaintance with Egyptian tomb paintings, can conjure up a mental image of clean-shaven men wearing white linen kilts, and women with heavy eye make-up and jet black hair clad in long white shifts. We are able to picture the Nile, and to place it on a map, with Thebes famous for its Karnak temple at its southern end, and the Pyramids to the north. Even in the case of Mesopotamian cultures we are likely to have some recollection of seeing statues of sheepskin-clad Sumerians or heavily bearded Assyrians, and be able geographically to place them as having lived between the great rivers Tigris and Euphrates.

But ask anyone to envisage Turkey's ancient inhabitants – whether for the period immediately after the Flood, or for several millennia after – and it is a very different matter. Indeed, making things difficult even for the specialist is that for any millennium between the Flood and the Christian era it is impossible even to give a single all-embracing name to the country's peoples, let alone to picture them. This is largely because they were never one people, but comprised independent, variegated tribes each with their own distinctive traits, customs and so on. Adding to the unfamiliarity, most lay-persons, if they were quizzed concerning Turkey's geography, would be hard-pressed to name even a single one of the country's rivers, let alone to place this on a map.

In order to begin to comprehend Turkey as the home of some surprisingly civilised peoples living both before and after the Black Sea Flood, we need to try to 'see' the country as it was back in ancient times in at least something of its geographical and cultural diversity. It may be useful then to call upon the most ancient literary account to attempt this – even though in all likelihood this dates millennia after the immediate post-Flood period – while also drawing upon whatever relevant archaeological findings may be available.

The ancient literary account in question is the famous Greek legend of Jason and the quest for the Golden Fleece. The *Argonautika* or story of Jason was already old in the time of Homer, in whose *Odyssey* it was described as 'common knowledge' or 'world-famous',[1] references to it elsewhere in *Iliad* and *Odyssey* indicating widespread familiarity. According to the Greek archaeologist Christos Doumas its origins may stretch back to the 4th millennium BC, and derive from quests to find out the secrets of metal smelting and forging from the earliest peoples to have developed these crafts.[2] The earliest surviving complete version, however, derives from the 3rd century BC Alexandria librarian Apollonios Rhodios,[3] and may well have suffered distortions in the course of its being handed down through the generations. The story describes how Jason, his vessel the *Argo* and its trusty crew of Argonauts made their way up Turkey's west coast, through the Dardanelles and Bosporus, and then eastwards along Turkey's Black Sea coast to Colchis, on the Sea's south-eastern shores. It gives us some interesting glimpses of the arguably ancient peoples they encountered along the way.

In the course of the Argo's voyage northwards up Turkey's western coast the Argonauts reportedly visited the island of Lemnos, where they were attacked by armed women, consistent with the island's reputation for forceful females mentioned in the last chapter. They then went on to the now equally familiar island of Samothrace, where they were reportedly initiated into the mysteries of the Great Mother Goddess, thereby giving them some much-needed divine protection as mariners. Next they cleverly eluded the king of Troy's hold over the Dardanelles strait by rowing through this at night, safely reaching the Sea of Marmara.

After some adventures with two smallish kingdoms on the shores of this Sea, their next hurdle, in negotiating the Bosporus strait, was the Cyanaean rocks, the burst-through point where the Bosporus joins the Black Sea. Apparently in Jason's time these rocks had the fearsome reputation of driving together and crushing any vessel that tried to pass between them. Given that Cyanaean means 'blue', and that other writers describe the same rocks as 'Wandering' and 'Clashing' this may well have derived from icebergs washed down from Russia's great rivers tending to accumulate in the Black Sea at this point, with inevitable danger to any shipping.[4]

The Argonauts' typically clever ruse to avoid this danger was to release a dove ahead of their vessel as a decoy. This brought the rocks together, then as they parted the Argonauts rowed through before the next closure. According to the legend the ruse so fazed the rocks that they never clashed again.

For us, however, the more interesting aspect is that, in common with the Noah family of Flood stories, this part of the Jason story has as its basis a bird that was apparently kept captive on board as a help in danger. A 5th century BC Buddhist text offers a reason for this:

Long ago ocean-going merchants were wont to plunge
forth upon the sea on board a ship taking with them a
shore-sighting bird. When the ship was out of sight they
would set the shore-sighting bird free. And it would go to
the east and to the south and to the west and to the north
and to the intermediate points and rise aloft. If on the
horizon it caught sight of land thither it would go, but if
not it would come back to the ship again.[5]

The use specifically of a dove in such circumstances, in both
the Noah and the Jason stories, is also of interest since this
bird was regarded as especially sacred to the Great Mother
Goddess.[6]

Once through the mouth of the Bosporus and safely into
the Black Sea, Jason's *Argo* is described as turning right,
travelling along the coast in an easterly direction. Had they
turned left and had their voyage been as early as the 5th millennium BC they might have come across an interesting
culture on the Black Sea's now Bulgarian shores. It was only
in 1972 that a tractor driver named Raicho Marinov, excavating a trench near what is today the attractive Bulgarian
city of Varna made a remarkable find. He uncovered several
pieces of shiny metal that turned out to be part of the oldest
hoard of gold ornaments that have yet been found anywhere
in the world, deriving from just one of some three hundred
graves in a cemetery that dated back to *c*.4500 BC. Notably,
some of the ornaments featured bulls.

No one had previously suspected any culture of this kind
to exist in Bulgaria, certainly at so early a period, and curiously Bill Pitman in *Noah's Flood* paid no attention to it
amongst his various projected Flood survivors' migration
routes. Yet as further archaeological investigation revealed,
back in the 5th millennium BC Lake Varna, which is today an
inland lake, had been a bay of the western Black Sea that
reached some 21 kilometres (13 miles) inland and provided a
natural harbour for ships.[7] And around its shores Bulgarian

archaeologists found settlements specialising not only in gold-working but also in copper, these early metal-smiths very likely obtaining their raw metal for this latter by travelling up the River Danube to Rudna Glava in former Yugoslavia, site of the world's oldest known copper mine. This Varna metallurgical culture was not, however, long-lived. For reasons that are yet again thought to have been related to sea-level changes (and this interpretation was made before anyone had learned of Ryan and Pitman's Black Sea hypothesis), the settlements became abandoned c.4000 BC. The Varna metal-smiths' onward destination is unknown.

Yet curiously, when the Argonauts turned right rather than left for their coasting along the Black Sea, they too quickly came upon specialist metal-workers. Although the nature of the Jason legend's narrative makes any determination of precise locations mostly impossible, among the peoples apparently to be found along Turkey's northern coast in the Argonauts' time were Chalybians, who neither tilled the soil nor tended flocks. Instead, according to the *Argonautika*, these earned their livelihood by 'hacking into the stubborn earth for its iron ores', carrying out their work 'amid sooty flames and black smoke'.[8] Also mentioned are Tibarenians, a people similarly accredited by ancient sources as having been the first known iron-workers.

In fact the reason behind this duplication of names is very straightforward, as well as highly intriguing. For *chalybs* is the word that the ancient Greeks used for 'iron', Chalybians thereby simply being a name that the Greeks would have given to any iron-working people, regardless of whatever name the people themselves might actually have used. Tibarenians, on the other hand, is not a Greek-derived word, yet it is one that we came across earlier in this book. For if we recall that long list of non-Sumerian words for professions that became absorbed into the Sumerian language from an earlier, arguably pre-Flood language (see p.152) the word that the Sumerians had acquired for metal-worker was *tibira*. This raises some profound implications. Arguably the language that the Sumerians had absorbed on their arrival in southern Mesopotamia had indeed come from the Black Sea. It had been spoken there by some culture more advanced than theirs. Arguably it was the language both of the Çatal Hüyük people, and of at least some of those peoples who, post-Flood, settled afresh around and about the Black Sea's new coastlines.

But this is far from all, since as we noted in the last chapter one of the most enigmatic of the mid 3rd millennium BC Dorak discoveries was an iron sword that dated from two and a half millennia earlier than the recognised inception of the Iron Age c.1000 BC. And from the few vague details of where the Dorak tombs were located they would seem to have been somewhere in the environs of the picturesque and historic present-day Turkish town of Bursa, lying just south of the Sea of Marmara. In this context it is surely rather more than coincidence that only a little over a hundred miles east of Bursa are to be found the coastal towns of Eregli and Zonguldak, which to this day boast a reputation as homes to Turkey's biggest iron works. Eregli's indeed, have been described in recent decades as the biggest in the Middle East.[9]

And though of course this has come about only within the last century or so, due to the plenitude of coal-mines in this region, there is much to suggest that such resources might well have given the district its iron-working primacy in ancient times too. For Eregli in particular has had a very long history, its name, a Turkish corruption of its classical period name Heraclea,[10] linking it with one of the mythological hero Heracles' worst labours, descending deep into Hades (the underworld) somewhere in Eregli's vicinity to bring out the three-headed, hundred-eyed dog Cerberus.

Could this have been a garbled account of a journey down a very ancient coal-mine? Certainly Eregli existed well before the coming of the Greeks. In the Jason story it figures under the name Mariandyne, a variant on the Sumerian 'Marienna', also Myrine, one of the many names that were given to the Great Mother Goddess,[11] to whom the town was most likely dedicated by its original pre-Greek inhabitants.

Frustratingly, as yet we know little of Eregli's archaeology at this early post-Flood period, let alone that of whatever counterpart it may have had on the pre-Flood coastline some 21 kilometres (13 miles) out into the Black Sea.[12] Among the little archaeology that has been done, at Ahlateli Tepecik, 64 kilometres (40 miles) east of present-day Izmir, a 4th millennium BC site has been revealed. Here, even the relatively simple fishing folk were buried with such varied items as copper-bronze daggers and pins, a lead bar, gold earplugs and assorted silver ornaments.[13] The gold was apparently panned locally in the river Pactolus, in antiquity a well-known source for this, though today it is but a small tributary of western Turkey's River Gediz, or Hermus. At the very least, therefore, it is clear that peoples in the northwestern sector of Turkey had very early on developed some advanced metallurgical skills.

Had there been any Argonauts around in the late 6th millennium BC to wander far to the south of Eregli, then eventually they would very likely have found themselves at Hacilar. Like Çatal Hüyük, which lies 160 kilometres (100 miles) or so to its east, Hacilar became abandoned during the immediate pre-Flood mini Ice Age drought. Then it was reoccupied when climatic conditions improved, and between 1957 and 1960 it was investigated by James Mellaart, immediately before he began his Çatal Hüyük excavations. At the post-Flood levels Mellaart found rectangular houses along the lines of the pre-Flood ones at Çatal Hüyük. There also appeared in the post-Flood period what he described as a 'sophisticated painted pottery' 'first-rate, and of much higher quality than the earlier Çatal Hüyük ware.'[14] Great Mother Goddess figurines found in many of the houses, some of these suggesting her seated on leopards,[15] showed that she was still very much the centre of worship, just as she had been before the Flood.

Another settlement not far from Hacilar and certainly populated by the 3rd millennium BC was Beycesultan near the headwaters of western Turkey's River Maeander. This featured temples arranged in pairs, again with horns of consecration reminiscent of those at Çatal Hüyük and the Vinca sites. Novel features, however, were twin *stelae* or gravestone-like slabs (perhaps representative of the mysterious Cabeiroi twins), through which the sacrificial offerings may have been passed. Also certain shrines featured a single isolated wooden pillar or post of some again undetermined cultic significance.

As mentioned in an earlier chapter Çatal Hüyük's eastern mound became abandoned for good at the onset of the c.6000 BC mini Ice Age, and by digging the odd test trench Mellaart determined back in the 1960s that it was the west mound which then became resettled at some later date. For some complex political reasons, however, Mellaart was never able to return for a full excavation, and it has been only recently that fresh archaeological excavations were begun again at both the Çatal Hüyük mounds, this time under the direction of Cambridge University archaeologist Ian Hodder.[16] From Hodder's first probings of the west mound he has turned up graves of the classical period in the upper levels, and at its lowest levels pottery with geometric markings suggesting some relation to the culture which had occupied the east mound. However it is too early at present for any definitive dating, or for any firm deductions to be drawn.

Returning to the coastal route taken by the *Argo* one

definite port of call was 'Sinope in Paphlagonia', readily identifiable as precisely the same Sinop from which Ballard made his remarkable underwater discoveries in September 2000. Today the fertile plain immediately to the south of the town abounds in fields of wheat, corn and flax, with cattle breeding and fishing thriving a little further to the east. That it was much the same in antiquity was attested by the 1st century BC Roman geographer Strabo, who was born in the vicinity, and who enthused over its fertility, particularly its numerous herds of cattle, and horses. So all the indications are that the Sinop hinterland would have been a congenial enough territory for peoples displaced by the Black Sea Flood, leading us to expect that some at least remained there.

As at Eregli, Sinop has so much modern-day habitation overlying where ancient remains might be expected that little significant archaeology has been done. At Ikiztep, near Bafra a little to Sinop's east the earliest occupation levels have been dated to c.5350–5300 BC, readily attributable to early post-Flood settlement. The black, burnished pottery from these levels, initially supposed to have been from the Early Bronze Age, has incised or white painted decoration and elaborate shapes, and can be found westwards to the Sea of Marmara, in the very same region that we have already suggested to have been inhabited by early post-Flood metalworkers.[18] It bears no resemblance to anything found at either Çatal Hüyük east or west, but arguably could derive from equally advanced cultures that had previously been living around the freshwater Black Sea and had become displaced by the Flood.

In the main however it is necessary to look inland for some clue as to what standard of civilisation may or may not have existed where actual remains have yet to be found. And just over 160 kilometres (100 miles) due south of Sinop one particularly interesting site is Alaca Hüyük, located at the great bend of the Kizil Irmak river (in ancient times the Halys), not far from where the later Hittite invaders of Turkey would build their capital of Hattusas (Boghazköy). It was at Alaca Hüyük that in the 1930s Turkish archaeologists discovered 13 tombs apparently dating from the second half of the 3rd millennium BC, therefore near contemporary with the Dorak burials, also with the building of the pyramids in Egypt, and with the high period of Sumerian civilisation. Much as at Dorak and Çatal Hüyük, the Alaca Hüyük artefacts showed very advanced metal technology, one of the town's notables being buried with a gold-hilted dagger, the blade of which was again made of iron. Again the artefacts exhibited a strong aesthetic sense, and styling of the familiar Anatolian type. Notable amongst this styling was a striking 'fiddle' or 'violin' shape to representations of the human figure, with the chest and hips being rendered in a stylised and exaggerated way. There were also echoes of motifs earlier found at Çatal Hüyük, notably a cult of the Great Mother Goddess, some of the 'fiddle' figures being reminiscent of Çatal Hüyük's 'goddess in childbirth' wall reliefs; ornaments made in the semblance of twins, clearly reminiscent of the Cabeiroi [fig 24]; ornamental stags; and numerous oxen skulls indicative of a persisting bull-cult.

According to Greek mythology Sinop was founded by Amazons,[19] whom the 4th century BC Greek orator Lysias accredited with being the first to use (as distinct from make) iron weapons. In tune with this, the Argonaut myth described the *Argo*, immediately after its leaving Sinop, as sailing past 'the country of the Amazons'. Other classical writers likewise described the Amazons as living in the environs of the river Thermodon, today readily identifiable as the Terme Çay, which flows into the Black Sea about 160 kilometres (100 miles) east of Sinop, by the Turkish town still called Terme.[20] The Argonaut story also mentions another Amazon landmark in the vicinity – an island with a stone temple that

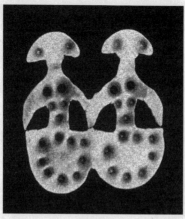

Fig 24 Fiddle-figure style ornaments in the shape of twins – the Cabeiroi? – as found in a 3rd millennium BC tomb at Alaca Hüyük

was founded by the Amazon Antiope.[21] This is identifiable as the island of Giresun Adasi. On this, there stands to this day a ruined roofless stone temple that is said to be visited every May by local women to celebrate fertility rites. However since we will later see evidence for the Amazons having been comparatively late arrivals in this territory, our more immediate concern is with other Flood survivors who may have settled early along this Black Sea coast.

A further people referred to in the Jason legend and elsewhere were Mossynoichians, described as living in well-elevated dwellings made of wood, a logical choice in view of the abundance of local timber. According to the *Argonautika*, these greatly offended later Greek sensibilities by their publicly indulging in sexual intercourse 'without blame, on the public highway, not even blushing to couple there',[22] this practice arguably relating to the Great Mother Goddess's Sacred Marriage rites. The Mossynoichians may possibly have been the same people elsewhere referred to as Moschians or 'calf-men', arguably from their adherence to the bull-cult that we have seen to be so prevalent. Assyrian annals of the late 2nd millennium BC called them Mushki, though later, when some of them had moved to western Anatolia, they also became referred to as Brigians or Phrygians.

These Moschians or Phrygians, who would later move into western Turkey, certainly regarded themselves as a pre-Flood people. According to their folklore their king Nannakos, who lived before the time of the Flood, saw that this was about to happen and gathered his people in sanctuaries to weep and pray. The age of Nannakos subsequently became a proverbial expression for great antiquity and lamentations.[23] The fact that, even among the Greeks and Egyptians, they had a reputation for being a very ancient people indeed – and specifically older than the Egyptians – is evident from the Turkish-born historian Herodotus.[24] He told a story of how one Egyptian king conducted a special test to determine whether the Egyptian or Phrygian language was the older, only to find that it was the Phrygian.[25] As Moschians they even found inclusion in the biblical book of Genesis, chapter 10 in which, immediately following the story of Noah's Flood, are listed the nations springing from Noah's son Japheth:

> 'Gomer, Magog, the Medes, Javan, *Tubal*, *Meschech*, [italics mine] Tiras'.[26]

Since an earlier Genesis chapter mentioned Tubal as 'ancestor of all who work copper and iron',[27] scholars acknowledge here a reference to north-western Turkey's earlier mentioned iron- and copper-working Tibarenians.[28] In which case the Meschech appearing alongside them must be the Moschians, later to be known as the Phrygians.[29]

The so-called Hurrians have long been thought to have been later insurgents into eastern Turkey.[30] However, the latest archaeological findings, as at Tell Mozan in what is today north Syria, just south of Turkey's south-eastern border, show them to have established there an impressively large city, anciently known as Urkesh, as early as the 3rd millennium BC, and therefore at least as early as the earliest ancient Egyptian dynasties.[31] Though the Hurrians remain sufficiently mysterious that their language, embodied in pictographic inscriptions on numerous seals, is barely understood, their word for coppersmith was *tab-iri* (one who has cast copper), thereby yet again indicating that this word, clearly related to the *tibira* import word into Sumerian and the 'Tibarenians' of the Argo myth hold an important clue to the post-Flood distribution (and languages) of pre-Flood peoples. Of possibly related relevance, scenes from Hurrian daily life as found on some of the seals from Tell Mozan/Urkesh show women with pigtail hairstyles similar to those seen on the near-contemporary Dorak figurines from west Turkey, while the male and female costuming bears resemblances to equivalents in Sumerian art. Since some of Tell Mozan's oldest levels have yet to be excavated, clearly much remains to be discovered.

Although Mount Ararat lies too far inland for it to feature in the Argonauts' voyage, our easterly sweep of Turkey in the post-Flood period would be incomplete without reference to it in view of the biblical Flood story's specific description of Noah's ark as having come to rest somewhere on the Mount Ararat range. A Black Sea boat loaded with families and livestock may not have actually washed up on the slopes of Ararát, but it is not unreasonable to suggest that some survivors might have made their way to the safety of its high ground. Certainly from the fact that biblically Noah was not described as having moved away from the Ararat region, the logical inference is that he and his family remained somewhere in its vicinity after having survived the Black Sea Flood.

Here it may be relevant to note that no less than four

Sumerian myths refer to an as yet undiscovered ancient city called Aratta that is thought to have been located somewhere in this same Ararat region. According to one Sumerian epic,[32] when Enmerkar, lord of the southern Mesopotamian city of Uruk, needed timber, gold, silver, lapis lazuli and precious stones for a temple that he was building to the Sumerian Great Mother Goddess[33] he sought to obtain these materials from Aratta. To reach this city, which was apparently particularly devoted to the same Great Goddess, seven mountains needed to be crossed. This has led scholars to suggest its location to be either in the Ararat district, or in the environs of nearby Lake Van, both of these areas comparatively little explored archaeologically due to modern-day political unrest. Certainly a city somewhere in this general region would have made an ideal entrepot. Modern-day Chechen writer Lyoma Usmanov has even suggested that the very name that the nearby present-day Chechens know themselves by, Noxçi or Noahkhchi, also certain local placenames such as Nakhichevan,[34] may have the same origin as the biblical Noah.[35] For this author at least, Mossynoichians or Moschians likewise sounds phonologically close.

According to the Genesis version of the Flood story, one of the first things that Noah – 'a tiller of the soil' – did after safely alighting on Mount Ararat was to become 'the first to plant the vine' for winemaking.[36] In which case it may be rather more than coincidence that the first known vine cultivation took place very shortly after the Black Sea Flood, and in the broad vicinity of Mount Ararat, a region in which the ancestor of the modern, cultivated grape vine notably grew wild. Tradition has it that up to 1840 there existed on Mount Ararat's slopes a vineyard that was planted by Noah.[37] Whatever the truth of this, certainly the oldest definite traces of wine so far found have been dated back to c.5400 BC, as soon after the Black Sea Flood as makes little difference. These traces were found on a potsherd excavated in the 1970s at Hajji Firuz Tepe near Lake Urmia, which although today in Iran, lies little more than 160 kilometres (100 miles) from Ararat.[38] A jar that was found near the potsherd was also found to have contained a similar wine, this also featuring a long narrow neck capable of being stoppered in order to check airborne bacteria from turning the wine vinegary.

Just to Ararat's north lie what are today Georgia and the Transcaucasus, regions likewise thought to have been very early centres of winemaking. In the proceedings of a high-powered conference on the history of winemaking held in 1991 in California's Napa Valley, great regret was expressed that no delegate from Transcaucasia had been able to attend since:

> many modern interpreters of wine history suggest that Georgia has yielded the earliest evidence of winemaking in the world, based on the excavation of domesticated grape seeds, silver-encased vine-cuttings and Neolithic [Late Stone Age] pottery vessels decorated with grape appliqués.[39]

Exactly as we noted in our earlier discussions of animal and plant domestication, there has to have been someone who manipulated the transition from the grapevine's wild ancestor *Vitis vinifera* subsp *sylvestris* to the cultivated plant. While in nature the wild vine has plants of separate sexes, the random union of which will produce fruits of equally wildly variegated quality, the viniculturist's job is to select and propagate only those plants possessing hermaphrodite characteristics. This will enable them to be self-pollinating, after which the grower can concentrate on obtaining a consistent fruit quality. So yet again someone back in the 6th millennium BC appears to have understood the sexual or genetic principles involved, prompting us to have a yet healthier respect for the know-how of the priestesses behind the Great Mother Goddess's fertility cult.

Returning to the Argonauts' voyage, after their long coasting steadily due eastwards, the natural lie of the coast would eventually have impelled them northward, towards the imposing ice-capped peaks of the Caucasus range of mountains. At the first river mouth they came across – that of the Phasis, today called the Rhion – they would have been in the kingdom of Colchis, today the former Soviet republic of Georgia.

According to Greek mythology it was on Mount Elbrus in Georgia's Caucasus mountains that Prometheus, whose only crime was to teach mankind most of its arts and sciences, was punished by the gods by being left exposed on a rock for vultures to peck at his vitals. If this reminds us of the pre-Flood Çatal Hüyük custom of exposing the dead to vultures, further curiosity is that the Jason story specifically tells us that much the same was being practised in post-Flood Colchis. After the beaching of the *Argo*, the Argonauts' overland route to the Colchean city of Aea took them past a cemetery, where they observed male corpses, wrapped in un-tanned ox-hides, left exposed on the tops of willow-trees for birds of prey to eat the flesh. This, to us, grisly custom, was apparently specially reserved for men, women, by contrast being accorded a more normal burial.[40] On the Argonauts' meeting up with king Aetes of Aca,[41] they also encountered his witch-like daughter Medea, a priestess of the Great Mother Goddess.[42] So clearly this post-Flood culture on the Black Sea's south-eastern shores, whatever its date, had some intriguing affinities with that of pre-Flood Çatal Hüyük.

And as we have seen of other post-Flood peoples living in the Black Sea's environs, Colchis likewise had a metallurgical reputation. The famous 'Golden Fleece' that the Argonauts sought would seem to have had its origin in the fleeces used to pan for the gold that washed down from local rivers, Colchis' the Phasis, being now the Rion, and the regions around it including mines producing gold, silver, iron and copper. Arguably, therefore, the Colcheans, just like the Tibarenians, were metal-workers. Once again, any supporting archaeology largely eludes us, though further up the coast of the Caucasus, just east of the Sea of Azov, there have been found royal burials dating from the 3rd millennium BC, exhibiting much the same culture that we have become familiar with further south. One such burial was at Maikop where excavations revealed the grave of a chieftain who had been buried beneath a magnificent canopy decorated with gold bulls on its carrying poles.[43] Furthermore, if we again return to Greek legend, on the Tauric Chersonese, a peninsula of rich cornfields jutting out into the Sea of Azov, there apparently lived the Tauri, or 'bull people' immortalised in the story of Iphigenia in Tauris.

From everything we have seen then, there remained scattered around the Black Sea a number of peoples exhibiting some strong affinities to the pre-Flood inhabitants of Turkey glimpsed at Çatal Hüyük. These post-Flood peoples were notably proficient in metal-work and strongly associated with a bull and Great Mother Goddess cult. Although some communities seem to have had kings, women often appear to have been the dominant ones. And there is not a single instance of a monarch being represented mowing down his enemies on a battlefield, or executing prisoners, themes that would be repeated *ad nauseam* amongst the later monarchs of Egypt and Mesopotamia. Not least of these peoples' individualities was their language, which was certainly not a member of the Indo-European family of tongues that from the 2nd millennium onwards would become so dominant all around the Mediterranean.

Yet the exact family to which that language belonged has so far eluded us. Furthermore, despite all that we have seen in and around Turkey there lingers an air of something that is still missing to the conundrum. It is as if there may have been a 'somewhere else' that perhaps some of the more advanced Flood survivors moved to in the wake of the catastrophe. A somewhere else that neither Bill Pitman, nor we, nor anyone else, have yet managed to account for.

CHAPTER 14

AN AFRICAN INTERLUDE?

Earlier in this book we touched on how post-Ice Age high-rainfall patterns had created a Saharan North Africa very different from its largely desert character of the last two thousand years and more. We noted that because of this, great lakes had formed over vast areas of the Sahara. And we learnt from the early north African artists who created the Tassili frescoes how these lakes, and their surrounding lush grasslands, attracted large herbivores such as antelope, sheep, hippopotamus and giraffe, together with human hunter-gatherers who preyed on them. The pioneering Henri Lhote, in trying to define broad epochs for the Tassili paintings, called this the 'Round-Headed' phase, after the round heads with which the hunter-gatherers were typically depicted.

But as Lhote duly noted, the Tassili rock paintings then began to exhibit a marked change to their subject matter, at a time which, though impossible to pinpoint precisely, appears to have been very shortly after the great c.6000 BC mini Ice Age drought and subsequent Black Sea Flood. Whereas previously the paintings had featured very few if any cattle, now suddenly they were full of great herds of

them,[1] clear evidence that north Africa, though rapidly
drying out, still had some very good grazing land. Lhote
called this the Tassili art's Bovidian phase.[2] He also noted
that the human figures depicted with the cattle were now
herds-people or pastoralists rather than the earlier hunters.
Just like the pre-Flood people of Çatal Hüyük, these were
Cattle People. They had clearly learned to domesticate their
cattle at much the same time as the Çatal Hüyük people, and
they also kept goats and domesticated sheep. Even the
Lowry style in which they were painted exhibited some
striking affinities to their Çatal Hüyük equivalents. And
some strife between these 'newcomer' herds-people and the
traditional hunter-gatherers was evident from one Bovidian
masterpiece, comprising no less than 135 human and animal
figures, in which several herds-people can be seen deter-
minedly resisting an attack upon their herd by hunter-
gatherer archers.[3]

Should we then infer some massive post-Flood migration
of Çatal Hüyük people and their cattle all the way to the
north Sahara? The rock paintings, though they exhibit a
variety of styles, suggest a continuity of artist-observers
from the Round-headed to the Bovidian phases, not a take-
over by any foreign artistic tradition. The Bovidian-period
cattle were depicted with such great fidelity to nature that it
can be seen they were of two different African species, the
African ox, or *Bos Africanus* and the *Bos brachyceros,* or
thick-horned ox. Of the depictions of herds-people it is possible to see that some at least of these were negroid, and
therefore of indigenous African stock. And there are no
signs of the introduction to Africa of anything resembling
Çatal Hüyük-type rectangular architecture.

Yet all this said, for the change from hunter-gatherer to
cattle raiser to have occurred in north Africa, apparently so
close to the time that cattle-domestication had pioneeringly
been achieved in Turkey, suggests something rather more

than coincidence. Whoever the newcomer pastoralists were, they kept their cattle in stone-built compounds. From paintings of women working in fields, they would appear to have cultivated some plants, though most likely on a rather smaller scale to their cattle-rearing. They were skilled and prolific in creating pottery. And since some paintings show some of them wearing proper garments, as distinct from animal skins, their skills may well have included weaving. From the pictorial evidence, therefore, all the indications are of a surprisingly advanced and variegated population, as if there were at least some well-informed outsiders of unknown provenance who had arrived to mix with, and comparatively peaceably settle amongst, an indigenous and far from necessarily backward African population. This prompts us therefore to look closely at whatever further evidence there may be for some very early and close across-the-sea connections between the peoples of north Africa and those of the Black Sea and Mediterranean Turkey.

For this, it is again important to consider the effects upon north Africa of the same general sea-level rise that had triggered the Black Sea Flood – the rise charted on our now familiar Shackleton and van Andel map (see p.79). As may be recalled, one result of this rise was that a very large chunk of what today would have been north-east Tunisia disappeared beneath the Mediterranean at some undetermined time between the end of the last Ice Age and the keeping of reliable written histories.

With this in mind, the Jason and the Argonauts myth again proves to be useful. This conveys that besides the van Andel-type oceanographic evidence there actually was some human memory of the geography of this part of north Africa having been significantly different only just a few millennia ago. For according to the Jason story (though details can again vary between versions), after the *Argo* had escaped from Colchis it made its way to Sicily, where the earlier-mentioned sea-going Rhodians had apparently established another of their colonies. From Sicily fierce winds drove the vessel across to the African coast,[4] where a huge wave tossed it some considerable distance inland, into terrain that had apparently already become desert. According to the story, Africa's Great Mother Goddess[5] then appeared to Jason in a dream, with instructions that the Argonauts should physically haul the *Argo* to a great lake called Lake Tritonis via which they would then be able to escape back to the Mediterranean.

Today there exists no such great lake anywhere along the north African coast, the sort of hard fact that so often gives myth-makers a very bad name. Yet there was nothing mythical about Lake Tritonis. This much at least is clear from the 6th century BC Greek geographer Scylax of Caryanda. He was an intrepid explorer who ventured as far as India, and although his writings have survived only in fragments, he specifically described Lake Tritonis extending in his time over an area of 2,300 square kilometres (900 square miles), that is, an average of some 48 kilometres (30 miles) across in all directions. A century later the similarly reliable historian Herodotus confirmed it as still partly extant in his time, describing it as a 'great lagoon', with a 'large river' (the Triton) flowing into it.[6]

But particularly valuable are Herodotus' descriptions of the surprisingly variegated peoples apparently still living in the Lake's vicinity. One of these was the 'Garamantes', whom Herodotus described as 'very numerous' in his time. They also featured in the Jason story, in which a Garamantan shepherd killed an Argonaut who tried to steal one of his sheep. And in 19 BC they figured in Roman history when the Roman general Balbus conquered them at an oasis to which they had retreated. According to some scholars the word 'Garamantes' has its root in 'Ker, Q're or Car', one of the names of the Great Mother Goddess, therefore at least redolant of some common heritage to the earlier-mentioned west Turkey-based sea-peoples, the Carians.

Other peoples mentioned by Herodotus as living in the Lake Tritonis' vicinity, the Machyles and Auses, apparently were also goddess-worshippers, and possessed some strangely Amazonian traits. Reportedly, each year they held a festival:

> ... at which the girls divide themselves into two groups and fight each other with stones and sticks; they say this rite has come down to them from time immemorial, and by its performance they pay honour to their native deity – which is the same as our Greek Athene.[7]

Another tribe, the Maxyes, living 'west of the [river] Triton and beyond the Auses', Herodotus described as living in ordinary houses and practising agriculture, to which he added laconically:

> They stain their bodies red *and claim to be descended from the men of Troy* [italics mine].[8]

So, albeit at a very late date, here we have specific reference to some otherwise obscure north African peoples having women as an unusually dominant and even martial sex, venerating a Great Mother Goddess, and claiming their roots in western Turkey. The further information that they painted their bodies red – which Herodotus noted also of a neighbouring people he called Gyzantes – inevitably recalls some similar tendencies we noted in Çatal Hüyük. Furthermore the ancient Egyptians, in 2nd millennium BC descriptions of the various north African tribes with whom they skirmished, called the westernmost of these the 'Meshwesh'. So there is at least a glimmer here (particularly bearing in mind that Egyptian hieroglyphs lack vowels), that Maxyes, Meshwesh and the Turkey-based Moschians of our last chapter could have been one and the same people.

It is though Diodorus Siculus – whom we may recall as the only known writer from antiquity aware that the Black Sea was once a lake – who has provided what is potentially the most illuminating information on Lake Tritonis and its early settlers. Diodorus, it should be pointed out, hailed from Sicily, just a brief ocean hop from the shores of Tunisian north Africa. He accredited his information to a lost book written by the 2nd century BC folklorist Dionysius Skytobrachion (Leather Arm) of Alexandria, and started by pointing out that:

> The majority of mankind believe that the only Amazons were those who are reported to have dwelt in the neighbourhood of the Thermodon river on the Black Sea.[9]

Here, of course, he was alluding to the same Terme area of Turkey's Black Sea coast that we noted as Amazon country in our last chapter. But as he went on:

> ... the truth is otherwise, since the Amazons of north Africa[10] were *much earlier in point of time* [italics mine] and accomplished notable deeds ... Now we are not unaware that to many ... the history of this people will appear to be a thing unheard of and entirely strange. For since the race of these Amazons disappeared entirely many generations before the Trojan War, whereas the women about the Thermodon river were in their full vigour a little before that time.[11]

According to Diodorus, these very early north African Amazons, were 'a race ruled by women' who practised 'the arts of war' while the men 'spent their days about the house'. They lived on an island:

> ... in the marsh Tritonis ... [which] was of great size and full of fruit-bearing trees of every kind, from which the natives secured their food. It contained also a multitude

of flocks and herds ... but grain the nation used not at all because the use of this fruit of the earth had not yet been discovered among them.[12]

As warriors the women were apparently highly successful, for as Diodorus went on, they:

... subdued all the cities on the [Lake Tritonis] island except the one called Mene, which was considered to be sacred and was inhabited by Ethiopian fish-eaters[13] and was also subject to great eruptions of fire [volcanoes] and possessed a multitude of the precious stones which the Greeks call *anthrax* [coal], *sardion* [carnelian] and *smaragdos* [a light green precious stone]. And after this they subdued many of the neighbouring Libyans and nomad tribes and founded within the marsh Tritonis a great city which they named Chersonessus [peninsula] after its shape. Setting out from the city of Chersonessus ... the Amazons embarked upon great ventures, a longing having come over them to invade many parts of the inhabited world.[14]

Now quite aside from the disbelief that Diodorus clearly anticipated in his own time, this is the sort of information that many historians and archaeologists of today understandably dismiss out of hand. For such sceptics even the one-time historical existence of a people led by warrior women called Amazons is a notion quite difficult enough to contemplate.[15] As for the idea that 'many generations before the Trojan War' such a female-dominated society might have founded a significant sized city on a lake in north Africa, and then mounted maritime expeditions from this, is simply preposterous. No such 'Amazon' city of Chersonessus has ever been found in north Africa. Nor anywhere on the Saharan landmass are there any volcanoes that might have been responsible for Diodorus' 'eruptions of fire'.

However given that Diodorus' Lake Tritonis was real enough, and that he was also uncannily right about the Black Sea, his description of the catastrophic fate of this lake, and by inference that of the city of Chersonessus likewise, surely deserves some closer consideration:

> The story is ... told that the marsh Tritonis disappeared from sight in the course of an earthquake, when those parts of it which lay towards the ocean were torn asunder.[16]

As we noted earlier from the Shackleton and van Andel map, it is a fact that sometime in the course of the geographical changes that were brought about by post-Ice Age sea-level rise, there was a major change in the north Africa land mass. A huge chunk of what otherwise would have become eastern Tunisia – very approximately, some 90,650 square kilometres (35,000 square miles) of it – disappeared beneath the Mediterranean. So what if this 'land' had in actuality been taken up largely by Lake Tritonis, this forming a lagoon with Chersonessus standing on an island in its midst?

Here particularly revelatory are Diodorus' mentions of an earthquake, also the 'great eruptions of fire' that reportedly occurred close to the seemingly so legendary Amazonian island on which Chersonessus stood. Volcanic and seismic disruptions invariably occur along the lines of instability that are found where the great tectonic plates that form the earth's crust collide. A study of north Africa's tectonic plate systems immediately reveals that between Sicily's south-western coast and Tunisia's major promontory east of Tunis there lies a particularly unstable plate line [fig 25]. Furthermore along this very same line there runs a series of volcanoes, of which today only the Italian island of Pantelleria stands above sea-level. The closely related archaeological facts are that some human remains have been excavated on Pantelleria, dating as early as the 6th

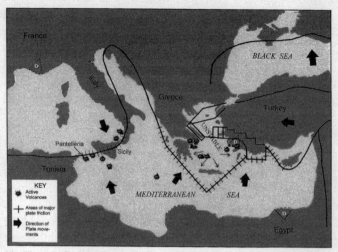

Fig 25 Map of north Africa and the eastern Mediterranean, showing the line of tectonic instability between Sicily and Tunisia. The stars denote active volcanoes, some now underwater. 'D': indicates a river delta

millennium BC, the Flood period. Also, the archaeologists found Pantelleria to be particularly abundant in obsidian, the volcanic glass that was so prized around Asikli and Çatal Hüyük, and indeed throughout the Late Stone Age world, during the immediate pre- and post-Flood periods. Some of this same obsidian has also been found on the Tunisian mainland,[17] other samples of it on Malta, which had no obsidian of its own.[18] So there can be no doubt that Late Stone Age peoples were attracted to this area.

This raises the question of whether Pantelleria had already become an island when it was first visited by these otherwise unknown humans back in the 6th millennium BC? Or did it, or one of its now underwater companions, then form part of the volcanic northern rim of a vast lagoon, Lake Tritonis, somewhere in the midst of which the Amazons built their city of Chersonessus, probably early in the post-

Flood era? Did a subsequent combination of sea-level rise and seismic activity then totally change the entire geography, destroying Lake Tritonis, and Chersonessus and its island along with it, leaving just Pantelleria as a lone remnant of what had gone before? Likewise, was the mere 2,300-square-kilometre (900-square-mile) 1st millennium BC Lake Tritonis, known to Scylax and Herodotus, just a remnant of the original Lake's dimensions, even this subsequently disappearing, for quite different reasons, in the course of the Sahara's ongoing desiccation? If the answers to the last three questions are 'yes' then Robert Ballard has awaiting him another underwater quest – the search for the north African Amazons' lost city of Chersonessus.

Whatever the exact circumstances may have been, Diodorus made clear that the Amazons were not wiped out by this natural disaster, but went on to invade other areas. One Amazon queen, Myrene, which we may recall as another variant on the name of the Great Mother Goddess, is reported to have led a group of her people westwards through the straits of Gibraltar, then voyaged with them southwards down the Atlantic coast of west Africa. There she captured the 'Atlantean' city of Cerne, only ultimately to be overcome by neighbouring Gorgons.

This may all sound far too outlandish to be credible, but one firm archaeological fact is that *someone* back in the Late Stone Age undeniably did venture beyond the straits of Gibraltar and then (any expeditions along the west African coast notwithstanding), voyaged at least 108 kilometres (67 miles) out into the open Atlantic. There they 'discovered' what are now called the Canary islands, islands which have never been joined to the African mainland throughout the entire existence of humankind, where some at least of these discoverers then settled.

This much is evident from the fact that when five hundred years ago the Spanish made what they supposed to be the first human discovery of the Canaries, they found that already long occupying the islands was a people called Guanche. Some of these had white skin with fair hair, others were darker-skinned and with black or brown hair. As determined by studies that were made in the early 1920s by the American physical anthropologist Ernest Hooton, there appear to have been at least three such migratory groups even before the Bronze Age, that is before the 4th millennium BC. The first group were pastoralists with sheep and goats but no cereals. The second group, which settled only in the southern Canaries, were brunette whites whose sole cultivated cereal was barley. The third group consisted of very tall, blonde whites.

Among the little that is known culturally of the Guanches, a cult of twins seems to have been prevalent. A pair of pre-Spanish statues found on the islands is in the form of twins.[19] Likewise a Spanish painting from the time of the discovery shows two light-skinned young men with long fair hair standing on twin mountain peaks.[20] Whatever connection any one or more of these groups may have had with Diodorus' Amazons, they all had to have made their journeys by boats capable of coping with the open Atlantic, a far more hostile marine environment than anywhere to be found within the Mediterranean.

A perhaps crucial further discovery made by Hooton was that one still extant north African group to which the Guanche seemed to bear some significant affinities was that of the Berbers of the Sahara. Individuals with light skin and red hair are not uncommon among these people to this day. It is also worth pointing out that Berber is not this people's own name for themselves, but rather a corruption of 'barbarian', the term that the ancient Greeks tended to use for anyone who did not speak Greek. The true name that the Berber people has always called both itself and the language spoken is *Amazigh*,[21] rather startlingly close to 'Amazon'.

Despite the Berbers/Amazigh having been all too little studied by western scholars, of their great antiquity there can be no doubt. In the family tree of the world's languages, their branch has been determined as part of the Afro-Asiatic language group which comprises the Semitic languages and ancient Egyptian, and this is thought to have formed at a very early stage. Closer to Sicilians, Spanish and Egyptians than to negroids such as Nigerians, Berbers are nonetheless very mixed anthropologically and are recognised to have been so for a long time.[22]

Before their forcible conversion to Islam in the 1st millennium AD, the Berbers seem to have shared with the Çatal Hüyük people the practice of 'sleeping with the dead' in order to communicate with them via dreams. Thus the Roman Pomponius Mela wrote of them that they 'consider the spirits of their ancestors gods ... and consult them as oracles, and having made their requests, treat the dreams of those who sleep in their tombs as responses.'[23] Likewise Michael Brent and Elizabeth Fentress, authors of the most recent authoritative book on the Berbers, have written of their ancient shrine of Slonta in the highlands of Cyrenaica:

> A bench, probably for sleeping, ran along one wall, while a separate chamber may have been used for the same purpose ... The funerary elements are mixed with fairly clear references to fertility – enlarged sexual members, for instance. The complicated iconography and the provision of space for sleepers to dream – the practice is called incubation – suggest that the sanctuary was used for communication with the dead and also suggests the role of the spirits in ensuring human fertility.[24]

Particularly significantly, however, before the Berbers' forcible conversion to Islam – which too often has led them to being supposed traditional patriarchally-minded Arabs – their most notable leaders were women. Thus when the

Arabs, fired by early Islamic missionary zeal, invaded the Sahara c.AD 700 the Berber resistance to them was led by a redoubtable queen, Kahina, who even temporarily succeeded in driving the invaders back before ultimately being defeated and killed. And before Kahina there was another major female leader called Tin Hanan, who lived around the 5th century AD, and whom the present-day Berber continue to regard as a particularly great ancestress.

For even to this day the Saharan Tuareg, one of the Berbers' major tribes, trace their lineage not by their fathers, but by their mothers and their mothers' mothers, a custom that anthropologists term matrilineal inheritance. As noted by Michael Brent and Elizabeth Fentress:

> Members of each Tuareg sub-group ... define themselves as the uterine descendants of a single eponymous ancestress. With this matriliny goes a relationship between men and women which for its equilibrium is unique in North Africa. Women control their own property, own the family tent, and can choose, or divorce, their husbands ... The new husband joins his wife in her tent and this will be their home as long as the marriage lasts ... The transmission and conservation of Tuareg culture is ... in the hands of the women ... The Tuareg women have little in common with other North Africans. They are not veiled or sheltered, may invite guests into their tents, and have a surprising freedom of behaviour.[25]

For most of us today this seems a strange and therefore distinctive custom, used as we are, despite so much emancipation, to the man being the assumed family head, and his giving his surname, not his wife's to their children, along with much else. Yet it is this Amazigh custom that also leads us straight back to the strongest possible association with Turkey's most ancient peoples. For amongst the ancient peoples in Turkey's south-western corner, Herodotus wrote of the Lycians:

Ask a Lycian who he is and he will tell you his name and his mother's then his grandmother's and great grandmother's and so on. And if a free woman has a child by a slave, the child is considered legitimate, whereas the children of a free man, however distinguished he may be, and a foreign wife or mistress have no citizen rights at all.[26]

Likewise with regard to the Carians of Turkey, whom we may recall that Herodotus specially featured as among the eastern Mediterranean's most outstanding mariners, the British scholar Sinclair Hood noted:

Among the Carians on the west coast of Anatolia [Turkey] succession was still through the mother in the fourth century BC.

Furthermore if we then look to what happened to the Amazons, as distinct from the Amazighs, following the loss of their power-base in Lake Tritonis and their military reverses in west Africa, this likewise leads us to Turkey. Diodorus recounted how the Amazon queen Myrene:

... conquered in war the races in the region of the Taurus [in eastern Turkey], peoples of outstanding courage, and descended through Greater Phrygia to the sea ... And selecting in the territory which she had won by arms sites well suited to the founding of cities, she built a considerable number of them and founded one which bore her own name [present-day Smyrna in western Turkey], but the others she named after the women who held the most important commands, such as Cyme [in western Turkey], Pitana and Priene [present-day Güllübahçe in western Turkey] ... She seized also some of the islands, and Lesbos in particular on which she founded the city of Mitylene, which was named after her sister.

Apparently the Amazons thereby gained the foothold in Turkey that we have seen them subsequently to have at

Terme on the Black Sea coast. There were however military reverses that obliged some of them to withdraw back to north Africa, these arguably being the present-day Berbers' ancestors.

What cannot be emphasised enough is that until Ryan, Pitman and Ballard produced their findings, few would even have contemplated giving such tales from Diodorus Siculus even a vestige of credence. And even now the great majority of scholars would understandably baulk at anything of this kind.

If Diodorus were right however – and that remains a very, very big 'if' – nothing less than the most fundamental revision is needed of where and how some crucial human developments happened during the two to three millennia between the Flood and the rise of the Egyptian and Mesopotamian civilisations. We would need to consider the presence in the geographically 'lost' part of Tunisia, without as yet any archaeological evidence to back it up, of a female-dominated 'missing link' culture. A culture which hitherto has been virtually unknown to scholarship, yet which acted as a springboard for people movements that appear else-where.

The great virtue of such a revision, however, is that it has some huge potential to explain, where previously so much has seemed inexplicable.

CHAPTER 15

EMPIRE OF THE GODDESS

Odd social habits — exogamy, totemism, public coition, can-
nibalism, tattooing, the participation of women in battle ...
obtained in Thessaly before the coming of the Achaeans,
and in classical times among the primitive tribes of the
southern Black Sea coast, the Gulf of Sirté in Libya,
Majorca (populated by Bronze Age Libyans) and North-
West Galicia.[1]

Robert Graves, *The White Goddess*

For Oxford undergraduates of my own early 1960s generation, a not unfamiliar sight browsing in a town bookshop or
dashing into a lecture theatre was the university's newly
appointed Professor of Poetry Robert Graves, then a white-
haired, rather florid-faced figure in his late sixties. To subsequent generations he is perhaps better remembered as
author of *I, Claudius*.

However, the work that Graves would perhaps have preferred to be remembered by, and which certainly gave him
the most difficulty, was one that he had newly amended and
updated in the early 1960s, *The White Goddess*.[2] Calling
upon some striking insights which his poetic nature had
given him into ancient myths from right across Europe,
western Asia and north Africa, Graves presented a most
erudite, though often densely tangled study of an all-powerful female deity. This deity's cult dated way back to prehistory's darkest mists, most certainly well before the Black Sea
Flood. Readily identifiable as the same as the Great Mother
Goddess whom we have already met at Çatal Hüyük in
Turkey, on the island of Samothrace, in Tunisian north
Africa and elsewhere, Graves' underlying thesis was that

she had been revered by widely scattered peoples under hundreds of different names and aspects. Then with the coming of new peoples with patriarchal as distinct from matrilineal preferences she became supplanted by masculine gods such as the Greek Zeus and the Biblical Yahweh.

And Graves was far from alone in formulating such a hypothesis. Quite independently a woman archaeologist, Lithuanian-born Marija Gimbutas (1921–94), took up much the same theme, in her case basing her argument on prehistoric artworks and artefacts which she observed to carry an intricate language of symbols attesting to the same Great Goddess.[3]

Apparent from all such researches is that the Goddess was a most complex, all embracing deity. Not least of the bewildering aspects to her were the number of different names that she went under, many of these only coming to light from the mythologies of later peoples, and many of them individualised aspects of her rather than her whole deity. Some peoples, too fearful of her even to address her by name, referred to her simply as 'the Throne'. To those living in Turkey she was Cybele, or Kubaba or Myrene or Hepat, depending on their district and epoch. To the Danaan Achaeans she was the triple moon goddess Danae. To the Sumerians she was Inanna. To other Mesopotamian peoples she was Belet-Ili (as in the Babylonian Gilgamesh Epic), then later Anath and Ishtar. To the early Egyptians she was Neith, then later Isis and Hathor. To the Canaanitic and Syrian peoples she was Astarte and Asherah. To the Greeks she could be Hera, or Rhea, also, in aspects, Demeter, Artemis, or Athene. The Greeks, it should be noted, regarded Athene as having been born in 'Libya', that is north Africa, the goatskin dress in which she was traditionally depicted in statuary being noted by Herodotus as typically Libyan female costume.[4] She was in the heavens as the moon, yet she was also earth and water. She was all the earth's trees, with some varieties particularly sacred to her, and she was also the fertility goddess of all animal, plant and marine life. She was responsible for birth, sex and death – and for rebirth as well.

According to Graves, at a very early period, certainly in Turkey, Greece and Syria, the annual calendar was divided into three seasons in the Goddess's honour. The first season, sacred to her in her childbirth aspect, had the lion or leopard as its emblem, instantly recalling that pre-Flood Çatal Hüyük statuette depicting her in childbirth flanked by leopards. The second season, sacred to her in her sex aspect, had the goat as its emblem, perhaps evocative of the fact that the goat was one of the first creatures which some ancient wise-woman – the original, ancestral 'goddess' – had manipulatively 'bred' using her observation-acquired genetics know-how. The third season, sacred to her in her death aspect, had the serpent or snake as its emblem, all three emblems later becoming combined in the mythical creature known as the chimera. Birds were also sacred to the goddess in her rebirth aspect, hence Çatal Hüyük's vulture wall-paintings,[5] the griffin, the phoenix, and so on. While bulls were also commonly associated with her, they always represented the male counterpart to her femininity, a femininity that was never subservient to such powerful animals, but always in control of them.

In this same vein the Goddess was certainly not any congenial, ever-loving deity, in the manner, say, of traditional Roman Catholics' Virgin Mary, even though prehistoric families kept statuettes of her in much the same way. Because she controlled fertility she could and did expect young women at her behest to surrender their virginity to strangers in her shrines, likewise as we shall see later, men serving as her priests to sacrifice their masculinity. Because she controlled death she could and did expect lives to be sacrificed to her, from chickens, to bulls, to new-born babies to (on occasion) young men of the highest birth.

And wherever ancient peoples worshipped the Goddess, her highest earthly representative was mostly not a male priest but instead a very womanly high priestess with many of the attributes of witch and oracle all rolled into one. In 'royal' societies the king's consort often assumed the role of high priestess, or vice versa. In the mythologies Medea at Colchis, Ariadne on Crete, and Iphigenia at Tauris were all typical high priestesses. When they spoke, it was the Goddess speaking through them. Their commands therefore, while the Goddess cult held sway, were far more powerful than those of any earthly king. Arguably their Late Stone Age direct antecedents were the wise women, full of the lore of herbs and plants, and of divination, that to this day are typically found amongst surviving hunter-gatherer communities.

In Marija Gimbutas' opinion, it was mostly during the period 7000–3500 BC, immediately before and after the Flood, that pastoralist and agriculturalist communities spread across a very large area shared between themselves this cult of the Great Mother Goddess, as a kind of lingua franca, and lived largely in peaceful co-existence with each other. And as we have already noted, aside from the Goddess-worshipping cultures in and around Turkey, one of the post-Flood societies adhering to this cult, also certainly one of the earliest and most ambitious to venture into the post-Flood fad for building megaliths, was that of Malta.

Archaeologically it is a fact that sometime between c.5000 and 4500 BC Malta and its neighbour Gozo saw the arrival of a first wave of a people who were already long-standing members of the Goddess empire. A second wave arrived c.3500 BC, creating the vast limestone shrines such as the Hal Saflieni Hypogeum. The strength of their devotion is evident from the fact that they cut such extraordinary monuments into hillside rock using just stone mallets and bone picks, also manipulating great blocks of stone weighing as much as 50 tons apiece. The similarities of Maltese Goddess statuettes to those found at Çatal Hüyük have already been noted (see fig 21, p.163), also their adherence to a similar bull cult.

Recalling the fact that the pre-Flood Çatal Hüyük people had lived without defence walls of any kind, these extraordinary Malta builders, who apparently brought just their skills to the island, seem similarly to have been able to exist in surprising tranquillity. In the words of Malta archaeologist J.D. Evans:

> Insofar as we can judge from the evidence, no more peaceable society seems ever to have existed. It is easy, of course, to delude oneself with pictures of a primitive Mediterranean paradise; nevertheless, the earth seems to have yielded the Maltese a living on fairly easy terms, for otherwise they would scarcely have had time or energy to spare to elaborate their strange cults and build and adorn their temples.[6]

And although Malta's temples were undoubtedly used for what we would describe as burial of the dead, all the indications are that their builders regarded them rather more as houses for their ancestors, meaning that they had some important functions for the living as well. In Marija Gimbutas' words 'sick people sought health, barren women sought pregnancy and devotees congregated and slept' in them. As suggested by the famous 'sleeping goddess' statuette found in the Hypogeum of Hal Saflieni (see pp.162–3), these slumbers were very likely in order for them to dream their being in touch with their dead loved ones. Of course, the pre-Flood Çatal Hüyük people did much the same in their houses, likewise the Berber/Amazigh in the shrines that they built just across the Sicilian Channel in north Africa.

So where might they have come from, the people who conceived, designed and executed the Malta shrines with such astonishing expertise? The best that modern-day experts can suggest is Sicily to which Malta was certainly joined before the post-Ice Age sea-level rises, though the exact millennium of its separation is undetermined. However Sicily can offer no convincing architectural antecedents to the Malta shrines. There are some rather vague Turkey connections additional to those earlier suggested. Excavations during the late 1930s by Professor John Garstang near Mersin on Turkey's south-east coast brought to light massive walls made of huge stone blocks that are thought to have been built as early as the 5th millennium, therefore just conceivably precursors to the Malta shrines. And that early post-Flood mariners from Turkey ventured as far as Malta is strongly suggested by the finding on Malta of a 'fiddle-shaped' bone idol in the style of west Turkey and its islands, dating from earlier than any of Malta's own works of art.[7]

Perhaps rather more pertinent, however, is that only just beyond Sicily across the Sicilian channel there lies Tunisia, which, as we have heard from Diodorus Siculus, sometime around the Flood period still included the area around Lake Tritonis and the lake itself until this disappeared into the Mediterranean. In the face of this disaster, and the ever-worsening desiccation of the Sahara, advanced agriculturalist peoples who had settled in north Africa would have had every incentive to migrate out of Tunisia and Libya northwards, to Sicily, Malta and beyond. Robert Graves, for one, was convinced of this from his study of the mythologies. And if they were seagoing peoples who had earlier arrived from somewhere else – such as post-Flood Turkey – then they would have had the seagoing means for this as well.

Whatever the exact circumstances, it is undeniable that between the 5th millennium BC and the 3rd millennium BC – in the immediately post-Flood period – an extraordinary fashion for building great stone tombs, temples, stone circles, dolmens and much else spread northwards across the coasts of western Europe like a virus. Great monuments of this kind appeared across the Mediterranean in Sicily and on Italy's heel, in Sardinia and Corsica, on Balearic islands such as Majorca, in southern Spain, along the Atlantic coast of Portugal, in north-west Galicia, on the north-west coast of France, in south-west England, on the east coast of Ireland, even as far as the Orkneys. And as the more open-minded of prehistorians are bound to admit, what exactly lay behind this phenomenon still represents a most extraordinary mystery.

Much controversy surrounds the radio-carbon dating of these megalithic monuments. This is for a number of reasons, including the differing decades in which datings were carried out[8] and the many uncertainties of dating stone monuments when stone itself cannot be dated.[9] The one prevailing impression, however, not least from the monuments' geographical distribution hugging coasts, is that this was a movement which spread by sea, extending northwards from north Africa.

And certainly the source of the movement was not the civilisations of Egypt and Mesopotamia, which had not yet got properly under way at this time. Instead, Tunisian and Libyan north Africa represented a rather more plausible springboard from which all else might have emanated. Also wherever the megalithic movement appeared it used local materials, and most likely a lot of local labour, rather than imposing new materials from outside. Again the prevailing impression therefore is that the movement consisted of the arrival by boat of peoples comprising specialists in different crafts and skills who then proceeded to bring these skills to a new community. Along with the arrival of these skills there followed the erection of the megalithic monuments, acting as markers of their missionary progress much as did the building of churches during the growth centuries of Christianity.

One quite definite fact is that this megalith building was

Goddess based. As Marija Gimbutas noted, several shrines, including some on Malta and Gozo, have ground-plans suggestive that they were designed to represent the body of the Great Mother Goddess in her Turkey-inspired exaggerated 'fiddle-shape' proportions.

In England, researches by Michael Dames have suggested that the extraordinary human-created 3rd millennium BC mound called Silbury Hill near Marlborough in Wiltshire was planned with incredible precision to represent the Goddess giving birth in a seated posture. The site, which covers five and a quarter acres, must have demanded tens of thousands of man-hours of labour. As first designed, the Silbury mound consisted of a water-filled moat dug out to represent the Goddess's body, the mound itself being her womb. During each July and August, a Late Stone Age *son et lumière* could therefore be staged, during which the moon, reflected on the waters of the moat, gave the impression to appropriately sited onlookers, that the Goddess was giving birth.[10] Even in outline – except it was here magnified several thousand fold – this Silbury Hill Goddess exhibits in her extremities much the same almost gross proportions that we have seen on the Çatal Hüyük and Malta Goddess statuettes.

In Ireland similar huge effort and meticulous planning went into the creation of the astonishing late 4th millennium BC monument known as Newgrange. Located near the river Boyne not far from Drogheda on Ireland's east coast, this, like the Malta temples, appears to have been built as a house of the ancestors. It also has an additional feature in that its corbel-vaulted interior chamber is perfectly aligned to be lit by the sunrise only on mid-winter's day. As frankly admitted by Irish specialists, no one knows who built to such exacting standards this or similar monuments in the Boyne locality. Except that they were a Late Stone Age people who had arrived in Ireland before the arrival of the Irish and had acquired some clever engineering and architectural skills from somewhere else. Irish folklore does not give much information, other than that they were built by the Tuatha Dé Danann – 'the people of the goddess Dana' – and that these were wonder-workers who were associated with the colour red.

The megalith-building movement even extended as far north as Skara Brae and Isbister in the Orkneys, where again an unknown, pre-Scottish people arrived around the beginning of the 4th millennium BC and built superbly crafted houses for their ancestors. Unlike in the case of the Irish monuments, the bones in some of these, as at Isbister, have survived, and these have been accorded the very best analysis. This has revealed, that the Isbister people, exactly like those from Çatal Hüyük, were excarnated or defleshed before their being laid in the ancestral bone house. In the words of excavator John W. Hedges:

> I personally favour the hypothesis that the dead were exposed on constructed platforms with excarnation being effected by decay, *carrion-feeding birds* [italics mine], maggots and the elements.[11]

Mixed with the human bones at Isbister, Hedges found bones of the white-tailed sea-eagle, which he regarded as their totem animal. This is reminiscent of the griffon vultures of Çatal Hüyük, suggesting that the sea-eagle similarly carried the souls of the deceased into eternity.

One further clue to these people who had ventured, in Stone Age boats, as far north as the Orkneys derives from the 7th century AD Christian historian Bede. According to him when boatloads of Picts first arrived in northern Britain they sought wives from a people then living in Ireland who seem to have been descendants of megalith-builders. These latter agreed to provide wives, but they imposed one condition 'that when any dispute arose they should choose a king

Fig 26 An example of the not yet fully understood spiral patterns that Marija Gimbutas noted as typifying objects and sites of the ancient Great Mother Goddess 'empire' from Turkey to the Orkneys. Featured here is the great stone at the entrance to the magnificent 4th millennium BC 'house of the ancestors' at Newgrange, near Drogheda, Ireland

from the female royal line rather than the male'.[12] Clearly the Great Mother Goddess-related custom of matrilineal inheritance that we have found traceable all the way back to sea-going peoples of Turkey such as the Carians had somehow been brought to this far-flung realm.

Marija Gimbutas has also pointed to any number of symbols on the megaliths, in particular spirals, lozenge or net patterns and similar, which can be found all the way from Turkey to the Orkneys [fig 26]. These she has confidently interpreted as the Goddess's international language.

During the 5th and 4th millennia BC, the Goddess can essentially only be glimpsed in the various interpretational ways that we have shown. But by the 3rd millennia BC, the curtain began very quickly to rise on the Egyptian and Mesopotamian civilisations and their introduction of proper writing. The Great Mother Goddess's empire was also now to be found virtually everywhere of importance.

She was certainly still being revered in Turkey as is quite apparent from an enormous stone statue to her, recognised as extremely ancient even in antiquity, which can still be found on Mount Sipylus, a little to the north-east of present-day Izmir, the ancient Smyrna. Ninety metres (three hundred feet) up on the mountain's north face is still discernible a 90-metre (30-foot) high relief statue that ancient sculptors carved directly out of the rock and which although heavily weathered unmistakably depicts her enthroned in the manner of the Çatal Hüyük childbirth statuette. As the Roman travel writer Pausanias described this back in the 2nd century AD:

> The Magnesians to the north of Mount Sipylus have the most ancient of all statues of the Mother of the Gods on the rock of Koddinos; the Magnesians say it was made by Tantalus' brother Broteas.[13]

Across on the Black Sea coast of Turkey, the Great Goddess-revering Amazons who had formerly settled at Lake Tritonis, and whom Diodorus Siculus described as ultimately voyaging to Turkey, will almost certainly have made this transition by the beginning of the 3rd millennium BC. Thereby they perhaps brought the Great Goddess back to where she began. Robert Graves noted that several ancient sources attested to their founding towns on Turkey's west coast which certainly bore Amazon – and Great Goddess-related – names in antiquity.[14] And the same sources also attest to the Amazons establishing slightly more permanent settlements at Thermodon on the Black Sea coast, though proper archaeology has yet to be carried out to determine this point firmly.

However, in line with Bill Ryan's hypothesised projections for the migrations that followed the Flood, the Great Goddess was quite definitely being venerated by the Sumerians in Mesopotamia by c.3000 BC, though more than likely she had already arrived there substantially beforehand via earlier cultures. Vividly attesting to just how the same cult could stretch across thousands of kilometres even in the 4th millennium BC are statues of worshippers from Hal Tarxien, Malta and from Tell Asmar, Sumer, both depicted in exactly the same attitude of religious devotion, and looking almost as if they could have been crafted in the same workshop.

In Sumer the Goddess went under the name Inanna, and was regarded as responsible for fertility and sexual reproduction, and also as a warrior, arguably a vestigial memory of some earlier Amazon connotations. Certainly it is thanks to the Sumerians, with their development of proper narrative writing, and advanced account keeping, that we are able to see just what enormous power the Goddess's temple wielded over the entire community. As modern-day scholars have confidently inferred, her temple owned all the people's growing land, and likewise all their herds of animals. Additionally it controlled the activities of craftsmen, traders, farmers, shepherds, fishermen, fruit gardeners and many others, a situation that we in our turn may strongly suspect had also pertained in the earlier megalithic societies.

One such temple of Inanna's that is known to have been erected towards the end of the 4th millennium BC, at the very start of the Sumerian era in Mesopotamia, was that at Uruk, the modern Warka in Iraq. Although this was almost certainly one of the most splendid temple complexes of its time, far more than just a single building, sadly all too little of it remains today. Nonetheless what has survived from it, thereby providing us with at least a glimpse of what has been lost of Goddess culture at its most imperial, is a superbly crafted alabaster pedestal vase, the Uruk Vase, preserved in the Iraq Museum, Baghdad [fig 27 overleaf]. Near its base and more than a metre high, is depicted a running stream of water from which a luxuriant crop of wheat and barley rises up through the earth, also a date-palm, with just above these a procession of rams and ewes. Above these are represented a procession of priests bringing great jars of food, wine and fruit offerings. The recipient of all this produce was either the Goddess herself, or her high priestess,

Fig 27 Detail from a massive 4th millennium BC Sumerian vase found at Uruk, showing naked priests bringing offerings to the horned Great Mother Goddess

who is portrayed standing fully clad, a horned head-dress on her head, while the priests scurried towards her as naked slaves.

One of British archaeologist Leonard Woolley's greatest discoveries at Ur was the grave of a Sumerian queen or high priestess, Puabi, who went to this accompanied by an entire retinue.[15] Particularly interesting was one of Puabi's richly jewelled head-dresses. As spotted only recently by University of Pennsylvania archaeobotanist Dr Naomi Miller, the diadem has pendants in the form of the male and female branches of the date palm. In nature, the date palm has male and female trees in roughly equal proportions, with only the latter bearing the fruit. In order to domesticate the palm, groves of female trees are hand-pollinated from a single male tree. As Inanna, specifically acclaimed in Sumerian texts as 'the one who makes the dates be full of abundance', clearly the high priestess performed this sexual function, no doubt as but one of a number of sacred 'mystery' duties.

Indeed further emphasising the sex aspect of the Goddess, she was more often represented unclothed rather than clothed, not only amongst the Sumerians but among the many others sharing the Great Mother Goddess religion. Towards the end of the 3rd millennium BC we find her on the Burney Relief depicted quite naked, standing on two lions, with four tiers of bulls horns on her head, and equipped with birds' wings and feet reminiscent of the Çatal Hüyük vultures.[16] This terracotta relief statue's body was apparently liberally coated with red ochre. The cultures of Ugarit and Canaan depicted her in much the same way, except that she might be holding snakes or supported by goats, all representative of her authority over all nature and its workings. On Minoan Crete, although the high priestess's skirt was full length, her bodice was left wide open, giving great emphasis to the exposed breasts.

In ancient Egypt, as in Sumer, all the indications are that in its dimly discerned beginnings, the Great Mother Goddess was the original, all-powerful deity, who again controlled all the land, crafts and occupations from her temple. The proliferation of other deities for which Egypt is well known did not come until later. In Egypt the oldest and most deep-rooted centre of her worship seems to have been the Nile delta city of Sais, the site of which up until a hundred years ago featured the remains of a vast and ancient temple made in mud-brick, remains which sadly modern-day Egyptian farmers have long since destroyed in their search for fertiliser.

But as ancient sources attest, before Egypt had even begun its dynasties, during the 4th millennium BC and earlier, Sais had been reputedly founded by a Goddess whose Egyptian name transliterates as Neith. In Egyptian art Neith was depicted with a red crown. Much later Herodotus would note that in his time, Neith's virgin priestesses at Sais annually staged Amazon-like ceremonial fights with each other, apparently for the role of high priestess.[17] And since several of the queens of Egypt's very first dynasty, among these Neithotep and Merneit, bore Neith's name,[18] the strong inference is that their husbands ruled through the queens' matrilineal royal or high priestessly status, not through any equivalent male right of inheritance. The same may be inferred in Sumer, where again incoming monarchs seem to have needed to marry the Goddess in the form of the queen or high priestess in order to acquire recognition of their own status.

Amongst fully Great Mother Goddess societies all the signs are that the king was as nothing compared to the high priestess queen, who appears to have been regarded as the human equivalent of the queen in the natural world of bee and ant communities. Thus while Great Mother Goddess communities certainly had kings, as Robert Graves for one noted, a dual or twin system of kingship was common.[19] In this system, each co-king married the high priestess but then reigned for 50 lunar months, or half a 'great year' before his twin reigned for the next 50 months. The king could only be a king by such a marriage with the Goddess, this being by definition a Sacred Marriage. To the Goddess, alias her high priestess, the king owed everything.

The twinship system, obviously redolent of the mythical Cabeiroi and those twin figurines found at Çatal Hüyük and elsewhere, undoubtedly accounts for why, in the mythology of cities and royal dynasties, it is often twins, or kings with alternating names who figure as their original founders. The most well-known instance of this, of course, is the case of Romulus and Remus, the legendary founders of Rome, for whom, certainly in Robert Graves' interpretation, the she-wolf who suckled them was an embodiment of the Great Mother Goddess. Among other examples, ancient Sparta had Castor and Polydeuces, Messenia and Idas and Lynceus while Tiryns had Heracles and Iphicles. Such twinship always seems to be a sign of the culture having originated from a Great Mother Goddess basis, whatever the system of kingship that might later come into being.

For later, very different systems of kingship there certainly were. As the 3rd millennium BC gave way to the 2nd, a much sharper wind blew through the now ancient, pre-Flood originating empire of the Great Mother Goddess, certainly in an alarming number of her former dominions. The era of male-dominated patriarchal societies – that in which we still exist to this very day – was beginning to make its forceful and often bloody entrance on to the stage.

CHAPTER 16

WHEN PATRIARCH MET MATRIARCH

Hittites once martially conquering the land, may then have married Hattian priestesses to gain a more secure legitimate right to the throne in the eyes of the conquered population.

Merlin Stone, *When God was a Woman*

While the Great Mother Goddess's matrilineal order prevailed, and her high priestesses controlled lands, animal herds and human occupations all the way from Iraq to the Orkneys, so too did much of the ethos of the social order that had prevailed before the Black Sea Flood. For as long as we are able to trace Great Mother Goddess peoples post-Flood, there is a very real sense in which we can continue to catch glimpses of the world that had existed before the Flood.

As we have already seen, the post 5600 BC period continued with occasional further watery encroachments, though by way of counter-poise increasing desiccation steadily rendered the Sahara less and less habitable. However what ultimately brought about the demise of the Great Mother Goddess Empire was neither an excess of water, nor the lack of it. Instead the prevailing historical understanding is that it was patriarchal-minded warriors who swept in from vaguely perceived territories east and north-east of the old Empire, bringing with them rule by the sword, and the Indo-European languages directly ancestral to the majority of languages spoken around Europe to this day.

This process of invasion and infiltration happened gradually in varying ways, in varying countries, over several millennia, and with far too many vicissitudes to chronicle coherently. For reasons that are not at all clear, around 2500 BC the culture that was responsible for the Maltese megaliths vanished as mysteriously as it had begun. Around 2100 BC, there appears to have been another serious drought phase which may well have triggered the collapse of Egypt's Old Kingdom and a general 'musical chairs' of people movements.

A late introduction to ancient warfare was the horse. Although archaeological findings suggest that it was first domesticated north of the Black Sea sometime around the 4th millennium BC,[1] it appears to have begun to be used militarily only from the 2nd millennium BC on. Ancient Greek authors attested the Amazons as amongst the first to exploit horseback riding, but whether this was in north Africa or at their later base on the Black Sea is by no means clear. It was around the early 2nd millennium BC that the rock art of the Sahara began to feature horseback riding and horse-drawn chariots being driven at a very fast gallop – amongst the earliest known occurrences of such images in art. Also at much this same time – and whether connected with the Saharan 'flying gallop' rock-paintings is undetermined – Semitic-speaking Canaanitic peoples with horses and donkeys moved into the Nile Delta.[2] By the 17th century BC, and arguably with the aid of the horsepower which the Egyptians lacked, these had temporarily established their own 'Hyksos' capital and kingdom in Lower Egypt, pushing the indigenous Egyptians further to the south.

Hard evidence remains far too elusive for any proper evaluation of just how the still semi-mythical Amazons and the historically and archaeologically well-attested Hyksos Canaanites of north Africa figured in the overall scheme of things. Nonetheless there can be absolutely no doubt that the 2nd millennium BC saw some serious jostling for power, along with relocations of whole peoples. The patriarchal-minded Hittites were a linguistically Indo-European warrior aristocracy said to have originated in the steppes of Central Asia who around the beginning of the millennium moved into large parts of central Turkey. Their language included many words still to be found in present-day English, for example *watar* for water and *dohter* for daughter. Similarly patriarchal Mycenaean warlords, priding themselves as 'sackers of cities' and speaking an Indo-European language directly ancestral to present-day Greek, assumed control of much of Greece. In Mesopotamia patriarchal Semitic-speaking Babylonians under Hammurabi (*c.*1792–1750 BC) took over from the non-Semitic-speaking Sumerians. In the Bible lands nomadic tribes of patriarchal Semitic herds-people attached the ramparted cities of the similarly Semitic Canaanites who had long been occupying the region as crop-growing farmers and cattle-breeders (chronicled in the biblical books of Joshua and Judges). To the west, Indo-European Celtic peoples took over from the old Goddess-worshipping megalith-builders. Whereas little more than a couple of millennia earlier cities had often been left without walls, indicative of considerable international harmony, now even the stoutest walls all too often failed to protect.

In artistic works the new Indo-European order's more enduring signs included male gods depicted with mountains as their thrones and thunder, lightning, fire and storm as their attributes. The Great Mother Goddess usually became assimilated into Indo-European pantheons but in a lesser capacity. Mortal kings now assumed far greater status and had themselves depicted regally enthroned, or mounted on chariots leading mighty armies into battle.

Our interest, however, concerns those non-Indo-European cultures where the pre-Flood Great Mother Goddess cult managed to survive, at least temporarily. And one such was certainly that of the Minoans of Crete. As earlier noted, the distinctive iconography of a Great Goddess, of bare-breasted high priestesses, of bulls and appreciation of the general beauty of nature survived on Crete to the mid 2nd millennium BC, with not a single statue or painting of an enthroned king anywhere in sight.

Just over a century ago the wealthy British scholar Arthur Evans purchased a patch of land just outside the modern-day Heraklion on Crete. Evans rightly suspected this to be the site mentioned in Homer's *Odyssey* as the 'mighty city of Knossos wherein Minos ruled'. When he dug into this he uncovered an extensive 'palace' belonging to a hitherto unknown culture that he duly termed 'Minoan' after Homer's king Minos. This name has stuck so well that 'Minoan' now automatically springs to mind with regard to artefacts of Crete's distinctive Bronze Age culture.

In the way that the period of English history when it was ruled by a line of kings called George is described as Georgian, so Minoan strongly suggests a nation ruled by one or more autocrats called Minos. Yet throughout the Minoan period on Crete, the heyday of which was the early 2nd millennium BC, while there may have been kings called Minos there is no evidence of any monarchy exerting absolute authority in the manner of Egyptian pharaohs with their tendency to carve their images and names on every available surface. Furthermore, of the two main ancient Cretan scripts that have been found, the younger one, 'Linear B' has been deciphered and found to be Greek, a language that came into the eastern Mediterranean only with the Indo-European invasions. The older script 'Linear A', on the other hand, has not been deciphered, and the language behind it is as yet undetermined. Raising the serious question of which of these two can or should be called the Minoan.

In an oft-quoted passage in the *Odyssey*, Homer represented his Greek hero Odysseus as saying of Crete and its inhabitants:

> Out in the dark blue sea there lies a land called Crete, a
> rich and lovely land, washed by the waves on every side,
> densely peopled and boasting ninety cities. Each of the
> races of the isle has its own language. First there are the
> Achaeans; then the Eteo-Cretans, proud of their native
> stock; next the Cydonians; the Dorians with their three
> clans; and finally the noble Pelasgians.[3]

Homer was writing of a time when the Greeks had already
taken over the island, and as he recognised, of his list only
the Eteo-Cretans were the island's genuine, original inhabitants, as the Greek term 'Eteo' expressly conveys. So Eteo-
Cretans has to be the better term than Minoan to use for the
original, non-Greek-speaking Cretans in whom we are principally interested for any links and language that might
stretch back to the time of the Flood. Likewise it is these
same Eteo-Cretans with whom we should associate the name
'Keftiu' or 'pillar people', and not the island's later Greek
invaders. Described by the ancient Egyptians as sea-going
peoples from out in the 'Great Green' – the Mediterranean
Sea – Egyptian artists depicted them dressed identically to
those featured in early 2nd millennium BC so-called Minoan
art found on Crete.[4]

For the Eteo-Cretans the cult of the column, whether as a
standing stone, a pillar or a tree was certainly very important, their shrines sometimes having as a special feature a set
of three pillars topped by doves, arguably representative of
the Goddess in her triple aspect. A gold ring found at
Knossos shows a male figure descending towards the
Goddess or her priestess from a tall column set in front of a
temple. [fig 28] As we may recall, this pillar motif was one
which seems to have crept into Mother Goddess cultures in
the wake of the Flood, one of the earliest instances being
found on Malta (see p.161), others at Beycesultan.
Understanding of the pillar's significance will emerge, but
later.

Fig 28 The pillar as an Eteo-Cretan cult object. Pillar before an Eteo-Cretan shrine as depicted on a gold ring found at Knossos

Fig 29 (left) Eteo-Cretan Great Mother Goddess on a hillock flanked by heraldic lions, standing before a temple decorated with horns of consecration. (right) The Goddess and attendants before a fruit-bearing tree, with a fiddle-shaped cultic figure of the kind found in post-Flood Turkey in the background

Quite commonly the Goddess was depicted directly on the lively seal-stones in which the Eteo-Cretans were proficient. In one of these she appears heraldically flanked by the lions or leopards first known from Çatal Hüyük, and in front of a shrine topped with the horns of consecration motif [fig 29 left], sculpted versions of which turned up in Arthur Evans' Knossos excavations. On a gold ring of Eteo-Cretan workmanship, but found on the Greek mainland, either the Goddess or her high priestess was depicted with attendants before a fruit-bearing tree [fig 29 right]. High in the background can be seen a fiddle-shaped figure of the kind known from Turkey's immediately post-Flood period, arguably an ancient cult statue of the Goddess that was continuing to be venerated all this while later. Always the costumes of the Goddess and her female attendants, though exposing their breasts, were of most elaborately tiered designs, and with clearly colourful and variegated patterning. In using such colourful materials the Eteo-Cretans were clearly far more closely related to the ancient cultures of Turkey than they were to the altogether plainer and mostly uncoloured costumes which predominated in pharaonic Egypt.

Again exactly as at Turkey's pre-Flood Çatal Hüyük, a particularly notable feature of Eteo-Cretan art was its delight in the natural world. Faience plaques found in repositories of the Palace of Knossos depict a wild goat nursing her young, also a cow with her calf, as typical examples of the Eteo-Cretans' superb observations of the animal world. Again recalling pre-Flood Çatal Hüyük, in Eteo-Cretan Crete the bull was evidently the most potent animal associated with the Goddess. Besides the horns of consecration motif repeatedly used by architects, artists excelled themselves in creating vases in the shape of a bull's head.

Furthermore, in the light of the 'cattle' cult at Çatal Hüyük, and of the later Greek legend that on Crete young men and women were sacrificed to some kind of bull-entity, one of Arthur Evans' most spectacular finds at Knossos was the bull-leaping fresco [fig 30]. In this young men and young women were depicted leaping over an enormous bull. Modern-day 'cowboys' who ride bulls at rodeos insist that such a practice is far too dangerous ever to be performed as mere clever acrobatics. Yet that the Eteo-Cretan performers were both young men and young women is quite clear from the Knossan artists' convention, exactly as at Çatal Hüyük, of using red to depict the skins of males and white for

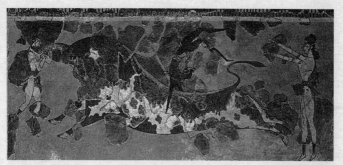

Fig 30 The famous Eteo-Cretan bull-leaping fresco, as discovered during Sir Arthur Evans' early 20th century excavations of the Palace at Knossos, Crete. This dates from the middle of the 2nd millennium BC. The central leaping figure is male, the figures to right and left are female

females. Redolant of Amazon cultures, clearly this was a society – quite unlike that of the Indo-European Greeks – in which women and men, on occasion at least, were expected to compete on equal terms. And a further notable feature, the significance of which will again emerge later, is that they were doing so without bladed weapons of any kind.

Yet the bull could also be a sacrificial victim, as again we have inferred from pre-Flood Çatal Hüyük. On a most interesting Eteo-Cretan sarcophagus found at Hagia Triada on Crete, a huge bull can be seen trussed up on an altar being offered up in sacrifice by what appear to be three priestesses [fig 31]. Closer inspection in fact reveals that one of these has the red skin of a man – even though he is unmistakably dressed as a woman.

Any bafflement posed by this 2nd millennium BC example of 'drag' is explained by reference to Greek mythology. Apparently even the macho mythological hero Heracles, when he was in western Turkey in the service of the high priestess Omphale, was required to dress up in female costume as a token of his subordination to her. According to Robert Graves,[5] this denoted an early stage in the more

Fig 31 Bull being offered up in sacrifice, from a 15th Century BC Eteo-Cretan sarcophagus found at Hagia Triada, Crete. Immediately behind the bull the pipe-playing 'priestess' is a man in female dress. Note also the spiral motif decorating the altar immediately in front of the right hand priestess, the cultic pillar immediately on front of this. At furthest right, just out of the picture as seen here, are horns of consecration

peaceful transitions from pre-Flood matriarchy to post-Flood patriarchy when the king, as consort, was privileged to deputise for the queen in ceremonies and sacrifices – but only on the condition that he wore her robes. Also worth noting is that the Hagia Triada male 'priestess' was depicted playing a rather distinctive double pipe, one reed of which was entirely straight, while the other curved like a trumpet at its end. This instrument will be found recurring later.

Arguably one of the most fascinating images to survive from the entire corpus of Eteo-Cretan art is the Ship Procession as found on a frieze in one of the rooms in the so-called West House on the Eteo-Cretan island of Thera 95 kilometres (60 miles) to the north of Crete [fig 32]. This provides a superbly lively and detailed glimpse of an Eteo-Cretan coastal town as it would have looked three and a half millennia ago. Indeed as a landscape it is reminiscent of the one with the volcano in the background as found at Çatal Hüyük.

In this instance, however, the mood is a very joyful one, suggestive of some special festival or celebration. A fleet of superbly designed vessels is depicted arriving at what would seem to have been the same Eteo-Cretan port where the fresco was found. Seated in an elaborate cabin on one of the arriving ships can be seen a young man, apparently the individual on whose behalf the voyage has been undertaken. At the port of the fleet's arrival, although both males and females are depicted watching from a building complex, the women are notably represented to a slightly bigger scale, as if they carry more importance.

All the indications are that the Eteo-Cretan town depicted was one under the tutelage of the Great Goddess.[6] A gold ring found at Tiryns on mainland Greece, but created in the Cretan style, shows much the same scene, with again a young male arriving by sea to be received by a woman, rather than vice versa. As deduced by Sweden's Gösta Säflund and other scholars, the young man would seem to have been a bridegroom who had come to marry his bride in her town.[7] So the fresco celebrates much the same Sacred Marriage rite that we saw in prototype at Çatal Hüyük, now apparently being carried on in Eteo-Cretan societies during the post-Flood era. Moreover, it was apparently being carried on along exactly the same matrilineal terms that we earlier noted to have been perpetuated by the Berbers, in that the bridegroom was expected to go to the bride's bed, rather than vice-versa.

Evident from the fine ships that are depicted in this same scene, also from elsewhere in Minoan art, is that the Eteo-Cretans enjoyed a confident mastery of the sea. Archaeologically this is corroborated from the fact that no sea-wall defences from the Eteo-Cretan period have been found at any of Crete's coastal cities such as Knossos, Mallia and Zakro. This suggests that when the Eteo-Cretans were at their height there was no other Mediterranean sea-power

Fig 32 The so-called 'Ship Procession' fresco found decorating the upper
wall of one of the houses on Thera buried by the volcanic eruption in the
mid-2nd millennium BC. Although here divided into two parts, in actuality
the fresco is one continuous scene depicting a flotilla of ships approaching
an Eteo-Cretan port (this latter seen to the right in the upper register).
From the general air of festivity one interpretation of the scene is that the
young man was a prince arriving to be married to a bride whose home was
at the port. In the multi-storey port building at upper right several women
can be seen in the upper floors watching the fleet's arrival

that posed any threat to them, the Egyptians, as we noted
earlier, having been little inclined to venture further than
their own river Nile.

This raises the issue of exactly what relationship may
have existed between the Eteo-Cretans, the earlier-mentioned
sea-faring peoples of western Turkey (whose vessels were
depicted on the Dorak sword), the Carians of south-
west Turkey, said by Herodotus to have manned Cretan
ships, and that other great seafaring people of antiquity
whom the Greeks, when they became literate, called
Phoenicians.

Phoenician literally means 'red people', from the Greek
word *phoinos*, for 'blood-red'. Though this may recall the
predilection for red in Çatal Hüyük, the more normal explanation is the Phoenicians' monopoly over manufacturing and

trading of a highly prized dye.[8] The term is, however, the Greek language equivalent of 'Canaanite', which in the Semitic language essentially means the same. The Canaanites/ Phoenicians, sometimes also called Syrians because of the Syrian corner of the Mediterranean they inhabited, were essentially the sea-going coastal variety of the Canaanite city-dwellers biblically described as occupying the inland region of what is now Syria and Israel before the coming of the patriarchal 'Israelites'. Indicative that this was a people highly developed in the skills of domesticating plants and animals, according to a 2nd millennium BC Egyptian tale, the story of Sinuhe, the Canaanites' land was:

> … a good land … Figs were in it, as well as vines. More abundant was its wine than water. Its honey was plentiful, its olives profuse. Every fruit was on its trees. Barley was there along with emmer wheat. There was no limit to its cattle.[9]

At least as early as the 3rd and 2nd millennia BC the Canaanites/Phoenicians' recognised heartland consisted of a string of ports established along the northern part of the easternmost sector of the Mediterranean from southern Turkey to the Lebanon. The ports in question included Rouad (Arwad), Byblos, Berytus (Beirut), Sidon and Tyre. For a variety of reasons – including sea-level changes and silting that have radically changed the coastline since ancient times – archaeologists have been able to learn little about these in their heyday except that their founders apparently chose off-shore islets or peninsulas for their locations, inevitably recalling Amazonian Chersonessus on Lake Tritonis.

For instance Arwad, the Arvad of Genesis, is a small off-shore island that is today almost entirely covered by modern-day housing, and therefore impossible to excavate. Sidon was built partly on an islet which Crusaders later converted into a fortress, this castle needing to be dismantled in order to gain access to any more ancient remains that might lie beneath. Tyre was built on a rocky island that stood half a kilometre (a third of a mile) offshore and although a 9th century BC Assyrian relief depicted it as a fine city, excavations have so far revealed few remains earlier than the Hellenistic period. Underwater investigations carried out by the pre-World War II archaeologists Antoine Pidebard and Gaston Jondet, also by Honor Frost in the 1960s, have indicated that to create these coastal ports the Canaanites/ Phoenicians cleverly utilised sandstone ridges that lay offshore just beyond and below the present shoreline. By quarrying parts of these ridges, and infilling elsewhere they created what were arguably the world's earliest artificial harbours. Tyre, for instance, has submerged reefs to the south which seem to have been reinforced to provide marina-like extra harbour space. From the consistent and clearly deliberate offshore nature of these ports it is evident that the Canaanite/Phoenicians were totally confident of their command of the sea, and feared attack only from the land, just as we have inferred of the Eteo-Cretans.

Though the Canaanites/Phoenicians were undoubtedly a literary people – their script is the direct ancestor of our own western alphabet – few narrative works of theirs have survived – at least in direct form. Largely responsible for this would have been the perishability of the materials on which they wrote, probably mostly papyrus, as used by the Egyptians, but in Canaan prone to the vagaries of a moister and therefore much less preservative climate. Nonetheless a 14th century BC cuneiform fragment of Tablet VII of the Gilgamesh story was found by chance in the 1950s on the site of the inland Canaanite metropolis of Megiddo. Likewise as recently as 1994 there turned up at Ras Shamra, the ancient Ugarit on the Syrian coast, a complete 12th century tablet, as yet unpublished, but said to be of local composition and drawing upon 'selected episodes' from the

Gilgamesh story.[10] So the Flood story was certainly part of their folklore.

Furthermore there can be no doubt that exactly as in the case of the Eteo-Cretans these were partly if not wholly Great Mother Goddess peoples. A very fine ivory from Ugarit shows the goddess between two goats, wearing a Cretan-style tiered skirt but otherwise bare-breasted. Though they certainly had some male deities such as Baal and El (quite likely acquired through mixing with other peoples), both of these were associated with bulls. Also in the biblical book of Kings, Sidon is specifically described as being devoted to Astarte (1 Kings 11: 5), one of the Great Mother Goddess's many personae. The biblical books also convey that the Canaanites/Phoenicians cult included veneration of trees and pillars, that some priests suffered emasculation as a sign of their devotion, while women celebrated the sex act in ways that the Bible editors condemned as flagrant prostitution.

Wall-paintings found in ancient Egyptian tombs, such as those of Nebamun and Sobek-hotep at Thebes, have provided some invaluable pictorial glimpses of the Canaanites/Phoenicians. Both male and female garments featured elaborate tiering, in the case of the women strikingly similar to the Eteo-Cretan high-priestess dress, while filet headbands rather reminiscent of the Çatal Hüyük Great Goddess statuette were also common. They were proficient in use of the horse-drawn chariot for land warfare, the biblical book of Joshua attesting to this in respect of the inland cities of Canaan, also notably describing them as using 'chariots of iron', a description long thought anachronistic.

Egyptian records show that they were very craft-oriented peoples long involved in working and trading in the fine timber that abounded in the Lebanese hinterland. As early as mid 3rd millennium BC their port of Byblos supplied 40 shiploads of cedar logs to the 4th Dynasty Egyptian king

Snofru for boat-building and other purposes. At the entrance to Snofru's burial chamber in the southern pyramid at Dahshur archaeologists found well-preserved props of cedar which most likely came from the same source. Cheops, builder of the Great Pyramid, almost certainly obtained the cedar-wood for his funerary boat from the same source, while 2nd Dynasty Egyptian alabaster vases found at Byblos indicate commercial ties going back even earlier. A millennium and a half later, when the biblical king Solomon wanted wood to construct his temple in Jerusalem, it was to Tyre's king Hiram that he turned as supplier of both raw materials and craftspeople.

It is also evident that the Canaanites/Phoenicians tree-felling and carpentry skills gave them a long-established and widely-recognised command, not only of temple-building, but also of the construction and navigation of seagoing boats. This latter they used to great effect, and mostly peacefully. For instance the Egyptians appear to have trusted them sufficiently that they allowed them to create an off-shore base for themselves in the form of the island of Pharos off what is today Alexandria. In 1916 the Frenchman Gaston Jondet reported finding a vast underwater harbour works that may well have been the remains of this.[11] Importantly, the individual Canaanite/Phoenician city-states appear to have operated a pact always to co-operate with each other, and never to fight between themselves.

When we recall the seagoing navy that was depicted on the c.2500 BC Dorak sword from northwest Turkey (see fig 22, p.177), likewise the numerous vessels depicted in Minoan art, the issue that has to arise is whether Canaanites/Phoenicians, Eteo-Cretans and western Turkey's seagoing peoples all might have represented one great seagoing confederacy of independent states who belonged to much the same cultural heritage, and whose allegiance lay not in any master-autocrat but in a religion dating back to the pre-Flood era.

There is much to indicate this. Egyptian painters some-times labelled typical Canaanite/Phoenician peoples as deriving from Keftiu,[12] suggesting that while all Eteo-Cretans were Keftiu, not all Keftiu were necessarily Eteo-Cretans. Among scholars there is no consensus where the Canaanites/Phoenicians might have originated. Balance-pan weights from the wreck of a Canaanitic ship found off Cape Gelidonya off south-western Turkey indicate that the standards of measure used amongst Canaanite/Phoenician cultures were also used on Cyprus, Crete and the Cycladic islands. Ships of Phoenician Tyre depicted on a 7th century BC Assyrian relief from the palace of Sennacherib are not only of essentially the same design as those on the north-west Turkish Dorak sword blade from nearly two millennia earlier, but also show women in an apparent commanding role on a majority of the ships. We may recall how the sea-going Carians of western Turkey were similarly matrilineal. The same spiral motif that earlier we noted on Malta and at Newgrange (see fig 26, p.225) features prominently on Canaanite temple bowls, on jewellery found at Troy, and in numerous examples of Eteo-Cretan art (e.g. on the right-hand altar in fig 31 reproduced on p.240).

Whatever the exact nature of their relationship, the matri-lineal societies of the Eteo-Cretans and related peoples on mainland Greece, Turkey's more indigenous peoples, and the Canaanites/Phoenicians were under threat. During the 2nd millennium BC all were to suffer patriarchal incursions that were to change them for ever.

As earlier mentioned, around the beginning of the 2nd millennium BC Canaanitic peoples had moved into Egypt's Nile delta region and had established a seaport capital there from which they commanded Lower Egypt with the aid of horse-drawn chariots. Dubbed 'Hyksos' by the Egyptians, it is quite possible that some of these had moved eastwards from north Africa, fleeing the drying Sahara.

Around 1500 BC these people suddenly found themselves confronted and ousted by the forceful New Kingdom pharaoh Ahmose, who had cleverly developed chariotry superior to theirs, and drove them eastwards into what is today Israel. Once there, both they and the Canaanites/Phoenicians long settled in the region became prey both to Egyptian invasions that led to their subjugation by Egypt, but also to fierce attacks from nomadic bands of patriarchal fellow-Semites, possibly one and the same as the Joshua-led Hebrews of the Bible. Largely thanks to Egyptian 'protection' the Canaanites/Phoenicians in the coastal cities such as Tyre, Byblos and Sidon temporarily survived rather better than their more land-based compatriots in cities such as Jericho.

In the case of the indigenous peoples of Turkey, the exact mix of those occupying the country during the 2nd millennium BC is very tangled. Amongst surviving textual sources are mentions of peoples or territories with names such as Partakhvina, Pala, Halasa, Isuwa, many of which it is near impossible even to locate, let alone to correlate with archaeological finds. The Hurrians, whom we mentioned earlier as possible descendants of Black Sea Flood survivors, were a people whose language was definitely not Indo-European but thought to be related to the present-day Caucasian languages Chechan and Lezgian. The clannish division of these into many subgroups, among these Kurti (Kurds?), Hatti, Mitanni, Urartu and Mushku (the latter clearly evocative of the Moschians) has undoubtedly further contributed to the confusion surrounding the relations of one people versus another. Perhaps harking back to their ancestral survival of the Flood, the Hurrian-type peoples seem to have preferred hilly terrain, and as noted earlier, some archaeological remains are coming to light. But certainly all too little is known about them compared to those who temporarily took them over, the Hittites.

Themselves previously largely unknown, the Hittites first came to modern-day attention in 1906 when the German scholar Hugo Wichkler discovered the site of their capital, Hattusas, at Boghazköy, east of Ankara, and strategically placed within the bend of Turkey's river Halys. While the Hittites have often been vaunted as controlling a major 'empire' James Mellaart stresses that this has been greatly exaggerated. Around 1900 BC they seem to have infiltrated into Turkey where Assyrian merchants had established trading posts called *karum*, only properly beginning to impose dynastic rule in the 17th century BC. Even when they did this they notably tried to do so within the framework of the old Mother Goddess religion, arguably in order to ensure their greater acceptance among the indigenous and still largely Hurrian populace.

Nowhere is this more clear than 3 kilometres (2 miles) north-east of the ruins of Hattusas, and some 180 metres (600 feet) above the surrounding plain. Here in the 13th century BC the Hittite king Hattushili III built Yazilikaya, a religious sanctuary against a spectacular setting of rocks. Although the gods depicted in the shrine's reliefs are identified by inscriptions in the Indo-European Luvian language, their actual names are Hurrian. This is thought to have come about because Hattushili's queen, Puduhepa, was the daughter of a Hurrian priest and as such, arguably a high priestess of the Great Goddess.

Accordingly at Yazilikaya Hittite artists sculpted a Sacred Marriage scene in which the storm or weather god Teshub was depicted colossus-style astride two mountains greeting his Great Goddess bride, who was represented perched on a lion, immediately reminiscent of the beasts of the Çatal Hüyük statuette. Behind the goddess was depicted the son of their union on another lion, with behind him two attendant goddesses and a two-headed vulture or eagle. More than likely the indigenous Queen Puduhepa, in whose honour the relief was carved, physically consummated her marriage to her consort at Yazilikaya, as their religiously ordained love-nest. It is also likely that Puduhepa would have cherished in her folklore the story of Nahmizuli, the Hurrian 'Noah' and his Flood and would have been as familiar with it as the present-day Sunday School pupil the biblical story of Noah.

In the case of the Eteo-Cretans, for them disaster struck initially in natural form, in the guise of a massive eruption of the island of Thera, on which Eteo-Cretan colonists had settled. Although the exact date and details of this catastrophe are still the subject of considerable controversy, falls of volcanic ash may well have had disastrous effects on the Eteo-Cretans' crops and grazing animals, causing prolonged famine. In such straitened circumstances, it is likely that they became forced into a virtual surrender of their island and their sailing fleet to the mainland-based, Greek-speaking Achaeans of Mycenaeans.

For certainly within a generation or so the Mycenaeans can be seen to take over on Crete, the Eteo-Cretans' 'Linear A' script, written in an as yet undetermined language, being adapted as 'Linear B' to record transactions in what a translation breakthrough in the 1950s revealed as the Mycenaeans' native Greek. And as evident from 'Linear B' tablets found at Pylos on the Greek mainland, the Mycenaeans began using their newfound literacy to record their acquisitions of slaves from Lemnos, Chios, Miletus, Halicarnassos and Cnidus, all 'Great Mother Goddess' territories around the west coast of Turkey where we may expect Eteo-Cretan seapower earlier to have been pre-eminent. The famous Greek attack on Troy, as enshrined in Homer's *Iliad* (and insofar as it can be considered historical, thought to have happened around the 13th century BC), almost certainly became possible through the same shift of seapower from Eteo-Cretan to Mycenaean.

Then around 1200 BC, possibly due to some fresh climatic

disaster (there are hints of yet another disastrous drought), the Near East was rocked by the famous, though still far from fully understood, 'Sea Peoples' invasions. The Hittites, never numerically strong and already weakened by an earlier defeat at the hands of the Egyptian pharaoh Ramesses II, seem simply to have disappeared, most likely swallowed up by the indigenous Hurrians. The Egyptians under Ramesses III, definitely attacked by the Sea Peoples, defended themselves with considerable vigour, and ultimately successfully, though they lost much of their earlier acquired Canaanitic territories in the process.

According to Ramesses III's official account of these events, the Sea Peoples were puzzlingly diverse. They included 'Libyans' (north Africans to Egypt's west), 'Lukka' (confidently identifiable as Lycians from Turkey's southwest corner), 'Sherden' (who may have hailed from Sardis, some 48 kilometres (30 miles) inland from present-day Izmir, though another school of thought suggests they were Sardinians), 'Sheklesh' (thought by some to have been Sicilians) and perhaps most notably 'Peleset' (who can be identified with confidence as the same 'Philistines' biblically described as having settled in the coastal parts of Israel). As pointed out by Robert Graves 'Peleset' or 'Prst' is yet another word meaning 'red men'.[13] And intriguingly, wherever the Philistines came from – their culture was far more advanced than the pejorative modern use of their name suggests – they brought knowledge of iron-working with them. Biblically they are described as commanding a monopoly of the process when they settled in the former Canaan (1 Samuel 13: 19). This inevitably calls to mind the mysterious iron-workers of northern Turkey, dubbed Tibarenians, whom we earlier noted to have been the first in the world to develop this form of technology.

In Turkey the power vacuum left by the eclipse of the Hittites seems to have been quickly filled by the Moschians or Phrygians, a branch of the Hurrians whom we earlier noted to have the reputation of being more ancient than the Egyptians. These established a dynasty of kings alternately named Midas or Gordius (evocative of the twins system), basing themselves at Gordion, modern-day Yassibüyük, in central Turkey, though achieving little prominence before the 7th century BC. According to Herodotus these particular Phrygians came from Thrace, but they were certainly adherents of the Great Mother Goddess peoples (Midas was said to be the Goddess's son by an unknown satyr, clearly indicative of matrilineality). Furthermore, from Homer we also know that they were allies to the Trojans during the Trojan War.

These details aside, the exact circumstances pertaining to the whole 'Sea Peoples' period remain so controversial and have eluded so many scholars that it would be folly to add to the speculation. But if we have been right that there was some kind of confederacy between the Canaanites/Phoenicians of north Africa and the Syrian coast of the eastern Mediterranean, the Carian and other sea-going peoples of the west Turkish coast, and the Keftiu of Crete and related islands, then a new question arises. What else might these peoples have had in common aside from shared weights and measures and the Goddess religion? In particular, might they have shared a common language, thereby giving us a clue to the language that was spoken around the Black Sea at the time of the Flood?

In the case of the north African and Canaanites/Phoenicians there is no mystery. Despite the loss of much written material, their language was undoubtedly a Semitic one, as known from a variety of inscriptions. However, mystery still surrounds the language of the Eteo-Cretans, the early peoples of the Turkish west coast, and the pre-Greek inhabitants of the Greek mainland. As remarked earlier, the Eteo-Cretans' 'Linear A' script has not been deciphered. The language of the matrilineal people living on the island of Lemnos, west of Troy, which survives on a single stele written in Greek characters, is similarly undetermined, except that it apparently exhibits affinities to the similarly poorly understood language of the Etruscans of Italy. And both in western Turkey, in mainland Greece and on Crete the names of certain ancient sites have endings that suggest they were formulated in whatever language the inhabitants of these places had spoken before the Indo-European invasions.[14]

In the case of Eteo-Cretan 'Linear A' one man, at least, claims that he has cracked the problem.[15] According to the veteran archaeologist Cyrus Gordon the Eteo-Cretan language of the 'Linear A' tablets was Semitic. And he says that he and those of his students who follow his lead are able to read it.

The intriguing element here is that nearly three decades ago James Mellaart, on the basis of the striking affinities between the Çatal Hüyük and Eteo-Cretan cultures, argued that the Eteo-Cretan language is likely to have been a direct descendant of that spoken in pre-Flood Çatal Hüyük.[16] Similarly worthy of note is that, according to present-day Chechens of Georgia, the ancient language that was spoken in Black Sea Colchis, where Jason and his Argonauts sought the Golden Fleece, was again a Semitic one.

So far, however, Gordon's decipherment claim has won precious few converts among fellow-scholars, even James Mellaart being among the dissidents. Besides which, looking for any common language, let alone a Semitic one, amongst the Black Sea Flood survivors, may well be the pursuit of a chimera. Seagoing peoples tend to be multilingual. Languages can change, while deep-seated cultural characteristics are retained, as many modern-day multi-cultural societies, including my own Australia, bear witness. Of far greater interest is the retention of such cultural characteristics, including folk-memories of the Flood, even as late as the 1st millennium BC, and these we will be studying in the penultimate chapter.

Overall the 2nd millennium BC, with its climatic disturbances, incursions of Indo-Europeans, Sea Peoples' movements, and much else, seriously further fragmented what had once been a most remarkable 'empire'. An arguably pre-Flood-originating empire that in its hey-day had extended across Europe, northern Africa and western Asia, and which had been unfortunate enough to suffer some untimely inundations, most notably the Black Sea Flood and related floodings to the Mediterranean coasts and islands. Also, possibly, the still semi-mythical Lake Tritonis.

This then raises the question – is it just conceivable that such an empire might have been remembered in some other ancient source, one quite aside from the famous Flood stories?

CHAPTER 17

'ATLANTIS' FACT OR FICTION?

There occurred violent earthquakes and floods; and in a single day and night ... the island of Atlantis ... disappeared into the depths of the sea.

Plato, *Critias*

From everything that we have put together so far, it should have become apparent that the 6th millennium BC pre-Flood society of northern Turkey and environs that became overwhelmed by the Black Sea burst-through has to have been considerably more advanced and interesting than anyone has previously anticipated. And key facets of it, such as the bull cult, the matrilineality, the manipulation of animal and plant reproductive processes and the emphasis on high standards of craftsmanship lingered even several millennia later.

When James Mellaart uncovered the pre-Flood inland town of Çatal Hüyük, and found it to have been so surprisingly developed, it struck him even then as unlikely that so many advances would have been made in isolation. There had to have been something wider behind it all. And, as we have seen, the post-Flood Goddess empire was a very wide one indeed. This in itself suggests that there is more that has not yet been discovered, whether because the clues lie beneath the Black or Mediterranean Seas or for other undetermined reasons which have not so far been brought to light.

All of which raises an interesting question. Could

something of the post-Ice Age sea-level disruptions – that is, the great Black Sea Flood, whatever may have happened to Lake Tritonis in Tunisian north Africa, and other localised watery disasters – have given rise not only to the Noah family of Flood stories, but also to the famous story of the drowning of Atlantis?

Back in the mid 4th century BC the Athenian philosopher Plato, in two of his dialogues, *Timaeus* and the unfinished *Critias* told a 'lost continent' story which he accredited to the earlier Greek statesman Solon, who died *c*.560 BC. Thirty years earlier, in around 590 BC, Solon had visited the then Egyptian capital Sais in the Nile Delta, which though virtually nothing of it remains today, had been a flourishing city as far back as the 1st Dynasty period. There Solon was befriended by Egyptian priests who belonged to the city's ancient temple of the goddess Neith, the very same 'red' goddess with Amazon-like attributes whom we noted earlier[1] as an early Egyptian *persona* of the Great Mother Goddess.

The priests of Sais told Solon how this goddess, as 'a lover both of war and wisdom' (and in their view a direct counterpart of the Greeks' Athene), in very ancient times had founded their city and had ordained its laws, crafts and professions. They also told him that as a result they possessed written records stretching back to the remotest antiquity, including of great floods and other disasters. Amongst these records there were references to 'an island situated in front of the straits which by you [the Greeks] are called the pillars of Heracles [the straits of Gibraltar]'.[2] This island was the seat of a 'great and wonderful empire' ruled by ten kings comprising five sets of twins. This empire ruled over 'the whole island and several others and over parts of the continent', its bounds being 'larger than Libya and Asia put together'. But then occurred:

... violent earthquakes and floods, and in a single day and night ... the island of Atlantis ... disappeared into the sea. For which reason the sea in those parts is impassable and impenetrable, because there is a shoal of mud in the way; and this was caused by the subsidence of the island[3]

One of the problems that hinder any serious discussion of 'Atlantis' is that for well over a century the story has been so bandied about by sensation-mongers that even to whisper it is likely to invite immediate alienation by scholars of any repute. In 1882 the American lawyer and politician Ignatius Donnelly in his best-selling *Atlantis: the Antediluvian World*[4] argued that Atlantis was a large island that before 9600 BC had stood out in the Atlantic beyond the straits of Gibraltar and was the original cradle from which all civilisation sprang. In Donnelly's view, all the main inventions of civilised society – agriculture, textile manufacture, the principles of navigation, writing, the compass, even gunpowder – originated in Atlantis. He stated that a great chain of underwater mountains, the mid-Atlantic ridge, still attested to Atlantis' one-time existence. The several parallels between civilisations on both sides of the Atlantic, such as pyramids, likewise suggested that these had their source in a central Atlantic master civilisation.

Subsequent scientific findings have fatally undermined Donnelly's claims. For instance, from geophysical evidence, we know that no human-populated super-continent could ever have stood on the mid-Atlantic ridge, which has been submerged beneath the Atlantic for at least 60 million years. And the Egyptian and Mexican pyramids are over three thousand years separated in time. Yet this has not deterred the writing of more than 2,000 subsequent books on the 'Atlantology' theme. Few peoples and places on earth have not been linked with the lost civilisation. As listed in E.S. Ramage's *Atlantis: Fact or Fiction?* these have included: 'the Goths, the Gauls, the Druids, the Egyptians and the Scyths

... the Mediterranean, the Sahara, the Caucasus, ... South Africa, Ceylon, Brazil, Greenland, the British Isles, the Netherlands and Prussia.[5] Currently Britain's Colonel John Blashford-Snell is said to be looking for it in Bolivia. Small wonder, therefore, that when Cesare Emiliani, the great pioneer of studies of the effects of post-Ice Age sea-level rises, even mildly suggested that these rises and the Atlantis story might possibly have been linked, the brickbats hurled by his scientific colleagues were dire indeed.

Exactly as in the case of the Noah family of Flood stories, it is of fundamental importance to treat Plato's story neither as holy writ on the one hand, nor as wholly 'rot' on the other. For instance, since Egyptian narrative writing did not begin until c.3000 BC, the Egyptian priests' information that the Atlantis disaster happened nine thousand years before their present should be rather more loosely interpreted as 'several millennia before 590 BC'. Similarly, while it is often assumed from the very word 'Atlantis' that Plato's text demands a location out in the Atlantic Ocean, the highly respected classics scholar J.V. Luce has emphatically pointed out that this is far from necessarily so:

> The name 'Atlantis' is a most deceptive guide. Atlantis is *not* derived from Atlantic. Linguistically both names are in the same generation, so to speak, like brother and sister, and both trace their parentage back to Atlas, the giant Titan who held the sky on his shoulders. In Greek they are adjectival forms of Atlas, meaning '(the island) of Atlas' and '(the sea) of Atlas' respectively ... So if you decide to use the name of Atlantis as a clue to its location, you must consider what was the original location of the mythical Atlas.[6]

Here the archaeological writer Peter James has recently and valuably contributed to this same argument.[7] From Greek mythology he has noted the location of various members of

Atlas' family. Atlas' most famous brother was Prometheus whose punishment by the gods – being fastened to a rock with an eagle pecking at his liver – took place in the Caucasus, that is, in the south-east corner of the Black Sea. As also related in the Greek myths, Atlas' mother was 'Asia', a word that ancient writers mostly understood to mean the kingdom of Lydia on Turkey's west coast and nowhere near the Atlantic. Likewise all but one of Atlas' seven daughters were similarly associated with the region now called Turkey, one, for instance, mothering Dardanus, the mother of the Trojan dynasty.

Furthermore, in Greek legend Atlas' father was named Iapetus, which as scholars such as Robert Graves and others have recognised, has to have been one and the same as Japheth, one of the three sons of the biblical Noah. According to Genesis chapter 10, Japheth's sons were 'Gomer, Magog, the Medes, Javan, Tubal, Meschech [and] Tiras'.[8] Amongst these Gomer has been recognised as ancestor of the Cimmerians of the Black Sea's northern, or Russian coast. Magog is regarded by the present-day Chechens as ancestor of a Black Sea tribe which split after the Deluge, some settling north of the Black Sea, the others north of the Caspian. The Medes are associated with the Kurds of the Caucasus.[9] Javan is understood to refer to the Greeks. Tubal we earlier determined to refer to the Tibarenians of Turkey's north coast. Meschech we likewise identified as the Moschians or Phrygians of Turkey. Tiras, although more obscure, may refer to the Tyrrhenians or Etruscans, a major 1st millennium BC power in Italy with some strong Goddess culture affinities, whose still far from fully understood language we have noted as having similarities to the ancient language of Lemnos, and who possibly originated in Turkey.

Overwhelmingly, therefore, the great majority of these peoples' locations were either on the fringes of the Black

Sea, or in its near vicinity. None of them were even remotely associated with the Atlantic. And even the Atlantis legend's reference to the Pillars of Heracles does not necessarily pinpoint the story to the environs of the Straits of Gibraltar. As again pointed out by Peter James, a late Roman writer, Servius, remarked in a commentary on Virgil's *Aeneid*: 'We pass through the Pillars of Heracles *in the Black Sea* [italics mine] as well as Spain'.[10] Here Servius seems to have meant the same Cyanean rocks at the Black Sea end of the Bosporus that we noted in an earlier chapter.

All this, however, is almost incidental to Plato's description of the main features of the 'Atlantean' civilisation, features which exhibit some striking affinities to those we earlier came to associate with the post-Flood Goddess cultures.

Notable, for instance, is the reported rule of Atlantis by 'five pairs of twin male children',[11] which inevitably recalls the strange twin figurines that were found at pre-Flood Çatal Hüyük and other sites, also the Cabeiroi-type twin kings that we found so repeatedly associated with Goddess cultures. Of the Atlantean twins, Atlas, as 'first-born of the eldest pair' was apparently the most senior, thereby qualifying him to inherit his mother's dwelling and the surrounding allotment which was the largest and the best'.[12] This unmistakably indicates a law of matrilineal inheritance, exactly as we have noted of Goddess cultures from Turkey to the Berber Sahara.

Both Atlas, as the most senior, and the nine other designated princes, were all, it seems, subject to predetermined written laws that governed their interpersonal behaviour. As the Egyptian priests told Solon:

There were many special laws affecting the several kings inscribed about the temples; but the most important was the following; they were not to take up arms against one another and they were all to come to the rescue if any one of their cities attempted to overthrow the royal house.[13]

Here is a mutual non-aggression pact between the Atlantean royals of exactly the kind that, as mentioned in the last chapter, is known to have existed between the Canaanite-Phoenician city-states, and which must have existed amongst the Eteo-Cretan city-states likewise, in view of their lack of sea-defences.

Solon's priestly informants also made it abundantly clear that, befitting Atlantis' island status, the Atlantean civilisation was very much a seagoing one. Further concerning the five sets of kingly twins they told him:

> All these and their descendants for many generations were the inhabitants and rulers of divers islands in the open sea; and also, as has been already said, they held sway in our direction over the country within the pillars [of Heracles] as far as Egypt and Tyrrhenia [Etruria].[14]

Because of the Atlantean empire's vast extent 'many things were brought to them from foreign countries', from which we may infer that the Atlanteans were far-ranging and enterprising traders, just as we know the Canaanite-Phoenicians to have been. Recalling from the last chapter the major harbour works that the Canaanite-Phoenicians carried out on their offshore island bases, the Atlanteans reportedly:

> ... beginning from the sea ... bored a canal of three hundred feet [90 metres] in width and one hundred feet [30 metres] in depth and fifty stadia in length, which they carried through to the outermost zone [of their island], making a passage from the sea to this, which became a harbour, and leaving an opening sufficient to enable the largest vessels to find ingress ... the docks were full of triremes and naval stores ... the canal and the largest of the harbours were full of vessels and merchants coming

from all parts, who, from their numbers, kept up a multitudinous sound of human voices, and din and clatter of
all sorts night and day.[15]

According to the priests of Sais, the Atlanteans 'dug out of
the earth whatever was to be found there,' a major local
resource for them apparently having been 'orichalcum
[copper ore] more precious in those days than anything
except gold'. Clearly, therefore, they were proficient metal-
workers. Furthermore:

> ... there was an abundance of wood for carpenter's work,
> and sufficient maintenance for tame and wild animals ...
> also whatever fragrant things there now are in the earth,
> whether roots or herbage or woods or essences which
> distil from fruit and flower, grew and thrived in that
> land; also the fruit which admits cultivation.

This enables us to infer that they were also skilled at woodworking, animal husbandry and plant cultivation.

According to the Sais priests the Atlanteans were builders
in stone, and experts in hydraulics:

> The stone ... they quarried from underneath the centre
> island, and from underneath the zones ... One kind was
> white, another black, and a third red ... Some of their
> buildings were simple, but in others they put together
> different stones, varying the colour to please the eye ...
> also they made cisterns, some open to heaven, others
> roofed over, to be used in winter as warm baths ... Of the
> water which ran off they carried some to the grove of
> Poseidon, where were growing all manner of trees of
> wonderful height and beauty, while the remainder was
> conveyed by aqueducts along the bridges to the outer
> circles.[16]

As noted by James Mellaart, white, black and red were the
three colours used in building decoration at Çatal Hüyük,

while for many authors the Atlantean plumbing systems have seemed strikingly similar to the proficiency in these things exhibited by the Eteo-Cretans.

The Atlanteans were also reportedly users of horse-drawn chariots for warfare:

> The inhabitants ... had leaders assigned to them according to their districts and villages. The leader was required to furnish for the war the sixth portion of a chariot, so as to make up a total of ten thousand chariots; also two horses and riders for them, and a pair of chariot-horses without a car, accompanied by a horseman who could fight on foot carrying a small shield, and having a charioteer who stood behind the man-at-arms to guide the two horses.[17]

This inevitably recalls the earlier-mentioned military use of horse-drawn chariots by Canaanitic peoples, both in north Africa and in their eastern Mediterranean coastal city-states. Reportedly the Atlanteans also had a stadium where horse races were staged.

The Atlantean empire's central temple was apparently dedicated to Cleito and Poseidon, parents of the royal dynasty. Here it is notable that Plato quoted Cleito's name before Poseidon's, suggesting that she was the more senior deity, and thereby corresponding to the matrilineal inheritance that we earlier noted among post-Flood Goddess peoples. In other respects, however, Plato, coming as he did from a patriarchal culture, seems to have focused rather more on the cult of Poseidon.

In line with the pillar-worship that we earlier noted amongst the same peoples, reportedly a central feature of the Atlantean cult was 'a pillar of orichalcum' (copper ore) which was situated in the middle of the island, at the temple dedicated to Cleito and Poseidon. The Atlantean dynasty's ancestors had apparently inscribed on the pillar the laws, such as non-aggression towards each other which even the kings were obliged to obey. And 'every fifth and every sixth year alternately'[18] this same pillar apparently had a key role to play in a special ceremony that the kings performed at the temple. As the priests of Sais told Solon:

> There were bulls who had the range of the temple ... and the ten kings, being left alone in the temple, after they had offered up prayers ... hunted the bulls, without weapons, but with staves and nooses. And the bull which they caught they led up to the pillar and cut its throat over the top of it so that the blood fell upon the sacred inscription

The bull's limbs were apparently then roasted as a sacrificial offering, while some of its blood was mixed with wine which the princes then drank as a libation, swearing to uphold their ancestral laws.

As scholars such as Robert Graves, J.V. Luce and others have rightly recognised, this description of the kings performing such a 'bull-sport' strongly evokes the rites depicted in the bull-leaping fresco at Eteo-Cretan Knossos. Just as somewhere within the sacred palace precinct at Knossos there must have been a special area where the Cretan bulls were given free range for the bull-leaping rites to take place, so apparently the temple on Atlantis – wherever Atlantis was – must have had much the same. Furthermore, exactly as in the case of the Eteo-Cretan bull-leapers, the Atlantean kings would appear to have had the limitation imposed on them that they should not use any bladed weapons in order to bring the bull to where it was to be sacrificed, only staves and nooses.

Scenes on two mid 2nd millennium BC gold cups found in a royal tomb at Vapheio near Sparta on the Greek mainland provide the most graphic illustration of this requirement [fig 33]. As pointed out by Robert Graves, Sparta was a

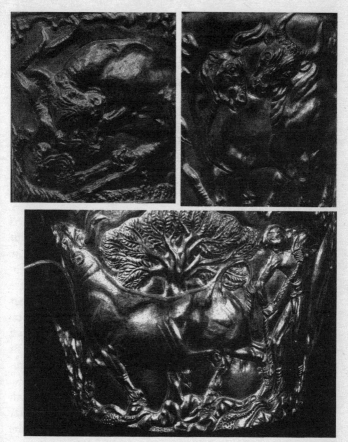

Fig 33 Capturing a bull Atlantean-style, using only 'staves and nooses'.
Scenes from two gold cups found at Vapheio, Sparta, showing (top left) the
hazards of the wrong method, and (top right) the use of an amorous cow,
thereby (lower picture) enabling the thus-distracted bull to be tethered
with ease

city-state where the twin kingship system – and equality of women in martial activities – survived even after Indo-European patriarchy had been imposed elsewhere. And whatever the relevance of this, the first of the two cups depicts two men (possibly twin kings) who had apparently rather disastrously tried to snare a wild bull in open country using only nets and ropes. We see them flying through the air like rag dolls, the bull having angrily tossed them for their temerity. The second cup, by contrast, shows the use of a different, and much more successful, approach to the same challenge. On this an amorous-looking cow has been deployed to attract and pacify the bull, which has enabled one man to tether it with ease.

Even without a word of explanatory inscription, it is evident from the scenes on these cups that sex, when intelligently used, will win out over brute strength. So for the society that produced the Vapheio cups, for the Eteo-Cretans, also for the still mysterious Atlantean culture, there would seem to have been a common understanding that when a bull was brought to sacrifice this should be done without the shedding of its blood. This inevitably raising the issue of whether this bull rite, with all its inherent dangers, might trace back to the earliest, arguably pre-Flood, times that cattle domestication was achieved.

In fact, there has come to light a specific west Turkey link to the Atlantean rite of sacrificing the bull on a pillar. Peter James discovered a coin that was minted at Troy during the Roman era, and which features a sacrificed bull hanging from a pillar, while to its left the coin-engraver depicted the goddess Athene as the deity to whom this huge creature had apparently been sacrificed. Troy's temple to Athene as this existed in classical times is known specifically to have been staffed by priestesses of the matrilineal Locrian people who had originated in Turkey. These were Great Mother Goddess worshippers who later moved on to southern Italy. So such clues strongly suggest that instead of the Atlantis story being a mere figment of Solon or Plato's imagination, it has to have had some basis, albeit dimly remembered, in a real Great Mother Goddess society that suffered a catastrophic inundation, though when and where remain far from clear.

For Peter James the resemblance between the bull cults of Troy and Atlantis seemed so 'undeniable'[19] that he felt the Atlantis story had to have its roots in western Turkey. In his view, as published just before the release of William Ryan and Walter Pitman's Black Sea Flood hypothesis, Atlantis was most likely the lost Phrygian city of Tantalus, which he located as a little to the east of Izmir on Turkey's west coast, in the environs of Mount Sipylus. This would appear to have been the same lost city mentioned by the early 2nd century AD Greek travel guide writer Pausanias, who in the course of a discussion on earthquakes remarked:

> A like fate [i.e. earthquake] befell a city on Mount Sipylus: it disappeared into a chasm, and from the fissure in the mountain water gushed forth, and the chasm became named Lake Saloe. The ruins of the city could still be seen in the lake until the water of the torrent covered them up.[20]

Certainly up to comparatively recent times there was a lake at the foot of Mount Sipylus, until this became reclaimed as agricultural land. So an ancient city could conceivably have been located in this region until its destruction and inundation by some seismic spasm for which the western Turkish region is notorious – though whether it was the fabled Atlantis is a very different matter.

However, before Peter James' 'Atlantis in Turkey' theory, several scholars were particularly struck by the resemblance between the bull rites described of the Atlantean kings and those that pertained in Eteo-Cretan Crete. As early as 1909, when Arthur Evans was creating headlines with his discoveries at Knossos, the scholar K.T. Frost of Queen's University, Belfast wrote an article to *The Times* in which he pointed out:

> The great harbour [of Atlantis] with its shipping and its merchants coming from all parts, the elaborate bathrooms, the stadium and the solemn sacrifice of a bull are all thoroughly, though not exclusively, Minoan; but when we read how the bull is hunted 'in the temple of [Cleito and] Poseidon without weapons but with staves and nooses' we have an unmistakable description of the bull-ring at Knossos, the very thing which struck foreigners most and gave rise to the legend of the Minotaur.[21]

Likewise Robert Graves wrote in the 1950s:

> Several details in Plato's account, such as the pillar-sacrifice of bulls and the hot-arid-cold-water systems in Atlas's palace, make it certain that the Cretans are being described, and no other nation.[22]

Despite Frost's and Graves' immense erudition a major difficulty to any identification of Atlantis with Eteo-Cretan Crete lay in the fact that there was no evidence for Crete ever having been swamped by flood in the manner described of Atlantis. However in the late 1960s the Greek archaeologist Spyridon Marinatos began excavations on the Aegean island of Thera, only to discover unmistakable evidence of a volcanic eruption *c.*1500 BC. This massively overwhelmed settlements that the Eteo-Cretans has established on the island. According to Dr James Mellaart there is even an as yet unpublished contemporary BC text from the territory of Arzawa in west Turkey describing displaced Therans being resettled on the island of Rhodes.[23] And from the scale of the catastrophe it can hardly not have had a major impact on Crete 97 kilometres (60 miles) to Thera's south. Since one of the most destructive accompaniments of such sea-based volcanic eruptions are great *tsunami*, or tidal waves which swamp surrounding coasts, here lay a logical explanation for how the Eteo-Cretans, if they were one and the same as the Atlanteans, might have suffered Atlantis' watery fate. Marinatos himself suggested this, and was swiftly supported by the Greek seismologist A. Galanapoulos, the classicist J.V. Luce and archaeologist Nikolas Platon all arguing much the same.

The third possibility for Atlantis, and one which half a century ago Robert Graves quite strongly fancied, has to have been the Amazonian city of Chersonessus, said to have been island-based in much the manner described of Atlantis. Although Chersonessus remains mythical, we may recall that Diodorus Siculus, the author who knew the Black Sea formerly to have been a lake, described this as having stood in the middle of Lake Tritonis in north Africa until its watery destruction sometime no later than the 3rd millennium BC. Earlier we inferred that at least some former inhabitants of the Black Sea region might have migrated to this 'lost' part of north Africa in the wake of the Black Sea Flood. Knossos excavator Sir Arthur Evans, without his being aware of any scientific evidence for the loss of part of the old Tunisian coastline, always believed that the more advanced Eteo-Cretans had hailed from Libya, a term which both for him and for the ancient Egyptians, would certainly have included Tunisia. When viewed from an Egyptian perspective, Tunisia is readily describable as 'before the pillars of Heracles' (before the straits of Gibraltar) just as related of Atlantis by the Egyptian priests who were Solon's informants. And even though as a people the Egyptians were not great navigators it is perfectly credible that the priests of Sais could and would have learned of a major seismic disaster along the very same north African coast on which they were located sometime back in their distant past.

Furthermore, Herodotus specifically described a people

called Atlantes and Atarantes, possible remnants of the Lake Tritonis disaster, as still living in the furthest western part of north Africa as late as the 1st millennium BC.[24] Diodorus Siculus, who as a resident of Sicily, arguably had reliable near-local knowledge, likewise described this same people as 'most civilised'. They were clearly not identical to Amazons, since according to Diodorus the latter initially fought with them. But since Diodorus described the Amazons as forming a close and amicable alliance with the Atlanteans at some point earlier than the Lake Tritonis disaster, Chersonessus could well have been both an Atlantean and Amazon city at the time of its watery demise. According to Herodotus, Poseidon was the co-deity with a war-like *persona* of the Mother Goddess in this Tunisian part of north Africa, just as Solon's priestly informants described of Atlantis's leading deities. Likewise the Sais priests' description of the horse-racing and chariot-racing that the 'Atlanteans' indulged in finds ready support in what Henri Lhote called the 'Flying Gallop' phase that formed a notable period of Tassili Fresco Saharan rock art. In Herodotus' time the north African peoples whom he called Garamantes – a name which Robert Graves suggested, like that of the sea-going Carians of Turkey, to have derived from the Great Mother Goddess Car – were reportedly still using four-horse chariots to hunt down swift-footed local aboriginals.

Arguably, therefore, the Atlantis story could well have originated in a 'lost' major metropolis of the Goddess empire founded by descendants of the Flood peoples, and which suffered a catastrophic inundation at some point post-Flood and before c.3000 BC when the Mediterranean swallowed a large part of Tunisia's then coastline. If there is any truth to this scenario, then some of those who survived the catastrophe might well have escaped to Crete, which was affiliated to the Goddess empire, to assimilate with, and enhance the culture of, the Eteo-Cretans.

Whatever the true answer, however, it is important, as advised from the outset, not to lay too much store on any one interpretation of Plato's Atlantis story. It is far too third-hand, and far too removed in time from that of the principal informant, Plato, for it to carry serious weight. Crucially, it lacks the support of any Egyptian text that might corroborate what the priests of Sais told Solon. So although it is conceivable that it embodies an otherwise lost memory of how and where some survivors of the Black Sea Flood may temporarily have relocated themselves in north Africa, or wherever, in the wake of the Flood event, this must be accounted all.

In the case of the Noah family of Flood stories, by contrast, we can be far more confident. It is a matter of firm fact that many of these stories had been committed to writing several hundreds of years before Plato was born, in texts that have survived. And given our knowledge of the Black Sea Flood as a real event, these texts had arguably been handed down from yet earlier oral traditions. The Sumerians and Babylonians had certainly long been preserving them in cuneiform. The Jews were writing them in the scrolls of their Torah. And the Greeks, the moment that they had formulated their alphabet, made clear that they knew the story too.

The question arises, therefore – as we now reach the 1st millennium BC, some five thousand years after the original Black Sea Flood – just how much of a memory of this now scientifically certain Flood event was still lingering on?

CHAPTER 18

THE LINGERING MEMORY

In order for any memory of the Black Sea Flood to have survived even in the rather vague form of the Noah family of Flood stories, there has to have been transmission from one generation to another. In the case of an event that happened as far back as *c.*5600 BC that transmission could certainly not have been via writing, even if the earlier-mentioned Tartaria tablets can be considered to be in a proper script, since it was still far too early for any lengthy narrative to be formulated as writing.

Yet we need have absolutely no doubt that story telling was well developed at the time of the Flood. As evident from ancient hunter-gatherer peoples who have survived to the present day, such as the Khoisan of southern Africa and the Aborigines of Australia, one of the most deep-rooted of all human customs is for stories from ancestral history to be told at tribal gatherings, accompanied by music. And there is no reason to believe that such a practice would have died with the shift to farming, indeed very much the reverse. As evident from the art of ancient Sumer, also from that of Eteo-Cretan Crete, of Canaan, and of ancient Greece the lyre was a well-established instrument amongst these cultures. So the telling of folk-tales to such an instrument's rhythms would have been a good and natural aide-memoire. In the case of the tales of Homer, scholars are agreed that several generations certainly heard these told in this way before their being committed to writing. And as evident from studies that have been made of traditional bards who remained active into the 20th century, oral transmission does not have to mean inaccurate transmission.

But with the development *c.*3000 BC of narrative writing as a means of preserving words long after they have been spoken, it was natural for those already so–minded to preserve their oral heritage to do so in more permanent form using this revolutionary new medium. And in the case of the Flood stories we saw in an earlier chapter how several different cultures certainly committed these to writing, the more difficult issue being exactly which memories were received directly, from unbroken cultural continuity, and which ones were more indirect.

As may be recalled, the principal peoples preserving Flood memories were several different west Asian groups, Sumerians, Babylonians and Hebrews, with their Utanapishti, Atrahasis and Noah Flood stories, while Europewise there was also the Greeks with their Deucalion and his wife Pyrrha 'the red one'. However, from the point of view of posterity the single individual of the 1st millennium BC with the most pivotal role in this was arguably the Assyrian ruler Assurbanipal of Nineveh (668–627 BC). In Assurbanipal's time the Flood story had already assumed a heightened topicality since only decades before his grandfather Sennacherib had forced his way into Babylon, massacred its inhabitants, razed its temple to the ground, and wreaked his own artificial Flood upon the city by diverting its canal water to flood all the streets, squares and houses.

In the event Sennacherib's immediate successor Esarhaddon rebuilt Babylon, no doubt retrieving what he could of its archives.¹ And certainly when Assurbanipal in his turn succeeded in 668 BC and decided to found a major library at Nineveh, it was to Babylon that he despatched one of his officials, Shadanu, in search of records of an archival nature. As Assurbanipal instructed Shadanu:

> See out and bring to me the precious tablets for which there are no transcripts extant in Assyria. I have just now written to the temple overseer and the mayor of Borsippa that you, Shadanu, are to keep the tablets in your storehouse, and that nobody shall refuse to hand over tablets to you. If you hear of any tablet or ritualistic text that is suitable for the palace, seek it out, secure it, and send it here.²

Aided by an army of scribes whose task it was to make copies and transcriptions from older originals, Shadanu assembled for Assurbanipal a most impressive library. This included what for the Assyrians were the world's most respected writings on history, genealogy, law, medicine, mathematics, astronomy, popular science, poetry and much more, though for them the library's life was very short. In 612 BC, only a few years after Assurbanipal's death, a Mede king appeared before Nineveh's walls, laid siege to the city, captured it, then razed it to the ground, leaving it just a heap of ruin, the library included. However, thanks to the Assyrians' use of tablets of baked clay the 'books' survived beneath the rubble for more than two and a half millennia, to be uncovered in the late 1860s by Hormuzd Rassam, an assistant of the pioneer British archaeologist Sir Henry Layard.

Amongst the more than 20,000 tablets retrieved by Rassam and others, for us the text of greatest importance and interest is undoubtedly the 'Epic of Gilgamesh', with its story of Uta-napishti and how he had survived the Flood. For as we learned in an earlier chapter this was the document that British Museum assistant George Smith found himself reading in 1872, thereby coming to the fundamental realisation that the Noah Flood story had survived in other forms beside the Bible's. Yet as also noted earlier, subsequent similar finds have made clear that the 7th century BC Assurbanipal tablets were comparatively young and by no means as unique as they had at first appeared to Rassam and Smith. With or without the Uta-napishti component the Gilgamesh story was definitely very widely known as far back as the 2nd millennium BC, for in the archives of the Hittites as found at Boghazköy a version was found written in Akkadian, the Semitic equivalent of Latin. Also in the same archives were Hittite and Hurrian language versions. Excavations at Sultantepe in northern Syria turned up yet another version on the story. And the earlier mentioned 2nd millennium BC cuneiform tablet fragment found at Megiddo in Israel shows that the Canaanites, as the Hebrews' predecessors in Israel, also knew of it.

Furthermore depictions of the story on Sumerian seals of the 3rd millennium BC show that it had to have originated yet further back into the past, just as we would expect if it were genuinely based on real events that had happened back in 5600 BC. In terms of actual surviving evidence the Sumerians have to have been among the earliest peoples to have preserved a memory of the Flood, befitting some of the world's earliest narrative writing deriving from that culture. Yet given that the Sumerians' own origins remain so mysterious even they still cannot provide us with a clear and direct lineage for the story's transmission all the way back to those who actually experienced the Flood c.5600 BC.

What, therefore, of the Hebrew compilers of the Bible who transmitted to us the Noah version of the Flood story? How did these come by the story? Was this directly or indirectly? As noted in an earlier chapter, the book of Genesis tale of Noah was but one of numerous elements of Hebrew ancestral history which existed in two or more independent earlier written strands which the Bible's compilers cleverly wove together at some point during the 1st millennium BC. Although the oldest surviving manuscript material from Genesis, in the form of fragments found amongst the Dead Sea Scrolls, dates around the 3rd century BC, the likeliest date for the actual binding together of the formerly independent written strands is thought to have been some four centuries earlier. According to one theorist[3] the compilation work was carried out by the priest Jeremiah who authored the biblical book of that name, and who lived in the late 7th, early 6th centuries BC.

The greater difficulty comes when trying to trace the strands substantially earlier in time. One of the few clues is that in the biblical 'P' strand, instead of God being referred to as *Yahweh*, as in the 'J' version, the word that was used is a plural form, *elohim*, literally 'gods'. The strong inference here is that the story originated in a culture dating from before Jewish monotheism, and in which there was worship of more than one god, and thereby arguably goddesses. In which regard goddesses certainly feature in both the Sumerian and Babylonian Flood stories, under the names Inanna and Ishtar respectively, both of these personae of the Great Mother Goddess.

Furthermore the particularly interesting feature of the Babylonian Flood story is that the goddess Belet-ili or Ishtar, in the course of her blaming the watery catastrophe upon her fellow-god Enlil, was represented as swearing by her jewelled necklace, the rainbow, that the gods should never forget this event:

> O gods, let these great beads in this necklace of mine make me remember these days and never forget them.[4]

Whereupon when we turn to the 'P' version of the Genesis story, that is, the one referring to the deity as *elohim*, we find that the rainbow element has survived in this:

God [*elohim*] said ... 'I now set my [rain]bow in the clouds
and it will be the sign of the covenant between me and
the earth. When ... the bow appears in the clouds, I shall
recall the covenant ... and never again will the waters
become a flood to destroy all living things. [Genesis 9:
12–15]

So although in both the ancient Babylonian and the biblical
versions the rainbow served the identical function as token
of a divine promise never to forget the flood, in the latter
version, any vestige of a goddess's involvement in the story
has been deliberately written out.

This is extremely interesting, since much of biblical
history from the Exodus to king David was characterised by
patriarchal Semites taking over, though far from completely
eliminating, the older-established Great Mother Goddess-
based religion and culture of the similarly Semitic
Canaanites-Phoenicians. Numerous passages of the Bible
hint at key features of this religion. In the course of the
Hebrews' Moses-led wanderings after their flight from
Egypt, some of their number reportedly created a 'golden
calf' idol around which they danced. And from time to time
Israeli archaeologists turn up Canaanitic examples of these,
in actuality 'young bulls' representative of the Canaanitic
god Baal. Around the period of the biblical king David, the
priest Samuel complained that many of the Israelites were
worshipping 'foreign god and Astartes'. So it is no surprise
that 'Astarte' or 'asherah' statuettes are again among the
commonest of Canaanitic cult objects turned up in Israel and
its environs. Furthermore, when in 1968 the American
archaeologist Paul Lapp was excavating at Taanach in northern Israel, he discovered an 11th century BC cult stand
depicting the Canaanitic pantheon, on which, besides a
'young bull', a sculpted Astarte can be seen frontally naked
between two lions, strikingly evoking the Çatal Hüyük
Great Mother Goddess.

During the earliest centuries of the 1st millennium BC, when the coastal Canaanites became re-labelled Phoenicians and the more inland Canaanites became absorbed into the 'Israelite' kingdoms of Israel and Judah, the post-Davidic rulers of these states repeatedly apostasised to the old Canaanitic religious practices, as evident from the Biblical books monotonously describing them doing things 'displeasing' to the patriarchal deity Yahweh. The book of Kings specified some of these practices as building 'pillars and sacred *asherah* [figurines evocative of the Great Mother Goddess] on every high hill and under every leafy tree' [1 Kings 14: 23]. According to 1 Kings chapter 18 Elijah challenged hundreds of priests of the Canaanitic Baal and Astarte cults to a competitive bull sacrifice. We hear also of the conducting of certain human sacrifices, the performing of cultic sex, referred to as prostitution, and wild dancing to tambourines. All of these were practices of the old Canaanitic religion.

So given the earlier-mentioned finding of fragments of the Gilgamesh story in Israel, as at Megiddo, there has to be a strong likelihood that the 'P' biblical Flood story was edited from a story earlier preserved by Canaanitic priests, who, as Semites and as Great Mother Goddess worshippers may well have had their own 'hot-line' back to the original events, just as we have earlier suggested.

Now as already established the classical Greeks certainly had their own seemingly independent Deucalion version of the Flood story. However their written versions have to have been much younger than those of their eastern counterparts, due to the Greek system of writing, known to have derived from that developed by the Canaanites or Phoenicians, not having even been developed until around the 8th century BC. Nor are there any prime Greek texts, such as the *Iliad*, that carry the story, in the manner of an Epic of Gilgamesh. Instead there are only very third-hand renditions in the works of relatively late mythographers such as Apollodorus and Ovid, the latter of whom was in any case Roman.

Yet, this being the case, how could the classical Greeks and Romans have acquired a Flood story so close in its details to the eastern versions? For this our attention must turn to a text that, although it has come down to us in Greek – specifically in Ionic Greek written in a deliberately 'Olde English'-type archaic style – actually sets the 'Greek' Flood Deucalion in a city just across Turkey's south-eastern border, in northern Syria.[5] The text in question derives from an author called Lucian who was born in Samosata (today Samsat in south-east Turkey), and lived under the Roman Empire of the 2nd century AD (see Documents Appendix, Part 1, Document 5). And what is fascinating about this version is that it may be the clearest description that we have from antiquity of a continuous commemoration of the Flood event all the way from the time of the original catastrophe of 5600 BC.

The city that Lucian associated with Deucalion and with commemoration of the Deluge is today called Membij. Little more than a dusty Syrian–Turkish border village, it has few lingering signs of its former glory. And not many people are likely even to have heard of it, not least since, due to its frontier status, the local military discourage anyone from going there. Back in the classical period, however, it was known as Bambyce, or in Greek Hierapolis, the 'holy city', and besides its being an important staging post on the great trading route between coastal Antioch and the Far East, for the eastern cult of the Great Mother Goddess it was the equivalent of an Islamic Mecca. Devotees were drawn to it from as far afield as Babylonia, Assyria, Cilicia, Phoenicia and Arabia. Although Lucian rendered the goddess's name as Hera, her real name in the local Semitic Syriac language was Tar'atha, and she was universally recognised as one and the same as the Great Mother Goddess or 'Great Mother of the Gods'. Other localised names for her were Atagartis or Athar'atha, and she was also readily identifiable with Cybele, Isis and others.

Because Lucian had been born less than 65 kilometres (40 miles) from Hierapolis/Bambyce, his detailed description of Tar'atha's temple and the cults practised there is one that can be regarded as reasonably trustworthy. According to him a wall surrounded the edifice, the necessity of which becomes obvious when we learn that within its perimeter tame lions, bulls, eagles, horses and bears all roamed freely, reminding us of the Eteo-Cretan and Atlantean bulls being allowed to do much the same. So the Great Mother Goddess's sobriquet as 'Mistress of the Animals' was certainly no mere empty title.

Also according to Lucian, two 60-metre (200-foot) high wooden pillars stood at the temple's north entrance, one of which bore a dedicatory inscription to the Great Mother Goddess. The goddess's statue, kept in an inner shrine but open to the air, was made of gold, and was borne on lions. On its head were rays and a tower, this latter a traditional head-dress for local women up to modern times. Since she had the attributes of several goddesses including Athene, Aphrodite and Selene, she was evidently the Great Mother Goddess in her most ancient triple form.[6]

Though the original cult statue will have been melted down long ago, the Archaeological Museum at Damascus fortuitously preserves a 3rd century AD funerary epitaph of one of the Hierapolis Goddess cult's male adherents, as found at the nearby site of Dura-Europos [fig 34]. This shows the devotee bestowing a wreath upon the Goddess's statue, which can be seen to represent her enthroned between two lions. Here, still being revered after nearly six thousand years, we have the very same deity whose statuette, similarly enthroned between two lions, but dating from before the Flood, was found by James Mellaart at Çatal Hüyük. Further noteworthy is that the Dura-Europos relief

Fig 34 Worship of the Great Mother Goddess as late as the 3rd century AD. Here a relief found at Dura-Europos, northern Syria, not far from Membij/ Hierapolis, shows a devotee crowning the goddess's statue, while above a bull can be seen being led for sacrifice. Represented seated between two lions, the goddess's statue is clearly a descendant of the pre-Flood Great Mother Goddess statuette found at Çatal Hüyük

shows a bull being brought to the Goddess for sacrifice, while on its crowning pediment is depicted an eagle, or possibly a vulture?

Lucian also tells us that inside the temple's precincts sacred, or cultic sex was practised, exactly as in the Canaanitic religion, though this element became censored for those aspects of the Syrian Goddess cult that became popular in Rome during the first centuries of the Christian era. We also learn that the temple high priest or *archigallus*, who was elected to his office for a year, wore purple robes and a tiara in the manner of a king. A Roman era funerary relief depicts one such individual, and among his accoutrements can be seen exactly the same pipe instrument with one curved reed and one straight one that we earlier saw being played by the male 'priestess' on the Eteo-Cretan bullsacrifice sarcophagus. Whether the Hierapolis officiant was expected to dress up in 'drag' for sacrificial ceremonies to his Goddess is unclear. But what he was certainly expected to do, as the ultimate sacrifice and token of his subservience to her, was to castrate himself publicly according to a specially prescribed rite.

To help the *archigallus*, and any others so minded to prepare for this, the Hierapolis temple's lower order of attendants apparently included musicians with pipes and flutes. There were also a number of women possessed by frenzy, all of whom reportedly indulged in wild dancing, to the accompaniment of tambourines and other musical instruments. This inevitably reminds us of the Canaanitic-type dancing biblically described as having been performed before the 'golden calf' (Exodus 32: 19). When daily sacrifice was made to the Hierapolis or Syrian Goddess, this was with 'violent musical accompaniment'. Since according to Lucian the dedication on one of the temple pillars was from the Syrian equivalent of the Greek wine god Dionysus, this and the frenzied nature of the dancing and music suggests a strong Dionysiac element to the Hierapolis temple cult. In turn this reminds us of the viticulture biblically described as being introduced shortly after the Flood, also the 'new wine sailor' meaning of the Greek Noah, Deucalion's name.

While Tar'atha or Atagartis was Hierapolis's principal deity, the temple's central shrine also apparently housed a statue of the storm god Hadad, borne on bulls. Of neighbouring Harran one historical source describes a procession of a sacrificial bull festooned with garlands and bells, escorted by singers and musicians, being held as late as the 9th century AD. Lucian described how at Hierapolis it was not uncommon for children to be sacrificed by their parents sometimes by throwing them to their death. The Canaanite/Phoenicians, Canaanites and Eteo-Cretans are all known to have done much the same in extreme circumstances continuing in the colonies at Carthage and elsewhere that the Phoenicians later founded in north Africa.[7] And intriguingly, according to Lucian, the Titan Atlas, now familiar to us from the Atlantis legend (or some Semitic equivalent to him), was among the more minor deities venerated at Hierapolis.

All of this is valuable enough in its own right as an authoritative account of how worship of the Great Mother Goddess, arguably directly descended from that practised at Çatal Hüyük before the Flood, persisted at least at certain far flung reaches of Turkey (and beyond) even as late as classical times. Hierapolis's citizens would seem to have been Moschians, later known as Phrygians, whom we first met in northern Turkey, just south of the Black Sea, only for these to become displaced and pushed south by the invading Indo-Europeans.

However in this instance Lucian's even more riveting information concerned the reputed founder of this particular Hierapolis temple. This he reported, as a fact apparently attested by 'the generality of the people', was none other than the Greek Noah, Deucalion – 'that Deucalion in whose

time the great Flood occurred'. Curiously, and quite uniquely, Lucian described Deucalion as 'ton Skuthea' — the
Scythian — which would seem to have been either Lucian or
some later copyist's mis-reading of 'Sisuthea', an attempt to
render the Babylonian 'Xisuthros', 'exceedingly wise',
thereby recalling the name of Noah's counterpart in the
Babylonian version of the Flood story.

Whatever, of the 'great Flood' Lucian first gave the
version of this story as he had heard it from the Greeks:

> The story goes as follows: This generation, the people of
> nowadays, was not the first, but that first generation all
> perished, and this is of the second generation which came
> from Deucalion and multiplied. Concerning the first
> humans, they say they were quite violent and committed
> wicked deeds, for they did not keep oaths, nor welcomed
> strangers, nor spared suppliants; and because of these
> offences, the great tribulation came upon them. Suddenly
> the earth spewed forth a flood of water and heavy rains
> fell and the rivers rushed in torrents, and the sea rose
> amazingly high, until all things were changed into water
> and all humans perished. Deucalion alone among men was
> left for the second generation because of his prudence and
> good works. And his deliverance came in this way. Into a
> great ark that he possessed he put his children and his
> wives, and thence he himself entered. And as he boarded
> there came to him swine and horses and lionkind and ser-
> pents and all beasts that live, every kind of creature that
> grazes upon the earth, two by two. And he welcomed
> them all, and none did him any harm, for among them
> there was great charity from the gods, and in a single ark
> they all sailed while the Flood prevailed.

As Lucian went on to explain, the people of Hierapolis,
being Aramaic, or Semitic-speaking Syrians, told their own
special localised version of the Flood story. According to

this, 'in their land' which in view of the Indo-European dis-
placements we may infer not to have been their actual
location in Lucian's time:

> ... a great chasm opened up and took in all the water, and
> when this happened, Deucalion set up altars and built a
> temple over the hole sacred to Hera [the great Mother
> Goddess].

As a good reporter of facts Lucian was at pains to stress that
in the course of a personal visit to Hierapolis he had viewed
this chasm for himself. In his words:

> I myself saw the hole, a quite little one, which is beneath
> the temple. If it was once large, and now has become such
> as it is, I do not know; but the one I saw is small.[10]

Now the idea of waters that had reputedly overwhelmed the
entire world pouring into a 'great chasm' that then became
quite 'small' and in a region as inland such as Membij is
quite clearly absurd. Indeed Lucian himself appears to have
been sufficiently puzzled by this that he could not be sure
he had fully understood the story. So it would make rather
more sense if the original chasm was the breaching of the
Bosporus and the pouring of the Flood into the waters of the
Black Sea lake, an event which the Hierapolitans, as long
since migrated descendants of survivors of this catastrophe,
were continuing to commemorate in symbolic form.

In his telling of the Hierapolitan version of the Flood story
Lucian made clear that it was the Syrian or Asiatic Great
Mother Goddess who was the deity being thanked for humanity's survival of the catastrophe. Indeed the whole point of
the Asiatic Deucalion, erecting such an outstanding temple,
was to thank her for this. It also happens to be the only
instance in all surviving Noah family of Flood stories of the
Great Mother Goddess being accorded such a high profile in
relation to the event, and is all the more significant for this.

Although Hierapolis was 160 kilometres (100 miles) or so from any ocean, the Goddess was clearly venerated there in her 'water' aspects as well as her more land-based ones, for according to Lucian the temple included statues of mermaids. It also apparently had in its proximity a lake with fish that were sacred to the Goddess, and which because they were never being caught for food, were so tame that they would even come when called by name.

Another unique feature of Lucian's description not to be overlooked is that it represented the only known example of the Black Sea Flood apparently still being commemorated well over five thousand years after the original event. In Lucian's words:

> In token of this story they do thus. Twice each year water from the Sea is brought into the temple. Not only priests, but the whole of Syria and Arabia brings it; and from beyond the Euphrates men go to the Sea and all bring water, that soon they pour out in the temple. And then it goes down into that hole; and even though the hole is small, nonetheless it takes in a great deal of water. And in doing thus they say that Deucalion established this custom for the sanctuary in memory both of that disaster and that divine favour.[11]

In this same regard, according to Lucian, the tall wooden pillars which stood to the temple's north had a very special function, again specifically related to the Flood. In his words: 'A man goes up one of these pillars twice a year and stays at the top of the pillar for the period of seven days.' Apparently he who did so wore a rope around his waist, and ascended 'as one climbs a date palm in Arabia or Egypt', with the help of projections up to the top. Once there he would lower another rope and hoist up wood, clothing and other objects in which he sat 'as it were in a nest'. Here he had to stay for seven days, and if he fell asleep scorpions would wake him up. What was the point of this exercise? In Lucian's words, though he remarked, he did not personally believe it:

> ... in token and memory of that tribulation, when men went into the mountains and into the great high trees for fear of the Flood.[12]

Although there is some confusion about the excessive height of the pillars at Hierapolis as given in Lucian's description, conceivably, in the light of his account, these may have been built to replicate the height that the Black Sea water-level rose as a result of the Flood of 5600 BC. Due to later Turkish invaders using the Hierapolis temple's stones for their own building purposes neither the pillars nor any other part can be seen at present-day Membij. However just over 48 kilometres (30 miles) to the north-east, at Urfa in Turkey, very much a sister-city to Hierapolis (and very possibly the true Ur of Abraham), there survive on the town's citadel two ancient stone pillars. These stand at the northern end of now badly ruined buildings that are thought to have belonged to a pagan temple. From an inscription on one of the pillars these date back to sometime before the 2nd century AD. Furthermore one of Urfa's principal sights is a lake of 'protected' fish that were already a tourist attraction as early as the 4th century AD[13] and seem to go back to very ancient times.[14] So although Urfa's temple would seem to have been a much lesser version of that at Hierapolis/Membij, it quite possibly provides at least a faint glimpse at what has otherwise been lost.

Intriguingly, the Turkey-born Strabo, in the course of some unresolved discussion concerning the Leleges people of Turkey and whether these were one and the same as the seagoing Carians or merely fellow-inhabitants, quoted an otherwise lost remark by the 8th century BC Greek historian and poet Hesiod. In this Hesiod had described the Leleges as peoples who were once given 'to Deucalion – peoples picked out of earth'.[15] Mostly, however, classical writers associated Deucalion with Greece rather than Asia. Thus we know that 2nd century AD Athenian tourist guides pointed out what they claimed to be Deucalion's grave near the grandiose Temple of Zeus east of the Athens Acropolis, and in the same temple's precinct they pointed out a small cleft in the ground which just as at Hierapolis was claimed as that down which the waters of the Flood had drained away. Yet if we ask who is likely to have been borrowing from whom, in all logic north Syria/Turkey-located Hierapolis, with its roots stretching back into a far greater antiquity than could ever be claimed by the Greeks, has to have priority.

Furthermore the region in which Hierapolis stood is particularly interesting because of its close vicinity not only to Urfa, already remarked as the likeliest candidate for the true Ur of the biblical Abraham, but also to Harran, which was quite definitely associated with the biblical Abraham (Genesis 11: 31). In ancient times all three of these towns were highly important cult centres for ancient pagan rites. Tall tomb towers or *naphsha*, some of these several storeys high, were used for the burial of the dead, possibly recalling the excarnation practised at Çatal Hüyük. And they also continued human sacrifice. As the pioneer anthropologist Sir James Frazer wrote in his *Golden Bough*:

> The heathen of Harran offered to the sun, moon and planets human victims who were chosen on the ground of their supposed resemblance to the heavenly bodies to which they were sacrificed; for example, the priests, clothed in red and smeared with blood, offered a red-haired, red-cheeked man to 'the red planet Mars' in a temple which was painted red and draped with red hangings.[16]

Does this not yet again remind us of the red that was daubed everywhere at pre-Flood Çatal Hüyük, and later on Malta?

Should we also just brush aside claims in Armenian folklore that the ruling hierarchy of the Membij, Urfa and Harran region originated from Armenia, that is from Ararat, or Noah's ark country? Recalling the Great Mother Goddess's lion throne is it just coincidence that before the Romans swept them from power the local dynasty of kings was that of Aryu, the Canaanite-Aramaic word for lion? Also that these kings alternated in name between Abgar and Ma'nu yet again, in the manner of the Great Mother Goddess's ancient twin kingship system? So could it be that in the region of Membij, Urfa and Harran there may lie some of the most important direct links to the 'Before the Flood' people, and what became of them? Frustratingly, these questions must remain rhetorical not least because the environs of Urfa, Harran and Membij have yet to receive the archaeological investigation that they deserve.

But whatever the answer the Urfa/Harran/Membij region was certainly not the only part of Turkey and its near-environs where remnants of the old pre-Flood Great Mother Goddess culture survived. For whereas amongst the patriarchal Greeks it was unthinkable for a woman to play a part in politics, or to engage in war, in the case of the kingdom of Lydia in western Turkey, Herodotus told of a forceful 7th century BC queen called Nyssia who, outraged when her husband King Candaulus showed her off naked in her bath, conspired with one of the Lydian ministers, Gyges, to have Candaulus assassinated. She then married Gyges to legitimise him, thereby determining that even despite the Indo-European invasions, in Lydia the priority of the matrilineal line continued to be strongly recognised.

Herodotus also tells how in 529 BC Tomyris queen of the east-Caucasus-based Massegetae, a people with sexual proclivities similar to those of the neighbouring Moschians or Phrygians, led her troops against Cyrus the Great of Persia, won the battle, then had Cyrus' head cut off and thrown into a skin.[17] Likewise Satyrus, tyrant of the Bosporus kingdom was defeated by an army led by the Maeotian princess Tirgatao. And in the Sea of Azov region of the Black Sea, Armage, the Amazon-like wife of a Sarmatian king, usurped her husband and led her troops on horseback in a successful invasion of the neighbouring kingdom, imposing a peace treaty between the Scythian peoples of the Crimea and the then Greek city of Chersonessus, now Sevastopol.[18]

Likewise at Halicarnassus in Caria, also in what is today western Turkey, the local ruler in 480 BC under the overall suzerainty of the great Persian emperor was one Artemisia, whose very name evoked yet another variant of that of the Great Mother Goddess. At the battle of Salamis in which the Persians and Halicarnassans fought side by side against the patriarchal Greeks, Artemisia commanded five triremes. Her action was thereby identical to that which we inferred of the Tyrian females who apparently commanded Phoenician war-ships when the Assyrians attacked Tyre in 701 BC. And as late as the 2nd century AD when the travel writer Pausanias wrote of the 'wonder of the world' Temple of Artemis at Ephesus on Turkey's west coast, one of the towns said to have been founded by Amazons, he described it as still fre-quented by Carians, Lydians and Amazons, all peoples whom we would associate with the Great Mother Goddess alliance.

Ultimately Christianity did much to follow up on Indo-European patriarchal practices in suppressing Great Mother Goddess ways, and therefore whatever had lingered on of the pre-Flood culture. It was none other than Abgar VIII of Urfa (AD 177–212) who – apparently on his becoming con-verted to Christianity – abolished the practice of priestly self-castration by imposing the cutting off of one hand as punishment.[19]

Christianity's later great purges of witchcraft that were

still being conducted as recently as three centuries ago would seem in part at least to have been directed against adherents of what was often called with rarely appreciated justice, the 'old religion'.

Yet even to this day there linger on traces of the world that clearly suffered huge losses, though was certainly not annihilated, at the time of the great burst-through of c.5600 BC. Thus at the modern Turkish village near the site of Çatal Hüyük there can still be seen houses with red hands painted on their doorways,[20] recalling those similarly daubed on the shrines in the town of eight thousand years ago. In central and eastern Anatolia, in the Caucasus and in the mountains of eastern Iran there are still to be seen villages in which dwellings are made without external doorways and with sole entry through the roof, in the manner of the then state-of-the-art dwellings being built eight thousand years ago at Çatal Hüyük,[21] Once a year Turkish women still travel by boat to the 'Amazonian' island of Giresun, off Turkey's north coast, to dance round and place offerings in a particular rock that they associate with fertility. In eastern Serbia girls still dress up in a national costume that features above their skirts a fringe that may well hark back to the Stone Age fertility goddess's string skirt.[22]

But for the ultimate proof of the advanced nature of the pre-Flood world, and the scale of the disaster that befell it c.5600 BC, much still has to rest on just how much may still lie awaiting discovery beneath those so problem-fraught waters of the Black Sea. And for this the world's eyes have to continue to look to Dr Robert Ballard and his roving submersibles.

CHAPTER 19

THE CONTINUING QUEST

He brought back a tale of before the Flood
Epic of Gilgamesh, translated by Andrew George

If anyone thinks that Robert Ballard's researches in the Black Sea are simply about proving that a Noah's Flood once occurred, then they have a very limited appreciation of the dynamics behind the Black Sea burst-through hypothesis. Supporting claims that 'The Bible was Right' is not what the findings are all about. The possibility that there was once a man who built a boat to save himself, his family and his livestock from a major watery catastrophe has certainly gained a considerably greater credibility than it might have enjoyed a decade or more ago. But whatever happened to this individual's life-saving boat, and whether he who built it was named Noah, or Uta-napishti, or Xisuthros or Deucalion, is still unknown and likely ever to remain that way.

Instead what Ryan and Pitman have so admirably established is that a massive Flood event within the time that humankind has been building boats is no longer a matter of myth, but one of firm scientific and historical fact. Most unexpectedly the setting in which this event occurred was not any territory with obvious biblical associations. Rather, it was northern Turkey and the environs of the Black Sea, the latter then a land-locked freshwater lake. Thanks to the science of radio-carbon dating the time at which this Flood event occurred can now be calculated with very reasonable precision as c.5600 BC, that is, during the Late Stone Age. And what Robert Ballard's submarine explorations with the robotic *Argus* and *Little Hercules* have equally determined is that there undoubtedly were human settlements established on the lake's northern Turkish rim just prior to this catastrophe. So 'birds, cattle, wild animals ... and human beings' in all likelihood perished in the cataclysm, much as described in Genesis 7: 22. Chiefly remaining to be resolved are the numbers, size and spread of those human settlements that became overwhelmed, also just what scale of advancement their inhabitants had reached three millennia before the ancient Egyptians had built their first pyramid or the Mesopotamians had constructed their first ziggurat.

Despite Robert Ballard and Fredrik Hiebert's so astonishing initial successes, it is in fact this latter part of their Black Sea quest that is almost bound to be far the most difficult and most protracted – though potentially also the most rewarding. As a setting for history's most famous Flood, the Black Sea may seem neither as deep nor as hostile as the Atlantic into which Ballard so successfully sent an earlier generation of submersibles in search of the *Titanic* and *Bismarck*. However, quite aside from the earlier-mentioned anoxic properties of the Black Sea's lower layers, even its upper layers pose some serious hazards.

Thus American newspaper columnists have recently labelled the Black Sea 'the dirtiest in the world'.[1] A Canadian tourist on a visit to the possibly 'Amazon' island of Giresun recently reported:

> The Black Sea is an open sewer and the floating garbage alarmed me as I feared the propeller might get fouled ...
> My fisherman pal informed me that there was a competition going on between Russia and Turkey [for] who could dump the most foul mess.[2]

Out of 26 species of Black Sea fish which were being landed in commercial quantities in the 1960s, there remain viable populations of only six. Whereas back in the 1930s the annual catch of sturgeon in the Sea of Azov averaged some 7,300 tons, by 1961 this had dwindled to 500 tons, and at the present day almost all production derives from fish farms.[3]

And besides the heavily polluted Black Sea itself, much of its surrounding dry land on which future archaeological research and exploration work is needed poses difficulties in the guise of the even murkier world of politics. For instance, close to the Sea's south-eastern corner live the Kurds, noted earlier as likely descendants of the post-Flood Hurrians who inhabited much the same region. A mountain-hugging, herds-keeping people, the Kurds' independence aspirations and their territory's rich reserves of chrome, copper, iron, coal and oil ensure constant feuding with their political masters Turkey, Iraq and Syria. Although like the Berbers, the Kurds mostly became converted to Islam, their folklore includes a Noah story according to which the Flood happened 4,490 years before the birth of Mohammed, that is c.3920 BC. Noah's Ark reputedly came to rest on Iraq's Mount Cudi following which a great city was built ruled by Melik Kurdim of the tribe of Noah. The Kurds even claim that it was Noah who invented the language that they speak. Yet for all such Flood-related promise, the Kurdish region remains a mostly no-go area for any researches, archaeological or folkloric.

Likewise the picturesque Caucasus region of the Black Sea, where Jason's Argonauts' Colchis is thought to have been located, poses similar difficulties because it has long been home to that ongoing thorn in Russian flesh, the Chechens. As the Chechens describe themselves:

This land has always been populated by ancient Shemite people, descendants of Shem [the son of Noah who was ancestor of the Semitic peoples], who have been invaded, through the centuries, by people of different races.[4]

The Russians are merely one of the region's more recent invaders. Following World War II during which the Chechens sided with the Germans, the Chechens suffered the full force of Russian vengeance when the Germans lost. Josef Stalin packed tens of thousands of their number off to his Siberian death-camps, and although in the 1950s the survivors were allowed to return to their homelands, their independence aspirations following the Soviet Union's 1991 collapse provoked renewed opposition. Armed conflict continues fiercely even while this book is being finalised, with no end to it in sight. With at least 45,000 Chechens killed and two million displaced, it is a Black Sea coast environment that is again hardly conducive to archaeological or folkloric exploration.

Yet as we saw earlier in this book, it was quite definitely from the Black Sea's environs rather than from Egypt or Mesopotamia that there emanated many of civilisation's most fundamental advances. Agriculture, animal husbandry, the weaving of textiles, house-building, town-planning, carpentry, pottery, metallurgy and the decorative arts, are merely among the first to spring to mind. And most significantly, such advances appear to have been developed in the region before the c.5600 BC date ascribed to the Black Sea Flood.

Thus as we learned from James Mellaart's pioneering archaeological findings, Çatal Hüyük's east mound in central Turkey was quite definitely a pre-Black Sea Flood metropolis which had achieved spectacular developments in these fields before its abandonment in around 6000 BC. And in all logic Çatal Hüyük could not have been the sole major repository of such advancements. There have to have been other, similarly advanced major early centres in and around the same locality, even though archaeology has not yet pinpointed where they were. The likelihood of some at least of these awaiting Robert Ballard's underwater probings therefore has to be very strong.

Yet even establishing beyond reasonable doubt that there definitely was a Flood which wiped out a number of advanced settlements around the Black Sea – and we have yet to reach that stage – would raise more questions than it answers. For in the wake of the Black Sea Flood much of the pre-Flood development seems to disappear only to re-emerge again three millennia later. So did all the advancement simply die out, only to be re-invented in strikingly similar guise after such a long interval? And if that seems unlikely, we then face the question of where it went in the interim.

In this book we have suggested that the key may lie in some of the Flood survivors spending a period in north Africa, only for this region, in its turn, to suffer desiccation and inundation that periodically sent them scattering further afield to Malta, Spain, France and Britain. Long before Ryan and Pitman's findings, and without having any concept of a Black Sea Flood as such, Robert Graves, working almost entirely from his poetic insights into myths, reached much the same conclusions. Yet such a hypothesis is hardly safe. Much of it remains conjectural and lacking key evidence.

In both the short and long term whatever insights will emerge from Robert Ballard's recent finds off Sinop, and his ongoing explorations, have to be awaited with huge interest. For instance we have yet to have confirmation of the preservative-versus-destructive quirks of the Black Sea environment in which the explorations are being conducted. While we now know that some of the wood, a material that in land-based archaeology normally perishes, has been almost miraculously preserved by the anaerobic conditions, this may not have been the case with any metal objects. Though these can often survive for millennia beneath soil, the Black Sea may well have caused them to dissolve completely.

These concerns aside, the 'wildest dreams', though far from impossible scenario, is that several 6th millennium BC 'Pompeiis' may lie at the bottom of the Black Sea awaiting the arrival of Ballard's robotic vehicles. Here it is important not to be too mesmerised by the Black Sea's southern or Turkish coast as the only one off which any such remains may be found. Çatal Hüyük excavator James Mellaart, now in his late seventies, has recently suggested that the worst of the Flood's impact upon human populations may have been felt upon the old freshwater Black Sea's western and north-ern coasts, that is, 'in present-day Bulgaria, Romania and the Ukraine, with their low-lying coastline.'[5] Certainly during the post-Flood millennia, and indeed well into the Christian era a variety of peoples seem repeatedly to have migrated from north of the Black Sea into the Near East and Europe without archaeologists having any clear concept of exactly where they might have been settled earlier. And it is an intriguing fact that the names of the northern rivers that flow into the Black Sea, the Danube and Don, also possibly the Dneiper and Dneister, suggest their origination in one of the Great Mother Goddess names Danae, from whom con-ceivably may also have sprung the early Irish megalith-builders the Tuatha de Danaan, or 'people of the goddess Danae'.

Yet if the Black Sea's north and west coasts have offshore exploration potential, it is important also not to neglect its east coast. For instance, in the area of the Black Sea beyond the mouth of the present-day river Rhion in Georgia, we should expect a substantial pre-Flood settlement in the vicinity of where the Rhion's long-submerged old river mouth would have met the old Black Sea freshwater lake before everything became changed by the Flood. This is because according to the Argonaut saga the post-Flood Colchean city of Aea stood on an equivalent spot, the Rhion in the Argonauts' time being known as the Phasis. This is but one of many areas of potential promise for Robert Ballard's underwater probings.

But whatever Stone Age Pompeiis may be awaiting rediscovery beneath the Black Sea, the fact that the Sea's old pre-5600 BC coastline would have been well over 1,600 kilometres (1,000 miles) in circumference has to mean the Ballard exploration task going on for decades at the very least, even if the finds from September 2000, when they are released, prove to be so spectacular that they generate unlimited funding for further researches. The pace of any future progress is further complicated by the fact that the Black Sea is far from alone among Robert Ballard's ongoing research interests, others, arguably equally demanding, including his searches for the lost Arctic exploration vessel *Endurance*, also for Japanese submarines that were sunk just before the World War II Japanese attack on Pearl Harbour.

Yet remembering that what prompted the Black Sea burst-through was a general world sea-level rise that affected the entire Mediterranean area, it is also important to think beyond just the confines of the present Black Sea. Because of the former Black Sea freshwater lake's land-locked nature there surely has to have been some major Stone Age port on the Mediterranean side of the Bosporus land-bridge which would have catered for the widespread international trading activities that we know to have existed prior to the 6th millennium BC. Perhaps this was sited on the Sea of Marmara between the Bosporus and Dardanelles straits, somewhere in the environs of the pleasant and favourably sited present-day port of Erdek. Perhaps it was in the vicinity of where the later various Troys would be built. All along Turkey's western coast, heavy silting at river mouths has served to confuse and obscure the locations of ancient ports, quite aside from the effects of sea-level rise and earthquake activity. So it would be rash indeed for anyone to claim that there is nothing further to be found in these areas, particularly given that political circumstances within Turkey have long made it difficult for foreign archaeological expeditions to work there.

With regard to the Dardanelles strait region, Ryan and Pitman understandably concentrated all their attention on the former Bosporus land-bridge as the focal point of the great burst-through of the Mediterranean that they determined happened c.5600 BC. But as indicated by the Shackleton and van Andel maps of the post-Ice Age Mediterranean, there must have been a similar land bridge on the western, or Mediterranean side of the Sea of Marmara at what became the Dardanelles strait. So when did the post-Ice Age sea-level rises cause a burst-through to happen in this region? And what were the attendant effects of this on any coastal settlements? As yet no one has any idea.

There are also many ancient settlement sites inland in Turkey and its near environs which have yet to be properly investigated. As noted earlier in this book the Cambridge-based archaeologist Ian Hodder is currently conducting major new excavations at Çatal Hüyük. Besides whatever may be learned from Hodder's probings into the large proportion of the pre-Flood east mound that James Mellaart's 1960s excavations left untouched, news is also awaited of whatever he may uncover of the phases of occupation of the post-Flood west mound.

With regard to the still mythical Amazons that are said to have settled on Turkey's northern coast, the Austrian Gerhard Poellauer has tentatively identified several ancient sites east of Samsun on the Black Sea as the Amazon strongholds of Themiskyra, Lykastia and Chadesia. One of these notably features a cultic niche that might well have served for memorial Flood rites, similar to those conducted at the Hierapolis Goddess Temple. From recent archaeological findings of firm evidence for tribes of Sauromatian women warriors north of the Black Sea,[6] there is nothing

inherently unlikely about similar tribes having existed on
the Black Sea's southern shores. But at present Pollauer has
conducted only exploratory surveys, and properly
definitive archaeological work is as yet awaited.

Likewise Eastern Turkey has numerous *hüyüks* or mounds
that are recognised as marking the sites of ancient settlements, yet which for a variety of reasons, but predominantly local unrest, have not so far been excavated. Present-day
towns such as Urfa, which as suggested earlier may have
been the site of the true 'Ur' of Abraham, could well have a
substantially more ancient past than has yet been determined. Again, however, these have not been properly investigated due to modern-day housing having been built
directly over where there may or may not be ancient
remains.

It is also important not to forget the opportunities for
related research that lie just a bit further afield than Turkey.
Arguably somewhere in north Africa, either beneath the
desert sand or underwater just off the east coast of Tunisia,
there may remain the site of the Amazon city that is said to
have stood on the equally long-lost Lake Tritonis. While as
yet the one-time existence of such a city is in the realms of
myth, determination of its existence could provide a vital
missing link between the early post-Flood cultures of
Turkey and those of Malta and environs. It would also at last
make sense of the huge amount of very early human occupation of north Africa that is so obvious from Henri Lhote's
Tassili frescoes, yet which so far has given up little
archaeological evidence of itself.

And quite aside from any vanishing of dry land into the
depths of the Mediterranean, just how easily things could
and did disappear even on land as a result of the rapidly des-
iccating North African environment is evident from an incident that Herodotus described in his *Histories*. Herodotus
reported an entire 50,000 strong army of the 6th century BC

Persian emperor Cambyses as having been lost without trace in Egypt's western desert after their having set out on a seven day march from Thebes to the Oasis of Ammon.[7] Although a recent news report has suggested that remains of this army might at long last have been found, this has yet to be confirmed.

But the vast and daunting detective work that is associated with uncovering the lost world of the Black Sea Flood does not have to be confined just to land and underwater archaeology. As William Ryan and Walter Pitman rightly noted in their ground-breaking *Noah's Flood*, present-day science also offers a fascinating range of other approaches.

For instance, following huge strides in recent decades, genetics can now be applied to tracing early cultures back to their roots using DNA samples taken from ancient bones. Pioneered by the Italian geneticist Luigi Luca Cavalli-Sforza,[8] such work is now being yet further developed by specialists such as Dr Bryan Sykes of Oxford University's Institute of Molecular Medicine. As Sykes has demonstrated from the famous 'Cheddar man' Stone Age skeleton, if DNA is extracted from an ancient skull it can be compared with similar genetic material as taken via mouth-swabs from present-day populations living in the same area in which the skull was found. From comparison of the DNA patterns, a living individual can be pin-pointed as a direct descendant of the owner of the ancient skull. Using much the same methods it should theoretically be possible to take DNA from the skulls of Eteo-Cretans and determine the extent to which these may or may not have been genetically linked to the people of Çatal Hüyük,[9] also to the Canaanites-Phoenicians and others. A great deal of groundwork needs to be done obtaining representative ancient remains, since all too often archaeologists have shown least interest in human bones in the course of their excavations, earlier generations of archaeologists having blithely thrown them away. In time, however, valuable and perhaps surprising genetic information may come to light by this means.

Another approach, again anticipated by Ryan and Pitman, has to be via the genetics of language. As early as 1786 British High Court judge Sir William Jones, an enthusiast for ancient languages, delivered a lecture in which he argued that there must have been 'some common source, which perhaps no longer exists'[10] which he hoped would explain 'the strong affinity between the Sanskrit, Persian, Greek, Latin, Celtic and German languages'. More than two centuries have elapsed since Jones made his observations, during which time understanding of the origins of linguistics has advanced leaps and bounds. Yet the fundamental truth of his remarks, and the deductive opportunities to which they give rise, remain undiminished. Just as genealogists can construct a family tree showing lineage back through time, so the same can be applied to the ancestry of languages. Italian and Spanish, for instance, can be shown to be direct descendants of Latin and English, with German rather less so. By working further back in time therefore it is possible to construct at least something of otherwise 'lost' ancestors of present-day languages.

Here a great point of interest inevitably concerns the language that was spoken by the pre-Flood inhabitants of Çatal Hüyük. This language we may infer to have been also that of at least some of those peoples who settled around the freshwater Black Sea lake before the great burst-through of c.5600 BC. We have seen hints of pre-Indo-European (and arguably pre-Flood), languages that may have been preserved in later cultures such as that of the Eteo-Cretans, also of the 1st millennium BC Phrygians, Lemnians and even possibly the Etruscans of Italy, all of whose languages remain as yet but minimally understood, if at all. It is important not to reject out of hand Cyrus Gordon's intriguing suggestion that the original Eteo-Cretan language may have been Semitic.

And it should not be overlooked – not least because as noted earlier the Chechens consider themselves descendants of the Semitic common ancestor Shem – that there are a bewildering number of tongues that continue to be spoken amongst the at least 50 different ethnic groups scattered amongst isolated valleys of the Caucasus. Conceivably one or more of these languages may hold vital clues to the language of the 'Before the Flood' peoples. In an age of ever increasing specialisation, however, finding someone with the right skills to span eight thousand years of linguistic development will be far from easy.

Ultimately, of course, by far the most convincing evidence – potentially catapulting many of the issues discussed in this book into the stratosphere of archaeological interest – must derive from whatever Robert Ballard and his archaeologist colleague Fredrik Hiebert may already have found, and may in future find, from their explorations and samplings amongst the human habitations so deep beneath the Black Sea.

For should they discover that the overwhelmed coastal settlements had advanced to a level at least equal to, if not greater than, that of Çatal Hüyük, and that they represented a substantial power-base, then the entire general understanding of how and where the earliest 'civilisations' began really will have to be radically revised. Out will have to go all the old misconceptions that 'civilisation began in Egypt' or that 'history began in Sumer'. Taking their place will have to be a new, albeit still far from perfect, understanding that the true cradle of civilised human development lay in the environs of Turkey and the Black Sea. Whatever the logistical difficulties of exploring this new region both underwater and on dry land, it now positively demands a far greater public interest and archaeological attention than it has hitherto been accorded.

Back in the 1970s James Mellaart remarked of the

extraordinary civilisation that he had found at Çatal Hüyük that it 'shines like a supernova among the rather dim galaxy of contemporary peasant cultures.' Much more recently – though notably just prior to Ryan and Pitman announcing their Black Sea Flood hypothesis – the prehistorian Richard Rudgley commented on James Mellaart's words:

> Future discoveries may well reveal that other bright stars [to that of Çatal Hüyük] once shone in the firmament of Neolithic civilization both in Anatolia and beyond.[11]

In the light of what Ballard's *Argus* and *Little Hercules* have already discovered, Rudgely's words could not have been more pertinent, or more prophetic. With little doubt at least some of those bright stars currently lie beneath the Black Sea's less than lustrous waters patiently awaiting their day of revelation. Others may lie as yet undiscovered on land in Turkey and its environs. Arguably Robert Ballard's quest for 'Noah's Flood' may hold more revelations about the origins of our civilisation than either he or his team archaeologist Fredrik Hiebert have yet dreamed.

NOTES AND REFERENCES

Author's Preface

[1] Mark Rose, 'Neolithic Noah', book review in *Archaeology*, 52 (January/February 1999).

Introduction

[1] Matthew 2: 1–19.

[2] The calculation of Christ's birth as 1 AD, derives from a miscalculation by the 6th century monk Dionysius Exiguus, who set the year as 753 years after the foundation of Rome.

[3] Different texts of the Bible offer slight differences to these numbers, for example, according to the Samaritan Pentateuch 1,307 years, according to the Greek Septuagint 2,242 years and according to an Ethiopian version 2,262 years. Ussher, a distinguished scholar for his time, opted for the Hebrew version as the most authoritative.

[4] These dates were inserted into at least the margins of printed copies of the Authorised Version of the Bible from 1701 onwards.

[5] Egyptologists divide into two schools for dating the pharaohs, some following a 'high' chronology, others a 'low' one. Both schools rely on such a mish-mash of assumptions that there is no cause for confidence in either system.

[6] This was not entirely new because some classical writers such as Hesiod and Lucretius had in this same way referred to periods earlier than their own.

Chapter 1

[1] There is an enormous literature for world myths amongst which world Flood stories can be found, but a useful introduction is Theodore H. Gaster, *Myth, Legend and Custom in the Old Testament*, New York, Harper & Row, 1969. See also Alan Dundes (ed.), *The Flood Myth*, Berkeley, University of California Press, 1988; Daniel G. Brinton, *The Myths of the New World*, New York, Greenwood Press, 1876 (reprinted 1969); E.T.C. Werner, *Myths and Legends of China*, Singapore, Singapore National Printers, 1922 (reprinted 1984); William Ramsay Smith, *Aborigine Myths and Legends*, London, Senate, 1930 (reprinted 1996).

[2] Frank Press and Raymond Siever, *Earth*, New York, W.H. Freeman & Co., 4th edn, 1986, p.254.

[3] ibid., p.255.

[4] C. Emiliani et al., 'Paleoclimatological Analysis of Late Quaternary Cores from the Northeastern Gulf of Mexico', *Science*, vol. 189 (26 September 1975), pp.1083–8.

[5] R.G. Fairbanks, 'A 17,000-year-old Glacioeustatic Sea Level Record: Influence of Glacial Melting Rates on the Younger Dryas Event and Deep-Ocean Circulation', *Nature*, 342 (1989), pp.637–42.

[6] E. Bard et al., 'U/Th and 14th C Ages of Corals from Barbados and Their Use for Calibrating the 14 C Time Scale Beyond 9000 Years BP', *Nuclear Instruments and Methods in Physics Research*, B52 (1990), pp.461–8.

[7] Worthy of note is that in the United States oceanographers of the Institute for Exploration and archaeologists at the Mashantucket Pequot Museum and Research Center are currently co-operating to investigate ancient submerged shorelines off Long Island and Block Island just east of New York. These are thought to have been settled by Palaeo-Indians some ten thousand years ago. The project is called 'Paleo-

Indians of the Ice Age'. See the Institute for Exploration website
www.if.org/ife/expeditions/PaleoIndians/index.cfm

[8] C. Emiliani et al., op.cit., p.1086.

[9] ibid.

[10] Quoted in Theodore H. Gaster, op.cit., after E.W. Nelson,
Eighteenth Annual Report of the Bureau of American Ethnology,
Part I, 1899, p.452.

[11] Quoted, with source, in Francis Hitching, *The World Atlas of
Mysteries*, London, Collins, 1978, p.164.

[12] Peter Bellwood, *Man's Conquest of the Pacific: The Prehistory
of Southeast Asia and Oceania*, Auckland, Sydney and London,
Collins, 1978, p.422.

[13] Quoted in Theodore H. Gaster, op.cit., p.99, after W.W. Skeat
and C.O. Blagden, *Pagan Races of the Malay Peninsula*,
Macmillan, London, 1906, ii, pp.355–7.

[14] ibid., p.100, after J. von Brenner, *Besuch bei den Kannibelen
Sumatras*, Würzburg 1894, p.218.

[15] ibid., p.101, after O.L. Helfrich in *Bijdragen Taal, Land – en
Volkenkunde van Nederlandsch Indië*, 71 (1916), pp.543 ff.

Chapter 2

[1] For very lucid discussion of this, including particular reference
to Genesis chapters 6–8, see Richard Elliott Friedman, *Who
Wrote the Bible?* London, Jonathan Cape, 1988.

[2] Translation from *The Epic of Gilgamesh*, trans. Andrew George,
London, Penguin Books, 1999. Although this particular
translation derives from the very latest scholarly readings,
Smith's understanding of the passage was very similar. See also
A. Heidel, *The Babylonian Genesis, the Story of Creation*, Chicago,
1951 for general detailed discussion of the Gilgamesh epic's Old
Testament parallels.

[3] Genesis 8: 6–10.

[4] For the purposes of textual consistency, here and elsewhere
when using the Andrew George translation I have replaced his
word 'Deluge' with the essentially identical 'Flood'.

[5] *The Epic of Gilgamesh*, trans. Andrew George, op.cit., pp.92–3.
The passage is from lines 106–29 of Tablet XI.

[6] T.C. Mitchell, *The Bible in the British Museum: Interpreting the Evidence*, London, British Museum, 5th impression, 1994, p.70.

[7] W.G. Lambert and A. R. Millard, *Atrahasis: The Babylonian Story of the Flood*, Oxford, Clarendon, 1969, pp.131 ff.

[8] The most complete version, from Sippar (Abu Habba), dates from the 17th century BC.

[9] For the Sumerian version see *The Epic of Gilgamesh*, trans. Andrew George, op.cit., also S.N. Kramer in J. Pritchard (ed.), *Ancient Near Eastern texts relating to the Old Testament*, Princeton, 1955, pp.42–4.

[10] See *Zeitschrift für Assyriologie*, 35 (1923), Leipzig.

[11] John Romer, *Testament: The Bible and History*, London, O'Mara, 1988, pp.30–1.

[12] Robert Graves, *The Greek Myths*, Harmondsworth, Penguin, 1955, vol. 1, p.141, note 3.

[13] Ovid, *Metamorphoses* I, 230 ff.

[14] H.J. Dresden, 'Mythology of Ancient Iran' in S.N. Kramer (ed.), *Mythologies of the Ancient World*, New York, Anchor Books, 1961, p.344.

[15] Theodore H. Gaster, *Myth, Legend and Custom in the Old Testament*, New York, Harper & Row, 1969, pp.94–5.

Chapter 3

[1] Sir Leonard Woolley, *Ur 'of the Chaldees': The final account, Excavations at Ur*, revised and updated by P.R.S. Moorey, London, Herbert Press, 1982, p.15.

[2] ibid. There is some confusion, however, since on the previous page Woolley describes the same pit as 'not more than 5 feet square'.

[3] See Moorey's up-dating remarks in Sir Leonard Woolley, op.cit., p.33.

[4] 'Abraham's Ur: Did Woolley Excavate the Wrong Place?', *Biblical Archaeology Review*, January/February 2000, pp.20 ff.

[5] Max Mallowan, obituary for Woolley in *Iraq*, 12 (1960).

[6] Cyrus Gordon in interview, quoted in 'Against the Tide: An Interview with Maverick Scholar Cyrus Gordon', *Biblical Archaeology Review*, November/December 2000, p.59.

[7] Molly Dewsnap Meinhardt, 'Woolley's Ur', *Biblical Archaeology Review*, January/February 2000, p.60.

[8] Quoted in W.G. Lambert and A.R. Millard, *Atra-hasis: The Babylonian Story of the Flood*, Oxford, Clarendon Press, 1969.

[9] Eugene Fodor and William Curtis, *Fodor's Turkey*, London, Hodder & Stoughton, 1971, p.291.

[10] James Bryce, *Transcaucasia and Ararat*, notes on a vacation tour, London, Macmillan, 1877.

[11] The last three examples are derived from information quoted in Francis Hitching's *The World Atlas of Mysteries*, London, Collins, 1978, p.167.

[12] Quoted from the English language edition of Navarra's book, *Noah's Ark: I touched it*, Logos International, 1974.

[13] Entry NPL-61 in *Radiocarbon* vol. 7, 1966.

[14] Tim Severin, *The Brendan Voyage*, London, Hutchinson, 1978.

[15] The site with the 'boat' structure is sometimes called the 'Durupinar' site in Ilhan Durupinar's honour.

[16] Ron Wyatt, *Discovered: Noah's Ark*, Nashville, World Bible Society, 1989.

[17] David Fasold, *The Ark of Noah*, New York, Wynwood Press, 1989.

[18] 'Bible Mysteries', *Popular Mechanics* (USA), December 1996, p.40.

[19] Ferrell Jenkins, 'From Tarsus to Mount Ararat', *Guardian of Truth*, 16 May 1996.

[20] Ron Wyatt, op.cit., p.12, no. 3, pp.7–8.

[21] John Morris, 'The Boat-Shaped Rock', *Creation Ex Nihilo*, vol. 2, no. 4, p.18.

[22] 'Bible Mysteries', *Popular Mechanics* (USA), December 1996, p.40.

[23] Quoted in Andrew A. Snelling, 'Amazing "Ark" Exposé', *Creation Ex Nihilo*, vol. 14, p.30.

[24] This and much of the subsequent information derives from personal correspondence with Professor Plimer.

[25] Fasold and Plimer argued that the non-scientific consumer was being duped with false evidence and information taken from others. The 1997 court ruling was that Roberts, by promoting his claim of finding the Akyayla 'ark', was in breach of

copyright, was engaged in misleading and deceptive conduct, and that his colleagues were unreliable witnesses. Fasold, like Wyatt, has died since the case was heard.

Chapter 4

[1] For an excellent account of Marsigli's experiments, see Neal Ascherson, *Black Sea*, London, Jonathan Cape, 1995, pp.1–3.

[2] D.A. Ross, E.T. Degens and J. MacIlvane, 'Black Sea: Recent Sedimentary History', *Science*, 170, no. 9 (October 1970), pp.163–5.

[3] Karlin is a geologist at the University of Nevada, Reno, Nevada. He reported his findings verbally to Walter Pitman, who described them on pp.160–1 of William Ryan and Walter Pitman, *Noah's Flood, The New Scientific Discoveries about the Event that Changed History*, New York, Simon & Schuster, 1998.

[4] As quoted in translation in BBC TV's documentary *Noah's Flood* produced in the Horizon series, 1998.

[5] Ryan and Pitman, op.cit., p.137.

[6] Jones actual quoted words were '7,540 years ago', but here for clarity they have been changed to the date (to the nearest decade) that they represented. Important to note is that such quoted dates carry with them margins of error of a century or more. By saying that the shells were all of the same date, Jones meant that they were the same within the parameters of his recognised margin of error.

[7] From transcript of BBC TV's documentary, *Noah's Flood*, op.cit.

[8] Ryan and Pitman, op.cit., p.234.

[9] In the *Horizon* series. For a transcript, see the BBC website www.bbc.co.uk/science/horizon/noahtranshtml

Chapter 5

[1] William Ryan, quoted in a report by Suzanne Trimel, 'Discovery of Human Artefacts Below Surface of Black Sea Backs Theory by Columbia University Faculty of Ancient Flood' posted in 'Earth Institute News' on the Columbia Earth Institute website (www.earthinstitute.columbia.edu), 13 September 2000.

[2] Gilgamesh Tablet X, lines 80–4, The Epic of Gilgamesh, trans. Andrew George, op.cit., p.78.

[3] 'Euxeinus qui nunc Axenus ille fuit'. See entry for axenos in Liddell and Scott, Greek English Lexicon, Oxford, Clarendon Press 1890, p.155.

[4] Ryan and Pitman, op.cit., p.104.

[5] Neal Ascherson, Black Sea, New York, Hill and Wang, 1995.

[6] Until post-Ice Age rising sea-level caused the Atlantic to break through the narrow strait beyond the Kattegat, the Baltic had been a freshwater lake similar to the Black Sea. So arguably it underwent a similar burst-through, the same hydrogen sulphide conditions pertaining to both.

[7] Ryan and Pitman, op.cit., p.146.

[8] Ryan and Pitman, on pp.146–7 of Noah's Flood suggest that the incoming salt water was deficient in oxygen. Neal Ascherson, author of Black Sea, was unaware of Ryan and Pitman's hypothesis at the time he wrote his book, instead attributing the hydrogen sulphide to a reaction between the fresh water of the rivers and what he supposed to have been the Black Sea's permanent sea-water composition. His explanation of the chemistry may be very pertinent: 'The inrush of organic matter from the rivers was too much for the bacteria in sea-water which would normally decompose it. They feed by oxidising their nutrients, using the dissolved oxygen normally present in sea-water. But when the organic inflow is so great that the supply of dissolved oxygen is used up, then the bacteria turn to another biochemical process: they strip the oxygen from the sulphate ions which are a component of sea-water, creating in the process a residual gas, hydrogen sulphide or H_2S.' (Neal Ascherson, op.cit., p.4)

[9] Robert D. Ballard, 'How we found Titanic', National Geographic, December 1985, pp.696–719.

[10] Robert D. Ballard, 'The Bismarck Found', National Geographic, November 1989, pp.622–35.

[11] Strabo, Geography, 12:3:11 trans. H.L. Jones, London, Heinemann, 1954.

[12] National Geographic news release, 3 October 2000.

[13] Quoted in the 1999 Black Sea Expedition Dispatch 10, 17

November 1999, posted on the *National Geographic* website
www.nationalgeographic.com

[14] Dwight F. Coleman, James B. Newman and Robert D. Ballard, 'Design and Implementation of Advanced Underwater Imaging Systems for Deep Sea Marine Archaeological Surveys', posted on the Robert Ballard Institute for Exploration website www.ife.org/ife/expeditions

[15] From Robert Ballard's log of 5 September 2000, quoted amongst the log entries is 'Witness History in the Making', posted on Robert Ballard's Institute for Exploration website www.ife.org

[16] *National Geographic* interview with Dr Fredrik Hiebert, 9 September 2000.

[17] Quoted in the 2000 Black Sea Expedition Dispatch 9, 9 September 2000, posted on the *National Geographic* website www.nationalgeographic.com

[18] *National Geographic* interview with Dr Fredrik Hiebert, op.cit.

[19] ibid.

[20] From Robert Ballard's log of Friday 22 September 2000, quoted amongst the log entries in 'Witness History in the Making' posted on Robert Ballard's Institute for Exploration website www.ife.org

[21] Quoted in the 2000 Black Sea Expedition Dispatch 12, 6 October 2000, op.cit.

Chapter 6

[1] Tjeerd H. van Andel, 'Late Quaternary sea-level changes and archaeology', *Antiquity*, 63 (1989), pp.736–7.

[2] C. Vance Haynes Jr, 'New World Climate', *Scientific American Discovering Archaeology*, January/February 2000, pp.37–9.

[3] Some suggest human beings hunted them to extinction, others that they were killed by some as yet undetermined changed environmental conditions.

[4] N. Kazanci et al., 'Paleoclimatic Significance of the Late Pleistocene Deposits of Aksehir Lake, West-Central Anatolia', Paper presented at The Late Quaternary in the Eastern

Mediterranean conference, Ankara, Turkey, 1997, as reported in Ryan and Pitman, *Noah's Flood*, op.cit., p.177.

[5] Ryan and Pitman, *Noah's Flood*, op.cit., p.177.

[6] Reports of Dr Miquel Molist of the Universitat Autonòma of Barcelona for the Spanish Archaeological Mission carrying out archaeological excavations in Tell Halula.

[7] See James A. Sauer, 'The River Runs Dry; Creation Story Preserves a Historical Memory', *Biblical Archaeology Review*, July/August 1996, p.55; also Farouk El-Baz, 'Boston University Scientist Discovers Ancient River System in Saudi Arabia', *Boston University News*, 25 March 1993, pp.1–2; also Farouk El-Baz, 'Gulf War Disruption of the Desert Surface in Kuwait' in *Gulf War and the Environment*, New York, Gordon and Breach, 1994.

[8] James A. Sauer, op.cit., p.57. See also J. Sauer and J.A. Blakely, 'Archaeology Along the Spice Route of Yemen', in David T. Potts, *Araby the Blest*, Copenhagen, Carsten Niebuhr Institute, 1988, pp.90–115.

[9] Henri Lhote, *The Search for the Tassili Frescoes: The story of the rock-paintings of the Sahara*, trans. Alan Brodrick, London, Hutchinson, 1960.

[10] Henri Lhote, op.cit., p.64.

[11] James Mellaart, *The Neolithic of the Near East*, London, Thames & Hudson, 1975, p.199.

[12] ibid., p.198.

[13] James Hughes (ed.), *The World Atlas of Archaeology*, London, Mitchell Beazley, 1985, p.171.

[14] Laurens van der Post, *The Lost World of the Kalahari*, London, Hogarth, 1980.

[15] Ronald L. Wallace, *Those who have Vanished: An Introduction to Prehistory*, Homewood, Illinois, Dorsey, 1983, pp.190–2.

[16] Laurens van der Post, op.cit., pp.12–13 and 215.

Chapter 7

[1] Colin Renfrew, *Archaeology and Language*, London, Jonathan Cape, 1987, p.168.

[2] For background to this and related rock engravings, see A.A.

Formozov, 'The petroglyphs of Kobystan and their chronology', *Rivista di Scienze preistorichi*, XVIII (1963), pp.91–114.

[3] For a detailed description of the process see Jane M. Renfrew, *Palaeoethnobotany: The prehistoric food plants of the Near East and Europe*, London, Methuen, 1973, pp.14–15.

[4] A.M.T. Moore and G.V.C. Hillman, 'The excavation of Tell Abu Hureyra in Syria: A Preliminary Report', *Proceedings of the Prehistoric Society*, 41 (1975), pp.50–77.

[5] These experiments were carried out by Jack Harlan in 1966. See Richard E. Leakey, *The Making of Mankind*, London, Michael Joseph, 1981.

[6] G. Hillman, 'The Plant Remains of Tell Abu Hureyra: A Preliminary report', in Moore and Hillman, op.cit., Appendix A, pp.70–3.

[7] M. Heun et al., 'Site of Einkorn Wheat Domestication Identified by DNA Fingerprinting', *Science*, 278 (November 1997), pp.1212–14.

[8] ibid., Letters section.

[9] Luigi Luca Cavalli-Sforza and Francesco Cavalli-Sforza, *The Great Human Diasporas: The History of Diversity and Evolution*, trans. Sarah Thorne, Reading (Mass.), Addison-Wesley, 1995, p.135.

[10] It can be seen being worn by the 'White Lady of Aouanrhet' dating from Lhote's 'Round Head' period. See Henri Lhote, *The Search for the Tassili Frescoes: The story of the rock-paintings of the Sahara*, trans. Alan Brodrick, London, Hutchinson, 1960, pl. 35, opposite p.88.

[11] E.J.W. Barber, *Prehistoric Textiles: The Development of Cloth in the Neolithic and Bronze Ages with special reference to the Aegean*, Princeton (N.J.), Princeton University Press, 1991, pp.126–7.

[12] Henri Lhote, op.cit., p.121.

[13] James Mellaart, *The Neolithic of the Near East*, London, Thames & Hudson, 1975, p.71.

[14] Gary O. Rollefson and Alan H. Simmons, 'The Life and Death of Ain Ghazal', *Archaeology*, November and December 1987, p.40.

[15] London *Times* report of a meeting of the American Association for the Advancement of Science, Monday 19 February 2001.

[16] V. Gordon Childe, *New Light on the Most Ancient East*, London, Routledge & Kegan Paul, 1952, p.26.

[17] Colin Renfrew, op.cit., p.168.

Chapter 8

[1] Denise Schmandt-Besserat, *Before Writing*, Austin, University of Texas Press, 1992, p.168.

[2] 'The origins of the Çayönü culture are obscure' James Mellaart, *The Neolithic of the Near East*, London, Thames & Hudson, 1975, p.54.

[3] U. Esin, 'Salvage Excavations at the Pre-Pottery Site of Asikli Höyük in Central Anatolia', *Anatolia*, 17 (1991), pp.123–64.

[4] Ryan and Pitman, *Noah's Flood*, op.cit., p.180, after ibid.; also U. Esin, 'Asikli, Ten thousand Years Ago: A Habitation Model from Central Anatolia' in *Housing and Settlement in Anatolia – a Historical Perspective*, Istanbul, Tarih Vakfi, 1996, pp.31–42.

[5] It is rarely realised that the Jomon culture of Japan, though quite backward in other respects, had begun producing the first pottery some two millennia earlier than the west.

[6] James Mellaart, op.cit., p.78.

[7] Today it is the Bunting Institute.

[8] Tzvi Abusch, 'Notes on a Pair of Matching Texts: A Shepherd's Bulla and an Owner's Receipt' in Martha. A. Morrison and David I. Owen (eds), *Studies on the Civilization and Culture of Nuzi and the Hurrians*, Winona Lake, Ind., Eisenbrauns, 1981, pp.2–3.

[9] For original source, see Denise Schmandt-Besserat, *Before Writing*, Austin, University of Texas Press, 1992, p.9.

[10] Gary O. Rollefson and Alan H. Simmons, 'The Life and Death of 'Ain Ghazal', *Archaeology*, November/December 1987, p.38.

[11] Denise Schmandt-Besserat, op.cit., p.36.

[12] Ronald L. Wallace, *Those who have Vanished, An Introduction to Prehistory*, Homewood (Ill.), The Dorsey Press, 1983, p.190; also Gina B. Kolatsa '!Kung Hunter-Gatherers: Feminism, Diet and Birth Control', *Science*, 13 September 1974, pp.932–4.

[13] In fact what is claimed as the world's earliest known representation of a boat, from *c*.17,000 BC or earlier, happens to

be a rock painting of the earlier-mentioned 'Bradshaw' people in the remote Kimberly region of north-west Australia. The four man craft can be seen to be being propelled by oars or paddles, with another oar apparently used for steering, and its prow is of a design that mariners recognise as suitable for coping with open sea.

[14] Judith Shackleton, 'Reconstructing past shorelines as an approach to determining factors affecting shellfish collecting in the prehistoric past', Geoff Bailey and John Parkington (eds), *The Archaeology of Prehistoric Coastlines*, Cambridge, Cambridge University Press, 1988, pp.11–21.

[15] Avraham Ronen, 'Besieged by Technology', *Scientific American Discovering Archaeology*, January/February 2000, pp.92–7.

[16] Thor Heyerdahl, *Early Man and the Ocean*, London, George Allen & Unwin, 1978, p.36.

[17] Avraham Ronen, op.cit., p.97.

Chapter 9

[1] James Mellaart, *Çatal Hüyük, A Neolithic Town in Anatolia*, London, Thames & Hudson, 1967, p.27.

[2] This system involves digging within a set grid-plan of measured squares. Because it seems a methodical way of working, it is often still used by archaeologists. However it tends to be over-rigid, hindering an overall view of the site excavated.

[3] James Mellaart, *Çatal Hüyük*, op.cit., p.55. An adze is a cutting tool with an arched blade set at right angles to the handle.

[4] One important qualification to this is that tombs such as at the Natufian site of Eynan on the banks of Lake Huleh in Galilee were often liberally coated with red ochre.

[5] As distinct from Ice Age cave and rock shelter decorations.

[6] For instance, two of the paintings, from shrine VII.21, imitate a stitched border. As Mellaart has pointed out (*Çatal Hüyük*, op.cit., p.152), 'On a painting this makes no sense unless a *kilim* provided its prototype.'

[7] See Alastair Hull and Nicholas Barnard, *Living with Kilims*, London, Thames & Hudson, 1988, p.35.

[8] James Mellaart, *Çatal Hüyük*, op.cit., p.177.

[9] However, as we noted earlier, further east Mount Ararat and its twin share this feature.

[10] Neil Roberts of the British Institute of Archaeology at Ankara, described in Ryan and Pitman, *Noah's Flood*, op.cit., pp.180–1.

[11] James Mellaart, *Çatal Hüyük*, op.cit., p.223.

[12] James Mellaart, *Çatal Hüyük*, op.cit., p.223.

[13] James Mellaart, *Çatal Hüyük*, op.cit., p.63.

[14] Levels IV and V in Mellaart's notation.

[15] ibid.

[16] James Mellaart, *Çatal Hüyük*, op.cit., p.87, p.186.

[17] ibid., p.220.

[18] ibid., p.211.

[19] Findings of Dr Andrea Cucina of the University of Missouri, Columbia, as reported in *New Scientist*, 11 April 2001.

[20] Level IX.

[21] Level VIA.

[22] James Mellaart, *Çatal Hüyük*, op.cit., p.217.

[23] D. Ferembach, 'Les Hommes du gisement néolithique de Çatal Hüyük', *VII Türk Tarih Kongresi (1970)*, 1972, pp.15–21.

[24] James Mellaart, *Çatal Hüyük*, op.cit., p.225.

[25] As remarked by Mellaart (*Çatal Hüyük*, op.cit., pp.182–3):
'The frequency with which the goddess is shown associated with wild animals probably reflects her ancient role as the provider of game for a hunting population and as patroness of the hunt. Her statuettes alone were found in the hunting shrine of Level III. Animal figurines, wounded or maimed in effigy during a hunting ritual, were found in pits near shrines VI.B.12 and IV.4, both of which contained plaster reliefs or statuettes of goddesses. Her association with possibly domesticated animals has been noted and her power over plant life and hence agriculture is clear not only from the numerous representations of floral and vegetable patterns, painted on her figure or in her shrines, but also from the association of her statuettes in heaps of grain and crucifers in shrine VI.A.44 (the Leopard Shrine) and the discovery of the birth-giving goddess in a grain bin in the Level II shrine. Here again the presence of the statue suggests a rite of sympathetic magic. The decoration of the

second shrine of Level III, ornamented entirely with floral patterns or textile designs, suggests that she was regarded as much as an agrarian deity as a patroness of weaving, innovations of supreme importance for the Neolithic Period.'
[26] James Mellaart, *Çatal Hüyük*, op.cit., p.64, p.136.
[27] ibid., pp.84 & 85, p.185.
[28] ibid., p.168.

Chapter 10

[1] Mellaart's calculations were for at least eight hundred years, but since he did not reach the very earliest levels of occupation, around a thousand years seems a reasonable guess.
[2] James Mellaart, *Çatal Hüyük*, op.cit., p.52.
[3] James Mellaart, *Çatal Hüyük*, op.cit., p.64.
[4] Nicholas Coldstream, 'Introduction to the Monuments and Early History of Cyprus' in Ian Robertson, *Blue Guide Cyprus*, London, A & C Black, 3rd edn, 1990, p.15 'After the desertion of these Aceramic Neolithic sites during the sixth millennium BC there follows a long period for which the record remains a blank'.
[5] James Mellaart, *The Neolithic of the Near East*, London, Thames & Hudson, 1987, p.66.
[6] Zeidan Kafafi, 'The Pottery Neolithic in Jordan in Connection with Other Near Eastern Regions', Adnan Hadidi (ed.), *Studies in the History and Archaeology of Jordan III*, Department of antiquities, Jordan and London, Routledge & Kegan Paul, 1987.
[7] James Mellaart, *The Neolithic of the Near East*, op.cit., p.67.
[8] F. Hole, K.V. Flannery, J.A. Nealy and H. Helbaek, *Prehistory and Human Ecology of the Deh Luran Plain*, Michigan, Ann Arbor, 1969.
[9] Andrew Smith, 'Origins of the Neolithic in the Sahara', p.85 in J. Desmond Clark and Steven A. Brandt (eds), *From Hunters to Farmers: The Causes and Consequences of Food Production in Africa*, Berkeley, University of California Press, 1984.
[10] M. Servant and S. Servant-Vildary, 'Les formations lacustres et les diatomées du Quaternaire récent du fond de la cuvette tchadienne', *Revue de géographie physique et de geologie dynamique*, 12 (1), 1970, pp.63–76.

[11] Faure H. et al., 'Formations lacustres du Quaternaire supérieur du Niger oriental: diatomites et âges absous', *Bulletin du Bureau de recherches géologiques et minières (Dakar)*, 3 (1963), pp.41–63.

[12] J.C. Stager and P.A. Mayewski, 'Abrupt Early to Mid-Holocene Climatic Transition Registered at the Equator and the Poles', *Science*, 276 (June 1997), pp.1834–6.

[13] S.J. Johnsen et al., 'Irregular Glacial Interstadials Recorded in a New Greenland Ice Core', *Nature*, 359 (1992), pp.311–13. The American expedition recovered the deepest ice core in the northern hemisphere, 3053 metres.

[14] K.C. Taylor et al., '"The Flickering Switch" of Late Pleistocene Climatic Change', *Nature*, 361, February 1993, pp.432–6.

[15] R.B.A. Alley et al., 'Holocene Climate Instability: A Large Event 8200 Years Ago', *Geology*, 25 (1997), pp.483–9.

[16] Eugene Fodor and William Curtis, *Fodor's Turkey 1971*, Hodder & Stoughton, 1971, p.361.

[17] Ian A. Todd, *The Prehistory of Central Anatolia I: The Neolithic Period*, Studies in Mediterranean Archaeology vol. LX, Göteborg, Paul Aströms Förlag, 1980, p.11.

[18] Ryan and Pitman, *Noah's Flood*, op.cit., p.185. This finding derives from Bulgarian researchers' analyses of pollen in Black Sea cores. This has refuted Oxford University prehistorian Andrew Sherratt's earlier contention that they were forest or woodland. In Ryan and Pitman's words: 'The emerged shelf of the Black Sea prior to the flood was not a forest or woodland, as reconstructed by Andrew Sherratt, but was in fact grassland and steppe ... The setting would have been like the Konya plain in Anatolia in the days of Çatal Hüyük prior to its desertion.'

[19] Ryan and Pitman, *Noah's Flood*, op.cit., p.234.

[20] ibid.

[21] ibid., p.236.

Chapter 11

[1] Ryan and Pitman, *Noah's Flood*, op.cit., p.188.

[2] In Andrew George's translation as used here (from p.126 of the Penguin edition, op.cit.) the term 'Stone Ones' is used for the stones. In N.K. Sandars' earlier (1960) edition the translation was

'things of stone'. Clearly neither translator had much of a clue as to what kind of objects the Epic writer could have been referring to. Although all versions refer to these mysterious stones, the particular passage here quoted in fact derives from a tablet that is thought to have come from Sippar, north of Babylon. It has been reliably dated to the 18th or 17th century BC, a millennium earlier than the Gilgamesh tablets found at Nineveh.

3 Samuel Noah Kramer, *The Sumerians, Their History, Culture and Character*, Chicago, University of Chicago Press, 1963, p.41.

4 ibid.

5 Remarks made in correspondence with the author, May 2001.

6 See Henri Frankfort, *The Art and Architecture of the Ancient Orient*, Harmondsworth, Penguin, 1954, p.1, fig. 1 and James Mellaart, *Çatal Hüyük*, op.cit., p.116, fig. 29.

7 N. Vlassa, 'Chronology of the Neolithic in Transylvania, in the Light of the Tartaria Settlement's Stratigraphy', *Dacia*, N.S., 7 (1963), pp.485–94.

8 M.S.F. Hood, 'The Tartaria Tablets', *Antiquity*, 41 (1967), pp.99–113.

9 Ryan and Pitman, *Noah's Flood*, op.cit., p.196, after M.A. Hoffman, *Egypt Before the Pharaohs*, New York, Barnes & Noble, 1979, pp.102, 181.

10 For excellent illustration and accompanying discussion, see Stuart Piggott (ed.), *The Dawn of Civilization*, London, Thames & Hudson, 1962, pp.102–3.

11 'To an archaeologist ... it would cause no surprise to learn that ... the language of Çatal Hüyük, Hacilar and Can Hasan may have been preserved in Crete well into the Late Bronze Age ...' James Mellaart, *The Neolithic of the Near East*, London, Thames & Hudson, 1975, p.282.

Chapter 12

1 Tjeerd H. van Andel, 'Late Quaternary sea-level changes and archaeology', *Antiquity*, 63 (1989), pp.733–45, p.736, fig. 3.

2 Philo Judaeus, 'On the Incorruptibility of the World', xxvi, in Philo Judaeus, *Works*, trans. C.D. Yonge, Bohn's Ecclesiastical Library, 4 vols, 1854.

[3] In his description of the Red Sea Diodorus remarked that he was 'drawing in part upon the royal archives preserved in Alexandria'. See Mostafa El-Abbadi, *Life and Fate of the ancient Library of Alexandria*, Paris, UNESCO, 1992, p.156.

[4] We hear of the Library being used by scholars up to the eve of Julius Caesar's military intervention in Alexandria in 48 BC. When Strabo stayed in Alexandria two decades later, the Library was no longer extant.

[5] Aidan and Eve Cockburn (eds), *Mummies, Disease and Ancient Cultures*, Cambridge, Cambridge University Press, 1980, pp.226–31.

[6] Diodorus Siculus, 55–6, as translated by C.H. Oldfather in *Diodorus of Sicily in Twelve Volumes*, Loeb Classical Library, London, Heinemann, and Cambridge (Mass.), Harvard University Press, 1939, vol. III, p.245 ff.

[7] Diodorus Siculus, op.cit., Book V, ch. 47, Oldfather trans. p.229. The Oldfather translation has been slightly edited here to break up overlong sentences, but can be consulted unchanged in the Documents section of the Appendix.

[8] 'The Cyeneae are two islets near the mouth of the Pontus [Black Sea], one close to Europe and the other to Asia; they are separated by a channel of about twenty stadia' Strabo, *Geography* 7: 6: 1, trans. H.L. Jones, London, Heinemann, 1924 (reprinted 1954), p.281. In an accompanying note Jones, the translator, refers to an authority who mentions one of the islets as visible in the 16th century, but 'is now submerged'.

[9] ibid.

[10] ibid.

[11] ibid.

[12] Robert Graves, *The Greek Myths*, Harmondsworth, Penguin, 1955, vol. II, p.130.

[13] For instance, in a fragment from Strabo's Book VII occurs the passage 'Many writers have identified the gods that are worshiped in Samothrace with the Cabeiri, though they cannot say who the Cabeiri themselves are, just as the Cyrbantes and Corybantes and likewise the Curetes and the Idaean Dactyli are identified with them', Strabo, *Geography*, trans. H.L. Jones, op.cit., vol. III, p.371.

[14] Stuart Rossiter, *Blue Guide Greece* (3rd edn), London, Ernest Benn, 1977, p.589.

[15] It was specifically called by the Greeks *gynaikokratumene*, which means 'ruled by women'.

[16] In Book VII of the *Iliad* Homer has the Trojan king Priam make a speech prefaced by 'Trojans, Dardanians and allies' – see E.V. Rieu translation, Harmondsworth, Penguin, 1950, p.141.

[17] Diodorus Siculus, Book V, 48, C.H. Oldfather trans., op.cit., vol. III, p.231.

[18] James Mellaart, 'The Royal Treasure of Dorak – A First and Exclusive Report of a Clandestine Excavation which led to the most Important Discovery since the Royal Tombs of Ur', *Illustrated London News*, 28 November 1959, pp.754 ff.

[19] Inferred from the likelihood that each oarsman had one oar, in the manner of later Viking longships.

[20] Homer, *Iliad*, E.V. Rieu trans., op.cit., p.62.

[21] Herodotus, *The Histories*, Selincourt trans., op.cit., p.82.

[22] Nicholas Reeves, *The Complete Tutankhamun*, Thames & Hudson, London, 1990, p.177.

Chapter 13

[1] Homer, *Odyssey*, XII, 70. The Greek expression used by Homer was *pasi melousa*, the literal meaning of which is 'of care (or interest) to all'.

[2] C. Doumas, 'What Did the Argonauts Seek in Colchis?', *Hermathena*, 150 (1991), pp.31–41.

[3] For an excellent recent edition see *The Argonautika by Apollonios Rhodios*, translated, with introduction, commentary and glossary by Peter Green, Berkeley, University of California Press, 1997.

[4] I owe this interesting suggestion to Robert Graves, who made it well before all the latest scientific findings concerning the aftermath of the last Ice Age. See his *The Greek Myths*, Harmondsworth, Penguin, vol. II, p.235.

[5] Professor I.W. Rhys Davids, *Journal of Royal Asiatic Society*, 1899, p.432. See also W.H. Schoff, *The Periplus of the Erythraean Sea*, 1912, pp.228, 229 (quoted in Hutchinson, *Prehistoric Crete*, Harmondsworth, Penguin, 1972, p.101).

[6] This is evident, for instance, in later Greek myths in which Athene and Hera, both aspects of the single primal female deity, on occasion assume the form of doves.

[7] *The Oldest Gold in the World – Varna, Bulgaria*, Jerusalem, Israel Museum, 1994; also Colin Renfrew, 'Ancient Bulgaria's Golden Treasures', *National Geographic*, July 1980, pp.112 ff.

[8] *Argonautika*, book II, lines 1005–8, see Peter Green edition, op.cit., p.105.

[9] Eugene Fodor and William Curtis, *Fodor's Turkey 1971*, London, Hodder & Stoughton, 1971, p.365.

[10] Actually Heraclea Pontica, i.e. Black Sea Heraclea.

[11] See Robert Graves, *The Greek Myths*, op.cit., vol. II, p.235.

[12] Since Eregli lies on a river mouth, if the former bed of this same river is traced out into the Black Sea to the former coastline, this might well prove to be the site of a pre-Flood settlement.

[13] G.M.A. Hanfmann (ed.), *Sardis from Prehistoric times: Results of the Archaeological Exploration of Sardis 1958–1975*, Harvard University Press, 1983, quoted in Peter James, *The Sunken Kingdom: The Atlantic Mystery Solved*, London, Jonathan Cape, 1995, p.218.

[14] James Mellaart, *The Neolithic of the Near East*, London, Thames & Hudson, 1975, p.114.

[15] James Mellaart, *The Neolithic of the Near East*, op.cit., p.115.

[16] Regularly updated information on the ongoing Çatal Hüyük excavations can be found at the excellent website www.catal.arch.cam.ac.uk

[17] Strabo, *Geography*, 12.3.11.

[18] Information provided to the author from Dr James Mellaart in personal correspondence, May 2001.

[19] Robert Graves, *The Greek Myths*, op.cit., vol. II, p.125.

[20] Gerhard Poellauer, 'Latest investigations in the Homeland of the Amazons at the river Thermodon', Klagenfurt, Austria. Available on the internet at ebooks.at

[21] Apollonius Rhodius, Book ii, 382–8, also ii, 1169–76.

[22] *Argonautika*, op.cit., book II, lines 118–25.

[23] Theodore H. Gaster, *Myth, Legend and Custom in the Old Testament*, New York, Harper & Row, 1969, p.87.

[24] Herodotus was born in Halicarnassus, on Turkey's west coast.

[25] According to Herodotus:

> The Egyptians before the reign of Psammetichus [of the
> 26th Dynasty – 7th century BC] used to think that of all
> races in the world they were the most ancient.
> Psammetichus, however, when he came to the throne,
> took it into his head to settle this question of priority,
> and ever since his time the Egyptians have believed
> that the Phrygians surpass them in antiquity and that
> they themselves come second.

As Herodotus' story continues, Psammetichus, assuming that there
had to have been one original language from which all others
descended, arranged for two babies to be brought up by a
shepherd living in an isolated spot. The shepherd was under strict
orders that no one should be allowed to utter a word in the babies'
presence. Psammetichus then waited to hear what would be the
first word that either baby would speak, which turned out to be
becos. This Psammetichus discovered to be Phrygian for 'bread'
from which he concluded that the Phrygians had to have been the
first civilised people, earlier even than the Egyptians. Whatever
we may make of the story, what it attests is that at least as far back
as the 7th century BC there was a perception that a Turkey-based
civilisation may have existed even earlier than the Egyptian
civilisation.

[26] Genesis 10: 2.

[27] Genesis 4: 22.

[28] Robert Graves, *The Greek Myths*, op.cit., vol. II, p.235, note 3.

[29] The same pairing in fact appears in the much later biblical
book of Ezekiel (38: 2,3), in which a king Gog, thought to be one
and the same as a Turkey-located king the Greeks called Gyges,
is described as 'paramount prince of Meshech and Tubal'.

[30] According to the entry on 'Hurrians' in the *Oxford
Encyclopaedia of Archaeology in the Near East*, (ed. Eric M.
Meyers, New York, Oxford University Press), published as
recently as 1997, only 'as early as 2000 BC'.

[31] Giorgio Buccellati and Marilyn Kelly-Buccellati, 'City of Myth:
In Search of Hurrian Urkesh', *Archaeology Odyssey*, May/June
2001, p.16 ff.

[32] Known as 'Enmerkar and the Lord of Aratta'.

[33] Here named Inanna.

[34] This is in an enclave of the Azeri people between Armenian territory and Turkey.

[35] Jaan Sepp, 'Caucasus – Europe Lost and Recovered', article on Chechen website www.idis.com/ChouOnline/native.txt

[36] Genesis 9: 20.

[37] It is said to have been destroyed by an earthquake.

[38] *Biblical Archaeology Review*, November/December, 1996, p.24.

[39] Patrick E. McGovern, Stuart J. Fleming and Solomon H. Katz, eds, *The Origins and Ancient History of Wine*, Philadelphia, University of Pennsylvania Museum/Gordon and Breach, 1995, p.xii.

[40] Robert Graves, *The Greek Myths*, op.cit., vol. II, p.237.

[41] Notably, he was reputed to be a son of Helius, just as the rulers of Rhodes were supposed to have been.

[42] Specifically, of the Great Mother Goddess's Hecate, or death aspect.

[43] E.D. Phillips, in his chapter on 'The nomad peoples of the Steppes' in Stuart Piggott (ed.), *The Dawn of Civilization*, p.321: 'These princely burials resemble in many respects others south of the Caucasus at Alaca Hüyük ... [and] their contents recall the treasures at Troy II in Asia Minor.'

Chapter 14

[1] 'Considerable changes took place *c.*6000 BC with the arrival of new peoples with a Neolithic economy based on domestic cattle', James Mellaart, *The Neolithic of the Near East*, London, Thames & Hudson, 1987, p.268.

[2] Henri Lhote, *The Search for the Tassili Frescoes: The Story of the rock-paintings of the Sahara*, trans. Alan Brodrick, London, Hutchinson, p.199 ff.

[3] Henri Lhote, op.cit., pp.70–1.

[4] The word used was 'Libya' which in ancient texts meant all Africa, rather than just the present-day north African country of that name.

[5] The 'Triple Goddess Libya'.

[6] Herodotus, *The Histories*, trans. Aubrey de Selincourt, Harmondsworth, Penguin, 1954, p.301.

[7] ibid., p.302.

[8] ibid., p.306.

[9] Diodorus Siculus iii, 52. I have here substituted 'Black Sea' for the 'Pontus' of the Loeb translation.

[10] Here the original text again uses the word 'Libya', for which I have substituted 'north Africa' for the same reasons stated in note 4 above.

[11] Diodorus Siculus, op.cit., iii, 52.

[12] ibid.

[13] The Loeb translation has 'ichthyophagi', for which I have substituted a translation the average reader will hopefully find more meaningful.

[14] Diodorus Siculus, op.cit., book iii, 53, 54.

[15] In fact, recent archaeological excavations have provided firm confirmation of the existence of warrior women north of the Black Sea. See for instance 'Warrior Women of the Eurasian Steppes', *Archaeology*, January/February 1997, pp.44–8.

[16] ibid.

[17] D.H. Trump, *The Prehistory of the Mediterranean*, Harmondsworth, Penguin, 1981, p.57.

[18] J.E. Dixon, J.R. Cann and Colin Renfrew, 'Obsidian and the Origins of Trade', *Avenues to Antiquity: Readings from Scientific American*, intro. Brian M. Fagan, San Francisco, W.H. Freeman, 1976.

[19] Ignatius Donnelly, *Atlantis: The Antediluvian World*, New York, Harper, 1883, p.xx.

[20] Reproduced in Thor Heyerdahl, *American Indians in the Pacific*, London, George Allen & Unwin, 1952, plate XXXIII, 1.

[21] Pronunciations differ betwen dialects. Michael Brett and Elizabeth Fentress, in their recent book on the Berbers (see next note), point out that the word by which the Berber describe themselves today is *Tamazight* if referring to their language, or *Imazighen* if referring to the people using it.

[22] Michael Brett and Elizabeth Fentress, *The Berbers*, Oxford, Blackwell, 1996, pbk edition 1997, p.4.

[23] ibid., p.35.

[24] ibid., p.210.

[25] ibid., pp.210–12.

[26] Herodotus, *The Histories*, op.cit., p.83.

Chapter 15

[1] Robert Graves, *The White Goddess*, London, Faber, 1961, p.51.

[2] Robert Graves, *The White Goddess*, A historical grammar of poetic myth, London, Faber and Faber, amended and enlarged edition, 1961.

[3] M. Gimbutas, *The Goddesses and Gods of Old Europe* and *The Language of the Goddess*.

[4] Herodotus, *The Histories*, trans. Selincourt, op.cit., p.305.

[5] In one shrine Mellaart observed griffon-vulture beaks emerging from the open nipples on a wall-statue of the goddess, then found these to belong to complete vulture skulls encased within the breasts. James Mellaart, *Çatal Hüyük*, op.cit., p.28 and figs 38 and 39.

[6] J.D. Evans, *Malta*, London, Thames & Hudson, 1959.

[7] Sibylle von Cles-Reden, *The Realm of the Great Goddess*, London, Thames & Hudson, 1961, p.97.

[8] Radio-carbon dating methods have undergone refinements, so that assumptions that were made in work carried out, say in the 1970s, would not be the same as those behind today's datings.

[9] Radio-carbon dating cannot be performed on anything of stone, and is only possible on organic materials, such as wood, bone, plant fibres, etc. In the case of stone monuments the archaeologist therefore has to find some organic remains that can be confidently associated with the time of the monument's foundation – not always easy.

[10] Michael Dames, *The Silbury Treasure: The Great Goddess Rediscovered*, London, Thames & Hudson, 1976.

[11] John W. Hedges, *Tomb of the Eagles: A Window on Stone Age Tribal Britain*, London, John Murray, 1984, p.134.

[12] Bede, *A History of the English Church and People*, trans. Leo Sherley-Price, London, Penguin, 1955, p.39.

[13] Pausanias, III, xxii, 7.

[14] See Robert Graves, *The Greek Myths*, op.cit., vol. II, p.128.

[15] See Leonard Woolley, Ur 'Of the Chaldees', op.cit., p.63 ff. Woolley called her 'Shubad' but her name has subsequently more accurately been rendered as 'Puabi'.

[16] In fact in this instance the bird is likely to be the owl, also regarded as an intermediary between the world of the living and the world of the dead.

[17] Herodotus, The Histories, book iv, 180. This custom is strikingly similar to the one that Herodotus had also noted of the Auses and Maxyes to the west, living around what remained of Lake Tritonis.

[18] James Mellaart, The Neolithic of the Near East, op.cit., p.271.

[19] In Greek mythology king Belus was the twin brother of Agenor, both being born of the goddess Libya by Poseidon. Belus bore twins Aegyptus (who was given Arabia and conquered Egypt) and Danaus (who was sent to rule Libya). According to Robert Graves (The Greek Myths, op.cit., vol. I, p.148) 'In the Mycenaean Age double-sovereignty was the rule: Sparta with Castor and Polydeuces; Messenia with Idas and Lynceus; Argos with Proetus and Acrisius; Tiryns with Heracles and Iphicles; Thebes with Eteocles and Polyneices.' At Sparta marriage to the Leucippides enroyalled the Spartin co-kings. The Leucippides were priestesses of Athene and Artemis, and given moon names, being the moon goddess's earthly representatives. Thus in vase paintings the chariot of Selene is frequently attended by the Dioscouri. [Graves, The Greek Myths, op.cit., p.251] For more about the Spartan system of joint kingship, see Herodotus, The Histories, op.cit., pp.378–9.

Chapter 16

[1] Marsha A. Levine, 'Dereivka and the problem of horse domestication', Antiquity, 64 (1990), pp.727–40.

[2] 'It should be mentioned that we found evidence that horses were kept at Tell el-Dab'a from the Early Hyksos Period', Manfred Bietak, 'Avaris and Piramesse, Archaeological Exploration in the Eastern Nile Delta', Proceedings of the British Academy, London, vol. LXV (1979), p.247.

³ Homer, *Odyssey*, 19, 176; translation from *The Illustrated Odyssey*, trans., E.V. Rieu, London, Rainbird, 1981.

⁴ Sir Arthur Evans, incidentally, thought the 'Minoan' costume to be of 'Libyan', i.e. north African, origin.

⁵ Robert Graves, *The Greek Myths*, vol. II, op.cit., p.167.

⁶ Gösta Säflund, 'Cretan and Theran Questions' (p.195) in Robin Hägg and Nanno Marinatos (eds), *Sanctuaries and Cults in the Aegean Bronze Age*, Acta Instituti Atheniensis Regni Sueciae, Series in 4°, XXVIII, Stockholm, 1981.

⁷ ibid., p.198 'There are, however, traces of a tradition according to which the bridegroom weds, or ravishes, the bride in her own quarters.' Säflund notably quotes king Minos's marriage to Dexithea at Keos, as recounted in Bacchyides, *Ode*, 1, 112–27.

⁸ This they produced from the *murex* sea-shell by what was a rather smelly process due to the shell only releasing the dye when dead and decaying.

⁹ A.M. Blackman, *Middle Egyptian Stories*, Brussels, Édition de la Fondation Egyptologique, 1932, pp.23:32, 24:5.

¹⁰ See *The Epic of Gilgamesh*, trans. Andrew George, op.cit., pp.138–40.

¹¹ Gaston Jondet, *Les ports submergés de l'ancienne île de Pharos*, ... 1916.

¹² Professor George Bass, 'Lessons from a Bronze Age Wreck' in *Archaeology Under Water*, New York, McGraw Hill, 1980, p.34.

¹³ Robert Graves, *The Greek Myths*, op.cit., vol. I, p.196.

¹⁴ In Crete, also in Greece and Turkey a number of place-names end in -ssos, -ndos or -nda, and -nthos or -ntha, as in Turkey where there are Halicarnassos, Labraunda, Assos and Perinthus; on mainland Greece where there are Corinth, Tirynas [accusative case Tirytha] and Mykalessos; and on Crete itself where there are Knossos, Tylissos, Karnassos, and Pyranthos. See R.W. Hutchinson, *Prehistoric Crete*, Harmondsworth, Penguin, 1962, p.56.

¹⁵ Cyrus H. Gordon, *Before the Bible: The Common Background of Greek and Hebrew Civilisations*, London, Collins, 1962.

¹⁶ 'The language of Çatal Hüyük, Hacilar and Can Hasan may

have been preserved in Crete well into the Bronze Age', James Mellaart, *The Neolithic of the Near East*, op.cit., p.282.

Chapter 17

[1] See chapter 15, p.230.
[2] This and subsequent quotes derive from the B. Jowett translation, *The Dialogues of Plato*, 3rd edn, Oxford, 1892, as reproduced in J.V. Luce, *The End of Atlantis: New Light on an Old Legend*, London, Thames & Hudson, 1969, pp.207 ff.
[3] ibid.
[4] Ignatius Donnelly, *Atlantis: The Antediluvian World*, New York, Harper & Brothers, 1882.
[5] E.S. Ramage, *Atlantis: Fact or Fiction?*, Indiana, Bloomington, 1978.
[6] J.V. Luce, op.cit., p.44.
[7] Peter James, *Sunken Kingdom: The Atlantis Mystery Solved*, London, Jonathan Cape, 1995.
[8] Genesis 10:2.
[9] See John Bulloch and Harvey Morris, *No Friends but the Mountains: The Tragic History of the Kurds*, London, Viking, 1992, p.56.
[10] Servius on Virgil's *Aeneid* XI, 262.
[11] Plato, *Critias*, 114.
[12] ibid.,
[13] ibid., 120.
[14] ibid., 114.
[15] ibid., 115 and 117.
[16] ibid., 116 and 117.
[17] ibid., 119.
[18] The reason for the alternating is stated by Plato as to give 'equal honour to the odd and to the even number'. This is an interesting point. In the Dorak figurines the amount of jewellery worn was notably an odd number on one arm, an even on the other.
[19] Peter James, op.cit., p.296.
[20] Pausanias, (trans. Frazer, 1898) VII, xxiv, 6–7.
[21] K.T. Frost, 'The Lost Continent', *The Times*, 19 February 1909;

'The Critias and Minoan Crete', *Journal of Hellenic Studies*, 33 (1913).

[22] Robert Graves, *The Greek Myths*, Harmondsworth, Penguin, 1955, vol. I, p.146.

[23] Personal correspondence with Dr Mellaart, who cites that Prof. A. Goetze as having been working on it before his death in the 1970s.

[24] Herodotus, *The Histories*, Selincourt translation, op.cit., p.304.

Chapter 18

[1] He would have been aided by the fact that the Babylonian (and Assyrian) practice of keeping records on baked clay tablets had the great advantage that such material could survive immersion in water, and even fire.

[2] Quoted in C.W. Ceram, *Gods, Graves & Scholars*, London, Gollancz, 1971, p.271.

[3] Richard Elliott Friedman, *Who Wrote the Bible?*, London, Jonathan Cape, 1987.

[4] *Epic of Gilgamesh*, trans. Andrew George, op.cit., p.94.

[5] Lucian 'Of the Syrian Goddess', text in the Loeb Classical Library series *Lucian*, vol. IV, English translation by A.M. Harmon, London and Cambridge, Mass., Heinemann & Harvard University Press, 1925, reprinted 1969. In order to convey the text's 'Olde Greek' character, Harmon rendered his translation in a mimicking of 14th century English. Since Lucian, for his part, had translated the Syrian deities names into Greek, for which Harmon then provided the Latin equivalents, trying to make the text accessible for the general reader is not easy.

[6] In Lucian's words, 'But when you look upon Hera [Atagartis] she presents great diversity of details, for although the whole could truly be considered Hera [Atagartis] nonetheless it contains something of Athene, Aphrodite, Selene, Rhea [Cybele] Artemis, Fortune [Nemesis] and Parcae [Moirai] [The Fates]'.

[7] Reliefs at the Temple of Ammon at Karnak, depicting the Egyptian pharaoh Merneptah attacking Canaanite cities, show this practice. See this author's *The Bible is History*, p.49. Excavations of an Eteo-Cretan temple at Arkhanes, near

Knossos, also revealed archaeological evidence of the sacrifice of a young man, apparently in an attempt to ward off an earthquake. See Yannis Sakellarikis and Efi Sapouna-Sakellariki, 'Drama of Death in a Minoan Temple', *National Geographic*, vol. 159 (1981), pp.205–22.

[8] For the Greek text, see the Loeb Classical Library edition of *Lucian*, op.cit., pp.350 ff. Harmon's 'Middle English' translation has here been rendered in modernised English.

[9] For the original Greek, see *Lucian*, op.cit., p.352.

[10] ibid.

[11] ibid. Another reference to the same rite occurs in the *Oration* attributed to Melito of Sardis, which is thought to have been written by an individual of the 3rd century AD local to the Hierapolis district. This reads: 'The Magi charged Simi, the daughter of Hadad, that she should draw water from the sea and cast it into the well [at Hierapolis/Mabbog], in order that the [unclean] spirit [i.e. a fresh flood] should not come up [and commit] injury' Quoted in J.B. Segal, *Edessa: The Blessed City*, Oxford, Clarendon, 1970, p.48, n. 4.

[12] *Lucian*, op.cit., p.380.

[13] A very early Christian pilgrim of this period, Egeria, mentions them in the course of her visit to Edessa. See John Wilkinson, *Egeria's Travels*, London, SPCK, 1972.

[14] According to Segal, there was also a lake of sacred fish at the temple of the Great Mother Goddess at Delos, and similar lakes were to be found at other temples in Palestine, Syria, Asia Minor and elsewhere. See Segal, op.cit., p.49.

[15] Strabo, *Geography*, 7.7.2. As remarked by Strabo 'He [Hesiod] seems to me to hint that from earliest times they [the Leleges of Turkey] were a collection of mixed peoples and that this was why the tribe disappeared'.

[16] Quoted in Robert Graves *The White Goddess*, op.cit., p.263.

[17] Herodotus, *The Histories*, trans. Selincourt, op.cit., p.10.

[18] For more details and further discussion see Neal Ascherson, *Black Sea*, op.cit., p.120.

[19] *Book of the Laws of Countries*, c.3rd century AD, 'when Abgar the king believed [in Christ] he decreed that anyone who castrated himself should have his hand cut off. And from that

day to this time no-one castrates himself in the country of Edessa', quoted in J.B. Segal, op.cit., p.56.

[20] Charles Burney, article on Çatal Hüyük in K. Branigan (ed.), *The Atlas of Archaeology*, London, Macdonald, 1982, p.138.

[21] James Mellaart, *Çatal Hüyük*, op.cit., p.68.

[22] E.J.W. Barber, *Prehistoric Textiles...*, op.cit., p.258.

Chapter 19

[1] Quoted from an un-named American newspaper in Neal Ascherson *Black Sea*, London, Jonathan Cape, 1995, p.257.

[2] Jane McLeod, quoted on the Internet 'Amazons Research' website www.myrine.at/Amazons

[3] Neal Ascherson, op.cit., p.259.

[4] Quoted in Chechen Internet website www.idis.com/Choul/Online/chechnya2.html

[5] Personal letter from James Mellaart, May 2001.

[6] Jeannine Davis-Kimball, 'Warrior Women of the Eurasian Steppes', *Archaeology*, January-February 1998, pp.44–8.

[7] Herodotus, *The Histories*, op.cit., p.185.

[8] Luigi Luca, Cavalli-Sforza and Francesco Cavalli-Sforza, *The Great Human Diasporas: The History of Diversity and Evolution*, trans. Sarah Thorne, Reading (Massachusetts), Addison-Wesley, 1995.

[9] At present the best we have is that the bones of both populations have showed a marked tendency to anaemia.

[10] Sir W. Jones, 'Third Anniversary Discourse On the Hindus', 1786.

[11] Richard Rudgley, *Lost Civilisations of the Stone Age*, London, Arrow Books, 1999, p.19.

BIBLIOGRAPHY

Alley, R.B., et al., 'Holocene Instability: A Large Event 6200 Years Ago', *Geology*, 25 (1997), pp.483–9

Apollonios Rhodios, *The Argonautika by Apollonios Rhodios*, trans. Peter Green, Berkeley (Ca.), University of California Press, 1997

Ascherson, Neal, *Black Sea*, New York, Hill and Wang, 1995 (first published Jonathan Cape, London, in the same year)

Bacon, Edward (ed.) *Vanished Civilizations: Forgotten Peoples of the Ancient World*, London, Thames & Hudson, 1963

Bailey, Geoff and John Parkington, (eds), *The Archaeology of Prehistoric Coastlines*, Cambridge, Cambridge University Press, 1988

Barber, E.J.W., *Prehistoric Textiles: The Development of Cloth in the Neolithic and Bronze Ages with special reference to the Aegean*, Princeton (NJ), Princeton University Press, 1991

Barber, Elizabeth Wayland, *The Mummies of Urumchi*, London, Macmillan, 1999

Bard, E., et al., 'U/Th and 14th C Ages of Corals from Barbados and Their Use for Calibrating the 14 C Time Scale Beyond 9000 Years BP', *Nuclear Instruments and Methods in Physics Research* B52 (1990), pp.461–8

Barich, B., *Archaeology and Environment in the Libyan Sahara*, Oxford, Oxford University Press, 1987

Baring, Anne and Jules Cashford, *The Myth of the Goddess: Evolution of an Image*, London, Viking, 1991

Bedrosian, Robert, 'Eastern Asia Minor and the Caucasus in ancient Mythologies',

[http://www.virtuatscape.com/rbedrosian/mythint.htm]

Bellwood, Peter, *Man's Conquest of the Pacific: The Prehistory of Southeast Asia and Oceania*, Auckland, Sydney and London, Collins, 1978

Bietak, Manfred, 'Avaris and Piramesse, Archaeological Exploration in the Eastern Nile Delta', *Proceedings of the British Academy*, London, vol. LXV, 1979

Bigalke, T., *A History of Tana Toraja*, U.S.A., Wisconsin University Press, 1981

Brett, Michael and Elizabeth Fentress, *The Berbers*, Oxford, Blackwell, 1996

Brice, W. (ed.), *The Environmental History of the Near and Middle East since the Last Ice age*, London and New York, Academic Press, 1978

Bright, John, 'Has archaeology found evidence of the Flood?' *Bulletin of the American School of Archaeology*, V, 4 (1942), pp.55–62

Brinton, Daniel G., *The Myths of the New World*, New York, Greenwood Press, 1876, reprinted 1969

Bulloch, John and Harvey Morris, *No Friends but the Mountains: The Tragic History of the Kurds*, London, Viking, 1992

Cavalli-Sforza, Luigi Luca and Francesco Cavalli-Sforza, trans. Sarah Thorne, *The Great Human Diasporas: The History of Diversity and Evolution*, Reading (Mass.), Addison-Wesley, 1995

Ceram, C.W., *Gods, Graves and Scholars, The Story of Archaeology*, London, Gollancz, 1971

Childe, V. Gordon, *New Light on the Most Ancient East*, London, Routledge & Kegan Paul, 1952

Clark, J. Desmond and Steven A. Brandt, *From Hunters to Farmers: The Causes and Consequences of Food Production in Africa*, Berkeley, University of California Press, 1984

Clark, J.G.D., 'Radiocarbon dating and the expansion of farming from the Near East over Europe', *Proceedings of the Prehistoric Society*, 21 (1965), pp.58–73

Cles-Reden, Sibylle von, *The Realm of the Great Goddess*, London, Thames & Hudson, 1961

Cockburn, Aidan and Eve (eds), *Mummies, Disease and Ancient Cultures*, Cambridge, Cambridge University Press, 1980

Coogan, Michael (ed.) et al., *Scripture and other Artifacts*, Louisville, Kentucky, Westminster/John Knox, 1994

Cowan, C. Wesley and Patty Jo Watson, *The Origins of Agriculture: An International Perspective*, Washington, Smithsonian Institution Press, 1992

Dames, Michael, *The Silbury Treasure: The Great Goddess Rediscovered*, London, Thames & Hudson, 1976

De Camp, L. Sprague, *Lost Continents*, New York, Dover, 1970

Diodorus Siculus, *Bibliotheca Historica*, trans. C.H. Oldfather, 12 volumes, London, Heinemann, 1935

Donnelly, Ignatius, *Atlantis: The Antediluvian World*, New York, Harper, 1883

Dundes, Alan (ed.), *The Flood Myth*, Berkeley (Ca.), University of California Press, 1988

El-Abbadi, Mostafa, *Life and Fate of the Ancient Library of Alexandria*, Paris, United Nations Educational, Scientific and Cultural Organisation, 2nd (revised) edition, 1992

Emiliani, C. et al., 'Paleoclimatological Analysis of Late Quaternary Cores from the North-eastern Gulf of Mexico', *Science*, 189 (26 September 1975), pp.1083–8

Esin, U, 'Salvage Operations at the Pre-Pottery Site of Asikli Höyük in Central Anatolia', *Anatolia*, 17 (1991), pp.123–64

——, 'Asikli, Ten Thousand Years ago: A Habitation Model from Central Anatolia', *Housing and Settlement in Anatolia: A Historical Perspective*, Istanbul, Tarih Vakfi, 1996, pp.31–42

Evans, J.D., *Malta*, London, Thames & Hudson, 1959

Fairbanks, R.G., 'A 17,000-year-old Glacioeustatic Sea Level Record', *Nature*, 342 (1989), pp.637–42

Fasold, David, *The Ark of Noah*, New York, Wynwood Press, 1989

Fodor, Eugene and William Curtis (eds), *Fodor's Turkey 1971*, London, Hodder and Stoughton, 1971

Frankfort, Henri, *The Art and Architecture of the Ancient Orient*, Harmondsworth, Penguin, 1954

Friedman, Richard Elliott, *Who Wrote the Bible?*, London, Jonathan Cape, 1988

Frost, K.T., 'The *Critias* and Minoan Crete', *Journal of Hellenic Studies*, 33 (1913)

Gaster, Theodore H., *Myth, Legend and Custom in the Old Testament*, New York, Harper & Row, 1969

Gilgamesh, *The Epic of Gilgamesh, The Babylonian Epic Poem and other Texts in Akkadian and Sumerian*, trans. Andrew George, London, Penguin Books, 1999

Gimbutas, Marija, *The Language of the Goddess: Unearthing the Hidden Symbols of Western Civilisation*, London, Thames & Hudson, 1989

Gordon, Cyrus H., *Before the Bible: The Common Background of Greek and Hebrew Civilisations*, London, Collins, 1962

Graves, Robert, *The Greek Myths*, Harmondsworth, Penguin, 1955, 2 vols

——, *The White Goddess, A Historical Grammar of Poetic Myth*, amended and enlarged edition, London, Faber & Faber, 1961

Hadidi, Adnan, (ed.), *Studies in the History and Archaeology of Jordan*, III, Department of Antiquities, Jordan and London, Routledge & Kegan Paul 1987

Hägg, Robin and Nanno Marinatos (eds), *Sanctuaries and Cults in the Aegean Bronze Age*, Acta Instituti Atheniensis Regni Sueciae, Series in 4°, XXVIII, Stockholm, 1981

Hedges, John W., *Tomb of the Eagles, A Window on Stone Age Tribal Britain*, London, John Murray, 1984

Heidel, A., *The Gilgamesh Epic and Old Testament Parallels*, Chicago, University of Chicago Press, 1949

Helbaek, Hans, 'First impressions of the Çatal Hüyük plant husbandry', *Anatolian Studies*, XIV (1964), pp.121–3

Herodotus, *The Histories*, trans. Aubrey de Selincourt, Harmondsworth, Penguin, 1954

Heun, M., et al., 'Site of Einkorn Wheat Domestication Identified by DNA Fingerprinting', *Science*, 278 (November 1997), pp.1312–14

Heyerdahl, Thor, *American Indians in the Pacific*, London, George Allen & Unwin, 1952

——, *Early Man and the Ocean*, London, George Allen & Unwin, 1978

Hole, F., K.V. Flannery, J.A. Nealy and H. Helbaek, *Prehistory and Human Ecology of the Deh Luran Plain*, Michigan, Ann Arbor, 1969

Homer, *The Iliad*, trans. E.V. Rieu, Harmondsworth, Penguin, 1950

——, *The Odyssey*, trans. E.V. Rieu, Harmondsworth, Penguin, 1946; also illustrated edition, Sidgwick & Jackson, 1980

Hood, M.S.F., 'The Tartaria Tablets', *Antiquity*, 41 (1967), pp.99–113

Hooton, E.A., 'The ancient inhabitants of the Canary Islands', *Harvard African Studies*, 7: 40–5

Hughes, James, (ed.) *The World Atlas of Archaeology*, London, Mitchell Beazley, 1985

Hull, Alastair and Nicholas Barnard, *Living with Kilims*, London, Thames & Hudson, 1988

Hutchinson, R.W., *Prehistoric Crete*, Harmondsworth, Penguin, 1972

James, Peter, *The Sunken Kingdom: The Atlantis Mystery Solved*, London, Jonathan Cape, 1995

Kramer, Samuel Noah, *Enmerkar and the Lord of Aratta*, Museum Monograph, University Museum, Philadelphia, University of Pennsylvania, 1952

—— (ed.), *Mythologies of the Ancient World*, New York, Anchor, 1961

——, *The Sumerians, Their History, and Character*, Chicago, University of Chicago Press, 1963

Kryzaniak, L., and Kobusiewicz, M. (eds), *Environmental Change and Human Culture in the Nile Basin and Northeast Africa*, Pozan, 1989

Lambert, W.G. and A.R. Millard, *Atra-hasis: The Babylonian Story of the Flood*, Oxford, Clarendon Press, 1969

Lang, M., *Palace of Nestor at Pylos in Western Messenia* vol. 2, *The Frescoes*, Princeton (NJ), Princeton University Press, 1969

Leakey, Richard E., *The Making of Mankind*, London, Michael Joseph, 1981

Levine, Marsha A., 'Dereivka and the problem of horse domestication', *Antiquity* 64 (1990), pp.727–40

Lhote, Henri, *The Search for the Tassili Frescoes: The story of the rock-paintings of the Sahara*, trans. Alan Brodrick, London, Hutchinson, 1959

Lisitsina, G.N., 'The Caucasus: A Centre for Ancient Farming in Eurasia' in W. van Zeist and W.A. Casparie, *Ancient Man, Studies in Palaeoethnobotany*, Rotterdam/Boston, 1984, pp.285–92

Lloyd, Seton, *Early Highland Peoples of Anatolia*, London, Thames & Hudson, 1967

Luce, J.V., *The End of Atlantis: New Light on an Old Legend*, London, Thames & Hudson, 1969

Lucian of Samosata, *Lucian*, in 8 volumes, trans A.M. Harmon, London, Heinemann and Cambridge (Mass.), Harvard University Press, 1925

McGovern, Patrick E., Stuart Fleming and Solomon H. Katz (eds), *The Origins and Ancient History of Wine*, Philadelphia, University of Pennsylvania Museum/Gordon & Breach, 1996

Maisels, Charles Keith, *The Emergence of Civilization: From hunting and gathering to agriculture, cities and the state in the Near East*, London, Routledge, 1990

Mallowan, M.E.L., 'Noah's Flood Reconsidered' *Iraq*, XXVI (1964), pp.62–82

Mattingly, David, 'Making the Desert Bloom: The Garamantian Capital and its Underground Water System', *Odyssey* (March 2000), pp.30 ff.

Mellaart, James, 'The Royal Treasure of Dorak – A First and Exclusive report of a Clandestine Excavation which led to the most important discovery since the Royal Tombs of Ur', *Illustrated London News* (28 November 1959), pp.754 ff.

——, *Çatal Hüyük, A Neolithic Town in Anatolia*, London, Thames & Hudson, 1967

——, 'Bronze Age and earlier languages of the Near East; an archaeological view', *Archaeological Theory and Practice*, London 1973, pp.163–72

——, *The Neolithic of the Near East*, London, Thames & Hudson, 1975

Mitchell, T.C., *The Bible in the British Museum: Interpreting the Evidence*, London, British Museum, 1988

Moore, A.M.T. and V.C. Tillman, 'The excavation of Tell Abu Hureyra in Syria: A Preliminary Report', *Proceedings of the Prehistoric Society*, 41 (1975), p.5077

Morrison, Martha A. and David I. Own (eds), *Studies on the Civilization and Culture of Nuzi and the Hurrians*, Winona Lake (Ind.), Eisenbrauns, 1981

Navarra, Fernand, *Noah's Ark: I touched it*, Logos International, 1974

Nützel, W., 'On the Geographical Position of as yet Unexplored Early Mesopotamian Cultures: Contribution to the Theoretical Archaeology', *Journal of the American Oriental Society*, 99 (1979), pp.288 ff.

Philo, Judaeus, *Works*, trans. C.D. Yonge, Bohn's Ecclesiastical Library, 4 vols, 1854

Piggott, Stuart (ed.), *The Dawn of Civilization: The First World Survey of Human Cultures in Ancient Times*, London, Thames & Hudson, 1961

Press, Frank and Raymond Siever, *Earth*, New York, W.H. Freeman & Co., 4th edn, 1986

Pritchard, J.B, *The Ancient Near East*, 2 vols, Princeton (N.J.), Princeton University Press, 1973

Reeves, Nicholas, *The Complete Tutankhamun*, London, Thames & Hudson, 1990

Renfrew, Colin, *Archaeology and Language*, London, Jonathan Cape, 1987

Renfrew, Jane M., *Palaeoethnobotany: The prehistoric food plants of the Near East and Europe*, London and New York, Methuen and Columbia University Press, 1973

Robertson, Ian, *Blue Guide Cyprus*, London and New York, A. & C. Black and W.W. Norton, 3rd edn, 1990

Romer, John, *Testament: The Bible and History*, London, Michael O'Mara, 1988

Ronen, Avraham, 'Besieged by Technology; The World's First Sect was a Straight-Laced Culture 8,500 Years Ago' *Scientific American Discovering Archaeology* (February 2000), pp.92 ff.

Ross, D.A., E.T. Degens and J. MacIlvane, 'Black Sea: Recent

Sedimentary History', *Science*, 170, no. 9 (October 1970), pp.163–5

Rossiter, Stuart, *Blue Guide Greece*, London, Ernest Benn, 3rd edn, 1977

Roux, Georges, *Ancient Iraq*, London, Allen & Unwin, 1964

Rudgley, Richard, *Lost Civilizations of the Stone Age*, London, Arrow Books, 1999

Ryan, William and Walter Pitman, *Noah's Flood, The New Scientific Discoveries about the Event that Changed History*, New York, Simon & Schuster, 1998

Schmandt-Besserat, D., *Before Writing*, Austin, University of Texas Press, 1992

Segal, J.B, *Edessa: 'The Blessed City'*, Oxford, Clarendon Press, 1970

Skeat, W.W. and C.O. Blagden, *Pagan Races of the Malay Peninsula*, Macmillan, London, 1906

Stager, J.C. and P.A. Mayewski, 'Abrupt Early to Mid-Holocene Climatic transition Registered at the Equator and the Poles', *Science*, 276 (June 1997), pp.1834–6

Stone, Merlin, *When God was a Woman*, New York, Dial Press, 1976

Taylor, K.C. et al., '"The Flickering Switch" of Late Pleistocene Climatic Change', *Nature*, 361, no. 4 (February 1993), pp.432–6

Todd, Ian A., *The Prehistory of Central Anatolia I: The Neolithic Period*, Studies in Mediterranean Archaeology vol. LX, Göteborg, Paul Aströms Förlag, 1980

Traill, David A., 'Priam's treasure, The Story behind the 4,000-Year-old Hoard of Trojan Gold', *Archaeology Odyssey* (July 1999), pp.14 ff.

Trump, D.H., *The Prehistory of the Mediterranean*, Harmondsworth, Penguin, 1981

van Andel, T.H. and Shackleton, J.C., 'Late Palaeolithic and Mesolithic coastlines of Greece and the Aegean', *Journal of Field Archaeology*, 9 (1982), pp.445–54

van der Post, Laurens, *The Lost World of the Kalahari*, London, Hogarth, 1980

van Zeist, W. and H. Woldring, 'Holocene Vegetation and

Climate of Northwestern Syria', *Palaeohistoria*, 22 (1980), pp.111–25

Vermaseren, Maarten J., *Cybele and Attis: The Myth and the Cult*, trans. A.M.H. Lemmers, London, Thames & Hudson, 1977

Vlassa, N., 'Chronology of the Neolithic in Transylvania, in the Light of the Tartaria Settlement's Stratigraphy', *Dacia*, N.S., 7, 1963, pp.485–94

Wallace, Ronald L., *Those who have Vanished, An Introduction to Prehistory*, Homewood (Illinois), Dorsey, 1983

Wilkinson, John, *Egeria's Travels*, London, SPCK, 1972

Wood, Michael, *In Search of the Trojan War*, London, Guild and BBC, 1985

Woolley, Sir Leonard, *Ur 'of the Chaldees'*, The final account, *Excavations at Ur*, revised and updated by P.R.S. Moorey, London, Herbert Press, 1982

Wyatt, Ron, *Discovered: Noah's Ark*, Nashville, World Bible Society, 1989

Zangger, E., *The Flood from Heaven*, London, Sidgwick & Jackson, 1992

APPENDIX

SOME KEY DOCUMENTS

PART I – THE NOAH FAMILY OF FLOOD STORIES

1: **From the biblical Book of Genesis, New Jerusalem Bible translation** (*New Jerusalem Bible, Darton, Longman & Todd and Doubleday & Company, Inc., 1985*) The 'J' strand is shown in ordinary type, the 'P' or Priestly strand appears in italics, following the separation of the strands adopted in Richard Elliott Friedman *Who Wrote the Bible?*, London, Jonathan Cape, 1988, p.54 ff.

Genesis, Chapter 6

... 5 Yahweh saw that human wickedness was great on earth and that human hearts contrived nothing but wicked schemes all day long. 6 Yahweh regretted having made human beings on earth and was grieved at heart. 7 And Yahweh said, 'I shall rid the surface of the earth of the human beings whom I created – human and animal, the creeping things and the birds of heaven – for I regret having made them.' 8 But Noah won Yahweh's favour.

9 *This is the story of Noah: Noah was a good man, an upright man among his contemporaries, and he walked with God. 10 Noah fathered three sons, Shem, Ham and Japheth. 11 God saw that the earth was corrupt and full of lawlessness. 12 God looked at the earth: it was corrupt, for corrupt were the ways of all living things on earth. 13 God said to Noah, 'I have decided that the end has come for all living things, for the earth is full of lawlessness because of human beings. So I am now about to destroy them and the earth. 14 Make yourself an ark out of resinous wood. Make it of reeds and caulk it with pitch inside and out. 15 This is how to make it: the length of*

the ark is to be three hundred cubits, its breadth fifty cubits, and its height thirty cubits. 16 *Make a roof to the ark, building it up to a cubit higher. Put the entrance in the side of the ark, which is to be, made with lower, second and third decks.* 17 *For my part I am going to send the flood, the waters, on earth, to destroy all living things having the breath of life under heaven; everything on earth is to perish.* 18 *But with you I shall establish my covenant and you will go aboard the ark, yourself, your sons, your wife, and your sons' wives along with you.* 19 *From all living creatures, from all living things, you must take two of each kind aboard the ark, to save their lives with yours; they must be a male and a female.* 20 *Of every species of bird, of every kind of animal and of every kind of creature that creeps along the ground, two must go with you so that their lives may be saved.* 21 *For your part, provide yourself with eatables of all kinds, and lay in a store of them, to serve as food for yourself and them.'* 22 *Noah did this; exactly as God commanded him, he did.*

Genesis, Chapter 7

1 Yahweh said to Noah,'Go aboard the ark, you and all your household, for you alone of your contemporaries do I see before me as an upright man. 2 Of every clean animal you must take seven pairs, a male and its female; of the unclean animals you must take one pair, a male and its female 3 (and of the birds of heaven, seven pairs, a male and a female), to preserve their species throughout the earth. 4 For in seven days' time I shall make it rain on earth for forty days and forty nights, and I shall wipe every creature I have made off the face of the earth.' 5 Noah did exactly as Yahweh commanded him.

6 *Noah was six hundred years old when the flood came, the waters over the earth.*

7 Noah with his sons, his wife, and his sons' wives boarded the ark to escape the waters of the flood.

8 (*Of the clean animals and the animals that are not clean, of the birds and all that creeps along the ground,* 9 *one pair boarded the ark with Noah, one male and one female, as God had commanded Noah.*)

10 Seven days later the waters of the flood appeared on earth.

11 *In the six hundredth year of Noah's life, in the second month, and on the seventeenth day of the month, that very day all the springs of the great deep burst through, and the sluices of heaven opened.*

12 And heavy rain fell on earth for forty days and forty nights.

13 *That very day Noah and his sons Shem, Ham and Japheth boarded the ark, with Noah's wife and the three wives of his sons,* 14 *and with them*

every species of wild animal, every species of cattle, every species of creeping things that creep along the ground, every species of bird, everything that flies, everything with wings. 15 *One pair of all that was alive and had the breath of life boarded the ark with Noah,* 16 *And those that went aboard were a male and female of all that was alive, as God had commanded him.* Then Yahweh shut him in.

17 The flood lasted forty days on earth. The waters swelled, lifting the ark until it floated off the ground. 18 The waters rose, swelling higher above the ground, and the ark drifted away over the waters. 19 The waters rose higher and higher above the ground until all the highest mountains under the whole of heaven were submerged. 20 The waters reached their peak fifteen cubits above the submerged mountains.

21 *And all living things that stirred on earth perished; birds, cattle, wild animals, all the creatures swarming over the earth, and all human beings.* 22 *Everything with the least breath of life in its nostrils, everything on dry land, died.*

23 Every living thing on the face of the earth was wiped out, people, animals, creeping things and birds; they were wiped off the earth and only Noah was left, and those with him in the ark.

24 *The waters maintained their level on earth for a hundred and fifty days.*

Genesis, Chapter 8

1 *But God had Noah in mind, and all the wild animals and all the cattle that were with him in the ark. God sent a wind across the earth and the waters began to subside.* 2 *The springs of the deep and the sluices of heaven were stopped up* and the heavy rain from heaven was held back. 3 Little by little, the waters ebbed from the earth.

After a hundred and fifty days the waters fell, 4 *and in the seventh month, on the seventeenth day of the month, the ark came to rest on the mountains of Ararat.* 5 *The waters gradually fell until the tenth month when, on the first day of the tenth month, the mountain tops appeared.*

6 At the end of forty days Noah opened the window he had made in the ark 7 and [he] released a raven, which flew back and forth as it waited for the waters to dry up on earth.

8 He then released a dove, to see whether the waters were receding from the surface of the earth. 9 But the dove, finding nowhere to perch, returned to him in the ark, for there was water over the whole surface of the earth; putting out his hand he took hold of it and brought it back into the ark with him. 10 After waiting seven more days, he again released the dove from the ark. 11 In the evening, the dove came back

to him and there in its beak was a freshly-picked olive leaf! So Noah realised that the waters were receding from the earth. 12 After waiting seven more days, he released the dove, and now it returned to him no more.

13 *It was in the six hundred and first year of Noah's life, in the first month and on the first of the month, that the waters began drying out on earth.* Noah lifted back the hatch of the ark and looked out. The surface of the ground was dry!

14 *In the second month, on the twenty-seventh day of the month, the earth was dry.*

15 *Then God said to Noah,* 16 *'Come out of the ark, you, your wife, your sons, and your sons' wives with you.* 17 *Bring out all the animals with you, all living things, the birds, the cattle and all the creeping things that creep along the ground, for them to swarm on earth, for them to breed and multiply on earth.'* 18 *So Noah came out with his sons, his wife, and his sons' wives.* 19 *And all the wild animals, all the cattle, all the birds and all the creeping things that creep along the ground, came out of the ark, one species after another.*

20 Then Noah built an altar to Yahweh and, choosing from all the clean animals and all the clean birds, he presented burnt offerings on the altar. 21 Yahweh smelt the pleasing smell and said to himself, 'Never again will I curse the earth because of human beings, because their heart contrives evil from their infancy. Never again will I strike down every living thing as I have done.

> 22 As long as earth endures:
>   seed-time and harvest,
>   cold and heat,
>   summer and winter,
>   day and night
>   will never cease.'

2: From the Babylonian Epic of Gilgamesh, translation by Andrew George, Tablet XI, lines 23–171 [*The Epic of Gilgamesh: The Babylonian Poem and Other Texts in Akkadian and Sumerian*, translated and with an introduction by Andrew George, London, Penguin 1999, pp.89–94]. Here italics indicate difficult or uncertain decipherments. Square brackets indicate words that can be confidently restored in passages where the tablet was broken. Italics within square brackets indicate restorations that are somewhat conjectural. Note that here Andrew George's word 'Deluge' has been retained, while for editorial consistency purposes 'Flood' has automatically been substituted wherever *Gilgamesh* passages have been quoted earlier in this book.

Tablet XI (beginning line 23)

   ' "O man of Shuruppak, son of Ubar-Tutu,
     demolish the house, and build a boat!
     Abandon wealth, and seek survival!
     Spurn property, save life!
Take on board the boat all living things' seed!

    ' "The boat you will build,
     her dimensions all shall he equal:
    her length and breadth shall be the same,
cover her with a roof, like the Ocean Below."

   'I understood, and spoke to Ea, my master:
    "I obey, O master, what thus you told me.
     I understood, and I shall do it,
but how do I answer my city, the crowd and the elders?"

    'Ea opened his mouth to speak,
     saying to me, his servant:
    "Also you will say to them this:
   'For sure the god Enlil feels for me hatred.

    ' " 'In your city I can live no longer,
     I can tread no more [on] Enlil's ground.
[I must] go to the Ocean Below, to live with Ea, my master,
   and he will send you a rain of plenty:

    ' " '[an abundance] of birds, a *profusion* of fishes,
    [*he will provide*] a harvest of riches.
In the morning he will send you a shower of bread-cakes,
   and in the evening a torrent of wheat.' "

   'At the very first glimmer of brightening dawn,
    at the gate of Atra-hasis assembled the land:
     the carpenter carrying [his] hatchet,
     the reed-worker carrying [his] stone,
[*the shipwright bearing his*] heavyweight axe.

    'The young men were…
    the old men bearing ropes of palm-fibre;
     the rich man was carrying the pitch,
    the poor man brought the … tackle. "

   'By the fifth day I had set her hull in position,
one acre was her area, ten rods the height of her sides.
At ten rods also, the sides of her roof were each the same length.
  I set in place her body, I drew up her design.

'Six decks I gave her,
dividing her thus into seven.
Into nine compartments I divided her interior,
I struck the bilge plugs into her middle.
I saw to the punting-poles and put in the tackle.

'Three myriad measures of pitch I poured in a furnace,
three myriad of tar I ... within,
three myriad of oil fetched the workforce of porters:
aside from the myriad of oil consumed in *libations*,
there were two myriad of oil stowed away by the boatman.

'For my workmen I butchered oxen,
and lambs I slaughtered daily.
Beer and ale, oil and wine
like water from a river [I gave my] workforce,
so they enjoyed a feast like the days of New Year.

'At sun-[*rise*] I set my hand [*to*] the oiling,
[before] the sun set the boat was complete.
... were very arduous:
from back to front we moved poles for the slipway,
[until] two-thirds of [the boat *had entered the water.*]

'[Everything I owned] I loaded aboard:
all the silver I owned I loaded aboard,
all the gold I owned I loaded aboard.
all the living creatures I had I loaded aboard.
I sent on board all my kith and kin,
the beasts of the field, the creatures of the wild, and members of
every skill and craft.

'The time which the Sun God appointed-
"In the morning he will send you a shower of bread-cakes,
and in the evening a torrent of wheat.
Go into the boat and seal your hatch!"-

'that time had now come:
"In the morning he will send you a shower of bread-cakes,
and in the evening a torrent of wheat.
I examined the look of the weather.

'The weather to look at was full of foreboding,
I went into the boat and sealed my hatch.
To the one who sealed the boat, Puzur-Enlil the shipwright,
I gave my palace with all its goods.

'At the very first glimmer of brightening dawn,
there rose on the horizon a dark cloud of black,
and bellowing within it was Adad the Storm God.
The gods Shullat and Hanish were going before him,
bearing his throne over mountain and land.

'The god Errakal was uprooting the mooring-poles,
Ninurta, passing by, made the weirs overflow.
The Anunnaki gods carried torches of fire,
scorching the country with brilliant flashes.

'The stillness of the Storm God passed over the sky,
and all that was bright then turned into darkness.
[He] charged the land like a *bull* [*on the rampage*],
he smashed [it] in pieces [*like a vessel of clay*].

'For a day the gale [winds *flattened the country*],
quickly they blew, and [*then came*] the [*Deluge*].
Like a battle [the cataclysm] passed over the people.
One man could not discern another,
nor could people be recognized amid the destruction.

'Even the gods took fright at the Deluge,
they left and went up to the heaven of Anu,
lying like dogs curled up in the open.
The goddess cried out like a woman in childbirth,
Belet-ili ['Lady of the Gods' – i.e. the Great Mother Goddess] wailed,
whose voice is so sweet:

"'The olden times have turned to clay,
because I spoke evil in the gods' assembly.
How could I speak evil in the gods' assembly,
and declare a war to destroy my people?

"It is I who give birth, these people are mine!
And now, like fish, they fill the ocean!"

The Anunnaki gods were weeping with her,
wet-faced with sorrow, they were weeping [with her],
their lips were parched and stricken with fever.

'For six days and [seven] nights,
there blew the wind, the downpour,
the gale, the Deluge, it flattened the land.

'But the seventh day when it came,
the gate relented, the Deluge *ended*.

The ocean grew calm, that had thrashed like a woman in labour
the tempest grew still, the Deluge ended.

'I looked at the weather, it was quiet and still,
but all the people had turned to clay.
The flood plain was flat like the roof of a house.
I opened a vent, on my cheeks fell the sunlight.

'Down sat I, I knelt and I wept,
down my cheeks the tears were coursing.
I scanned the horizons, the edge of the ocean,
in fourteen places there rose an island.

'On the mountain of Nimush the boat ran aground,
Mount Nimush held the boat fast, allowed it no motion.
One day and a second, Mount Nimush held the boat fast, allowed
it no motion,
a third day and a fourth, Mount Nimush held the boat fast,
allowed it no motion,
a fifth day and a sixth, Mount Nimush held the boat fast, allowed
it no motion.

'The seventh day when it came,
I brought out a dove, I let it loose:
off went the dove but then it returned.
there was no place to land, so back it came to me.

'I brought out a swallow, I let it loose:
off went the swallow but then it returned,
there was no place to land, so back it came to me.

'I brought out a raven, I let it loose:
off went the raven, it saw the waters receding,
finding food, *bowing and bobbing*, it did not come back to me.

'I brought out an offering, to the four winds made sacrifice,
incense I placed on the peak of the mountain.
Seven flasks and seven I set in position,
reed, cedar and myrtle I piled beneath them.

'The gods did smell the savour,
the gods did smell the savour sweet,
the gods gathered like flies around the man making sacrifice.

'Then at once Belet-ili arrived,
she lifted the flies of lapis lazuli that Anu had made for the courtship:
"O gods, let these great beads in this necklace of mine
make me remember these days, and never forget them!

> "All the gods shall come to the incense,
> but to the incense let Enlil not come,
> because he lacked counsel and brought on the Deluge,
> and delivered my people into destruction."

3: From Berossus, *Babyloniaka*, a lost history of Babylon written in Greek by the third century BC Babylonian priest Berossus, according to Alexander Polyhistor, a Greek of the first century BC. Greek text in F. Jacoby, *Die Fragmente der griechischen Historiker* III, C, pp.378–82. [English translation in W.G. Lambert & A.R. Millard, *Atra-hasis: The Babylonian Story of the Flood*, Oxford, Clarendon Press, 1969, pp.135–6]

The same Alexander, going still further down from the ninth king Ardates, as far as the tenth, called by them Xisuthros, reports on the authority of the Chaldean writings as follows: After the death of Ardates his son Xisuthros ruled for eighteen sars and in his time a great Flood occurred of which this account is on record:

Kronos appeared to him in the course of a dream and said that on the fifteenth day of the month Daisios mankind would be destroyed by a Flood. So he ordered him to dig a hole and to bury the beginnings, middles, and ends of all writings in Sippar, the city of the Sun(-god); and after building a boat, to embark with his kinsfolk and close friends. He was to stow food and drink and put both birds and animals on board and then sail away when he had got everything ready. If asked where he was sailing, he was to reply, 'To the gods, to pray for blessings on men.'

He did not disobey, but got a boat built, five stades long and two stades wide, and when everything was properly arranged he sent his wife and children and closest friends on board. When the flood had occurred and as soon as it had subsided, Xisuthros let out some of the birds, which, finding no food or place to rest, came back to the vessel. After a few days Xisuthros again let out the birds, and they again returned to the ship, this time with their feet covered in mud. When they were let out for the third time they failed to return to the boat, and Xisuthros inferred that land had appeared. Thereupon he prized open a portion of the seams of the boat, and seeing that it had run aground on some mountain, he disembarked with his wife, his daughter, and his pilot, prostrated himself to the ground, set up an altar and sacrificed to the gods, and then disappeared along with those who had disembarked with him. When Xisuthros and his party did not come back, those who had stayed in the boat disembarked and looked for him, calling him by name. Xisuthros himself did not appear to them any more, but there was a voice out of the air instructing them on the need to worship the gods, seeing that he was going to dwell with the gods because of his piety, and that his wife, daughter, and pilot shared in the same honour. He told them to return to Babylon, and, as was destined for them, to rescue the writings from Sippar and disseminate them to mankind. Also he told them that they were in the country of Armenia. They heard this, sacrificed to the gods, and journeyed on foot to Babylon. A part of the boat, which came to rest in the Gordyaean mountains of Armenia, still remains, and some people scrape pitch off the boat and use it as charms. So when they came to Babylon they dug up the writings from Sippar, and, after founding many cities and setting up shrines, they once more established Babylon.

4: From the Deucalion Flood story according to Apollodorus of Athens: The Greek scholar Apollodorus of Athens flourished c.140 BC, and is best known for his *Chronicle* of Greek history. The translation given here derives from Theodore H. Gaster, *Myth, Legend and Custom in the Old Testament*, New York, Harper & Row, 1969, p.84

Apollodorus, Book I.7, 2
Deucalion was the son of Prometheus. He reigned as king in the country about Phthia and married Pyrrha, the daughter of Epimethus and Pandora, the first woman fashioned by the gods. But when Zeus wanted to destroy the men of the Bronze age, Deucalion by the advice of Prometheus constructed a chest or ark, and having stored in it what was needful he entered into it with his wife. But Zeus poured a great rain from the sky upon the earth and washed down the greater part of Greece, so that all men perished except a few, who flocked to the high mountains near. Then the mountains in Thessaly were parted, and all the world beyond the Isthmus and Peloponnese was overwhelmed. But Deucalion in the ark, floating over the sea for nine days and as many nights, grounded on Parnassus and there, when the rains ceased, he disembarked and sacrificed to Zeus...'

5: From the Deucalion story acccording to Lucian of Samosata
Lucian of Samosata (c.120–180 AD) was born in Samosata, then in Commagene, Syria and now known as Samsat in Turkey. He was an orator and pamphleteer, notable for his cynicism. In the case of *Of the Syrian Goddess* in which his version of the Deucalion story appears, the original Greek text was translated in the 1920s by A.M. Harmon and was published in *Lucian* in eight volumes, trans. A.M. Harmon, London, Heinemann and Cambridge (Mass.) Harvard University Press, 1925. In a rather misguided attempt to convey the affectedly archaic style of Lucian's Greek, Harmon rendered his translation in Middle English. The translation given here is a

modernisation by Lilinah biti-Anat, with contributions from Harold W. Attridge and Robert A. Oden. It is available via the Internet at www.geocities.com/SoHo/Lofts/2938/deasyria2

Of the Syrian Goddess, Chapter 12

Most say Deucalion, called Sisythes [a variant of Xisuthros] founded the sanctuary. This is the Deucalion in whose time the great Flood befell. Of Deucalion I have heard a tale among the Greeks which they tell in honour of him, and the story goes as follows.

This generation, the people of nowadays, was not the first, but that first generation all perished, and this is of the second generation which came from Deucalion and multiplied. Concerning the first humans, they say they were quite violent and committed wicked deeds, for they did not keep oaths, nor welcomed strangers, nor spared suppliants; and because of these offences, the great tribulation came upon them. Suddenly the earth spewed forth a flood of water and heavy rains fell and the rivers rushed in torrents, and the sea rose amazingly high, until all things were changed into water and all humans perished. Deucalion alone among men was left for the second generation because of his prudence and good works. And his deliverance came in this way. Into a great ark that he possessed he put his children and his wives, and thence he himself entered. And as he boarded there came to him swine and horses and lionkind and serpents and all beasts that live, every kind of creature that grazes upon the earth, two by two. And he welcomed them all, and none did him any harm, for among them there was great charity from the gods, and in a single ark they all sailed while the Flood prevailed. So the Greeks say about Deucalion.

Chapter 13

But what happened after this, the inhabitants of the Holy City [i.e. Hierapolis] tell a tale at which we may rightly be amazed. How in their land a great chasm opened up and took in all the water, and when this happened, Deucalion set up altars and built a temple over the hole sacred to Hera [Atagartis]. I myself saw the hole, a quite little one, which is beneath the temple. If once it was large, and now has become such as it is, I do not know, but the one I saw is small.

In token of this story they do thus. Twice each year water from the Sea is brought into the temple. Not only priests, but the whole of Syria and Arabia brings it; and from beyond the Euphrates men go to the Sea and all bring water, that soon they pour out in the temple. And then it goes down into that hole; and even though the hole is small, nonetheless it takes in a great deal of water. And in doing thus they say that Deucalion established this custom for the sanctuary in memory both of that disaster and that divine favour.

Chapter 28
The place where the temple is situated is on a hill and it lies well within
the midst of the city, and two walls surround it. One of the walls is
ancient but the other is not much older than our own time. The
entrance of the sanctuary extends out to the north...and in that
entrance stand the pillars that Dionysus set up at a height of 300
fathoms. A man goes up one of these pillars twice a year and stays at the
top of the pillar for the period of seven days. And they say the cause of
his going up is this. Common folk believe that he speaks with the gods
on high and asks boons for all Syria, and the gods hear his prayers from
so near. But others believe that this is also done because of Deucalion,
in token and memory of that tribulation, when men went into the
mountains and into the great high trees for fear of the Flood.

[Author's note: One slight personal modification to this translation has
been in chapter 18 to substitute 'to the north', rather than use the translator's otherwise obscure phrase 'toward the Septemtryon']

PART II — FLOOD STORIES REFLECTING SEA-LEVEL RISE

1: From Philo Judaeus (c.20 BC–AD 50), an Alexandrian philosopher
who tried to reconcile the Bible with the works of Greek philosophers.
From Philo's On the Incorruptibility of the World [Philo Judaeus, Works,
trans C.D. Yonge, Bohn's Ecclesiastical Library, 4 vols, 1854Y]

On the separation of Sicily from Italy

Philo, On the Incorruptibility of the World, xxvi
Consider how many districts of the mainland, not only such as were
near the coast, but even such as were completely inland, have been
swallowed up by the waters; and consider how great a proportion of
land has become sea and is now sailed by innumerable ships. Who is
ignorant of that most sacred Sicilian strait, which in old times joined
Sicily to the continent of Italy? And where vast seas on each side being
excited by violent storms met together, coming from opposite directions, the land between them was overwhelmed and broken away...in
consequence of which Sicily, which had previously formed a part of the
mainland, was now compelled to be an island.

And it is said that many other cities have also disappeared, having been
swallowed up by the sea which overwhelmed them; since they speak of
three in Peloponnsos:

> Aigira and fair Boura's walls,
> And Helika's lofty halls

> And many a once renowned town
> With wreck and seaweed overgrown,

as having been formerly prosperous, but now overwhelmed by the violent influx of the sea.

2: From Diodorus Siculus *Biblioteca Historica* [*The Library of History*].

Diodorus Siculus was a 1st century BC Greek historian from Agyrium, Sicily who from his own statements made clear that he travelled in Egypt between the years 60 and 57 BC, where he researched in the royal library at Alexandria. He also spent some years in Rome. The last event recorded by him was in 21 BC. The translation that follows is that by C.H. Oldfather in *Diodorus of Sicily in Twelve Volumes*, vol III, p.227 ff, Loeb Classical Library, London, Heinemann, & Cambridge (Mass.), Harvard University Press, 1939

On the Black Sea having originally been a lake, and how sea-level rise affected the pre-Dardanelles island of Samothrace

Diodorus Siculus, *Biblioteca Historica*, Book 5, Chapter 47, 4

This island [Samothrace], according to some, was called Samos in ancient times, but when the island now known as Thrace came to be settled, because the names were the same, the ancient Samos came to be called Samothrace from the land of Thrace which lies opposite it. It was settled by men who were sprung from the soil itself...

The first and original inhabitants used an ancient language which was peculiar to them and of which many words are preserved to this day in the ritual of their sacrifices. And the Samothracians have a story that, before the floods which befell other peoples, a great one took place among them, in the course of which the outlet at the Cyanean Rocks was first rent asunder and then the Hellespont.

For the Pontus [Black Sea], which had at that time the form of a lake, was so swollen by the rivers that flow into it, that, because of the great Flood which had poured into it, the waters burst forth violently into the Hellespont and flooded a large part of the coast of Asia and made no small amount of the level part of the land of Samothrace into a sea. And this is the reason, we are told, why in later times fishermen have now and then brought up in their nets the stone capitals of columns, since even cities were covered by the inundation.

The inhabitants who had been caught by the Flood, the account continues, ran up to the higher regions of the island. And when the sea kept rising higher and higher, they prayed to the native gods, and since their lives were spared, to commemorate their rescue they set up boundary stones about the entire circuit of the island and dedicated altars upon which they offer sacrifices even to the present day. For these reasons it is patent that they inhabited Samothrace before the Flood ...

And ... they say that there were born in that land to Zeus and Electra, who was one of the Atlantids, Dardanus and Iasion and Harmonia. Of these children Dardanus, who was a man who entertained great designs and was the first to make his way across Asia in a makeshift boat, founded at the outset a city called Dardanus, organised the kingdom which lay about the city which was called Troy at a later time and called the people Dardanians after himself.

3: Diodorus Siculus, as translated by C.H. Oldfather in *Diodorus of Sicily in Twelve Volumes*, vol III, p.245 ff, Loeb Classical Library, London, Heinemann, & Cambridge (Mass.), Harvard University Press, 1939

On the island of Rhodes having been affected by floods

Diodorus, *Biblioteca Historica,* Book 5, Chapter 55
The island which is called Rhodes was first inhabited by the people who were known as Telchines; these were children of Thalatta [the Sea] ... And we are told that they were also the discoverers of certain arts and that they introduced other things which are useful for the life of mankind. They were also the first. Men say to fashion statues of gods, and some of the ancient images of gods have been named after them ...

Chapter 56
At a later time, the myth continues, the Telchines, perceiving in advance the Flood that was going to come, forsook the island and were scattered. Of their number Lycus went to Lycia and dedicated there beside the Xanthus river a temple of Apollo Lycius. And when the flood came the rest of the inhabitants perished – and since the waters, because of the abundant rains, overflowed the island, its level parts were turned into stagnant pools – but a few fled for refuge to the upper regions of the island and were saved, the sons of Zeus being among their number. Helius, the myth tells us, becoming enamoured of Rhodos, named the island after her and caused the water which had overflowed it to disappear ... And there came into being the Heliadae who were named after him [regarded by J. L. Myres to have been the early Minoan inhabitants of Rhodes] ... In consequence of these events the island was considered to be sacred to Helius.

The Heliadae, besides having shown themselves superior to all other men, likewise surpassed them in learning and especially in astrology; and they introduced many new practices of seamanship and established the division of the day into hours ...

Of their number Macar came to Lesbos, and Candalus to Cos and Eetis, sailing off to Egypt, founded there the city men call Heliopolis, naming it after his father; and it was from him that the Egyptians learned the laws of astrology. But when at a later time there came to be a flood among the Greeks and the majority of mankind perished by reason of the abundance of rain, it came to pass that all written monuments were also destroyed in the same manner as mankind; and this is the reason why the Egyptians, seizing the favourable occasion, appropriated to themselves the knowledge of astrology, and why, since the Greeks, because of their ignorance, no longer laid any claim to writing, the belief prevailed that the Egyptians were the first men to effect the discovery of the stars. Likewise the Athenians, although they were the founders of the city in Egypt men call Sais, suffered from the same ignorance because of the flood.

PART III — THE ATLANTIS LEGEND

From Plato's *Timaeus* and *Critias*. Plato (427–348 BC) was an Athenian philosopher who in the latter part of his life wrote a series of dialogues, in some of which his teacher Socrates features as leading the discussions. *Timaeus* and the unfinished *Critias* were two of these dialogues, both of these embodying references to the Atlantis legend, the latter carrying the greater detail. The translation given here is from B. Jowett, *The Dialogues of Plato* (3rd edition) Oxford, 1892, vol 3, as reproduced in J. V. Luce *The End of Atlantis: New Light on an Old Legend*, London, Thames & Hudson 1969, p.207ff

1) *Timaeus*, 20 d–27 a
Critias. Then listen, Socrates, to a tale which, though strange, is certainly true, having been attested by Solon, who was the wisest of the seven sages. He was a relative and a dear friend of my great-grandfather, Dropides, as he himself says in many passages of his poems; and he told the story to Critias, my grandfather, who remembered and repeated it to us. There were of old, he said, great and marvellous actions of the Athenian dry, which have passed into oblivion through lapse of time and the destruction of mankind, and one in particular, greater than all the rest. This we will now, rehearse. It will be a fitting monument of our gratitude to you, and a hymn of praise true and worthy, of the goddess, on this her day of festival.

Socrates. Very good. And what is this ancient famous action of the Athenians, which Critias declared, on the authority of Solon, to be not a mere legend, but an actual fact?

Critias. I will tell an old-world story which I heard from an aged man; for Critias, at the time of telling it, was, as he said, nearly ninety years of age, and I was about ten. Now the day was that day of the Apaturia which is called the Registration of Youth, at which, according to custom, our parents gave prizes for recitations, and the poems of several poets were recited by us boys, and many of us sang the poems of Solon, which at that time had not gone out of fashion. One of our tribe, either because he thought so or to please Critias, said that in his judgement Solon was not only the wisest of men, but also the noblest of poets. The old man, as I very well remember, brightened up at hearing this and said, smiling: Yes, Amynander, if Solon had only, like other poets, made poetry the business of his life, and had completed the tale which he brought with him from Egypt, and had not been compelled, by reason of the factions and troubles which he found stirring in his own country when he came home, to attend to other matters, in my opinion he would have been as famous as Homer or Hesiod, or any poet.

And what was the tale about, Critias? said Amynander.

About the greatest action which the Athenians ever did, and which ought to have been the most famous, but, through the lapse of time and the destruction of the actors, it has not come down to us.

Tell us, said the other, the whole story, and how and from whom Solon heard this veritable tradition.

He replied: In the Egyptian Delta, at the head of which the river Nile divides, there is a certain district which is called the district of Sais, and the great city of the district is also called Sais, and is the city from which King Amasis came. The citizens have a deity for their foundress; she is called in the Egyptian tongue Neith, and is asserted by them to be the same whom the Hellenes call Athene; they are great lovers of the Athenians, and say that they are in some way related to them. To this city came Solon, and was received there with great honour; he asked the priests who were most skilful in such matters, about antiquity, and made the discovery that neither he nor any other Hellene knew anything worth mentioning about the times of old.

On one occasion, wishing to draw them on to speak of antiquity, he began to tell about the most ancient things in our part of the world — about Phoroneus, who is called 'the first man', and about Niobe; and after the Deluge, of the survival of Deucalion and Pyrrha; and he traced the genealogy of their descendants, and reckoning up the dates, tried to compute how many years ago the events of which he was speaking happened. Thereupon one of the priests, who was of a very great age, said: O Solon, Solon, you Hellenes are never anything but children, and there is not an old man among you. Solon in return asked him what he meant. I mean to say, he replied, that in mind you are all young; there is no old opinion handed down among you by ancient tradition, nor any science which is hoary with age. And I will tell you why. There have been, and will be again, many destructions of mankind arising out of many causes; the greatest have been brought about by the agencies of fire and water, and other lesser ones by innumerable other causes.

There is a story, which even you have preserved, that once upon a time Phaëthon, the son of Helios, having yoked the steeds in his father's chariot, because he was not able to drive them in the path of his father, burnt up all that was upon the earth, and was himself destroyed by a thunderbolt. Now this has the form of a myth, but really signifies a declination of the bodies moving in the heavens around the earth, and a great conflagration of things upon the earth, which recurs after long intervals. At such times those who live upon the mountains and in dry and lofty places are more liable to destruction than those who dwell by rivers or on the sea-shore.

And from this calamity we are preserved by the liberation of the Nile, who is our never-failing saviour. When, on the other hand, the gods purge the earth with a deluge of water, the survivors in your country are herdsmen and shepherds who dwell on the mountains, but those who, like you, live in cities are carried by the rivers into the sea. Whereas in this land, neither then nor at any other time, does the water come down from above on the fields, having always a tendency to come up from below; for which reason the traditions preserved here are the most ancient. The fact is, that wherever the extremity of winter frost or of summer sun does not prevent, mankind exist, sometimes in greater, sometimes in lesser numbers. And whatever happened either in your country or in ours, or in any other region of which we are informed-if there were any actions noble or great or in any other way remarkable, they have all been written down by us of old, and are preserved in our temples.

Whereas just when you and other nations are beginning to be provided with letters and the other requisites of civilized life, after the usual interval, the stream from heaven, like a pestilence, comes pouring down, and leaves only those of you who are destitute of letters and education. And so you have to begin all over again like children, and know nothing of what happened in ancient times, either among us or among yourselves. As for those genealogies of yours which you just now recounted to us, Solon, they are no better than the tales of children.

In the first place you remember a single deluge only, but there were many previous ones. In the next place, you do not know that there formerly dwelt in your land the fairest and noblest race of men which ever lived, and that you and your whole city are descended from a small seed or remnant of them which survived. And this was unknown to you, because, for many generations, the survivors of that destruction died, leaving no written word. For there was a time, Solon, before the great deluge of all, when the city which now is Athens was first in war and in every way the best governed of all cities, and is said to have performed the noblest deeds and to have had the fairest constitution of any of which tradition tells, under the face of heaven.

Solon marvelled at his words, and earnestly requested the priests to inform him exactly and in order about these former citizens. You are welcome to hear about them, Solon, said the priest, both for your own sake and for that of your city, and above all, for the sake of the goddess who is the common patron and parent and educator of both our cities. She founded your city a thousand years before ours, receiving from the Earth and Hephaestus the seed of your race, and afterwards she founded ours, of which the constitution is recorded in our sacred registers to be 8,000 years old.

As touching your citizens of 9,000 years ago, I will briefly inform you of their laws and of their most famous action; the exact particulars of the whole we will hereafter go through at our leisure in the sacred registers themselves. If you compare these very laws with ours you will find that many of ours are the counterpart of yours as they were in the olden time.

In the first place, there is the caste of priests, which is separated from all the others; next, there are the artificers, who ply their several crafts by themselves and do not intermix; and also there is the class of shepherds and of hunters, as well as that of husbandmen; and you will observe, too, that the warriors in Egypt are distinct from all the other classes, and are commanded by the law to devote themselves solely to military pursuits; moreover, the weapons which they carry are shields and spears, a style of equipment which the goddess taught of Asiatics first to us, as in your part of the world first to you. Then as to wisdom, do you observe how our law from the very first made a study of the whole order of things, extending even to prophecy and medicine which gives health; out of these divine elements deriving what was needful for human life, and adding every sort of knowledge which was akin to them.

All this order and arrangement the goddess first imparted to you when establishing your city; and she chose the spot of earth in which you were born, because she saw that the happy temperament of the seasons in that land would produce the wisest of men. Wherefore the goddess, who was a lover both of war and of wisdom, selected and first of all settled that spot which was the most likely to produce men most like herself. And there you, dwelt, having such laws as these and still better ones, and excelled all mankind in all virtue, as became the children and disciples of the gods.

Many great and wonderful deeds are recorded of your state in our histories. But one of them exceeds all the rest in greatness and valour. For these histories tell of a mighty power which unprovoked made an expedition against the whole of Europe and Asia, and to which your city put an end. This power came forth out of the Atlantic Ocean, for in those days the Atlantic was navigable; and there was an island situated in front of the straits which by you are called the pillars of Heracles. The island was larger than Libya and Asia put together, and was the way to other islands, and from these you might pass to the whole of the opposite continent which surrounded the true ocean. For this sea which is within the Straits of Heracles (i.e. the Mediterranean) is only a harbour, having a narrow entrance, but the other is a real sea, and the land surrounding it on every side may be most truly called a boundless continent. Now in this island of Atlantis there was a great and wonderful empire which had rule over the whole island and several others, and over parts of the continent. And, furthermore, the men of Atlantis had subjected the parts of Libya within the columns of Heracles as far as Egypt, and of Europe as far as Tyrrhenia [Etruria in Italy]. This vast power, gathered into one, endeavoured to subdue at a blow our country and yours and the whole of the region within the straits; and then, Solon, your country shone forth, in the excellence of her virtue and strength, among all mankind. She was pre-eminent in courage and military skill and was the leader of the Hellenes. And when the rest fell off from her, being compelled to stand alone, after having undergone the very extremity of dangers, she defeated and triumphed over the invaders, and preserved from slavery those who were not yet subjugated, and generously liberated all the rest of us who dwelt within the pillars. But afterwards there occurred violent earthquakes and floods; and in a single day and night of misfortune all your warlike men in a body sank into the earth, and the island of Atlantis in like manner disappeared in the depths of the sea. For which reason the sea in those parts is impassable and impenetrable, because there is a shoal of mud in the way; and this was caused by the subsidence of the island.

2) *Critias*, 113–121

I have before remarked in speaking of the allotments of the gods, that they distributed the whole earth into portions differing in extent, and made for themselves temples and instituted sacrifices. And Poseidon receiving for his lot the island of Atlantis begat children by a mortal woman, and settled them in a part of the island, which I will describe.

Towards the sea, half-way down the length of the whole island, there was a plain which is said to have been the fairest of all plains and very fertile. Near the plain again, and also in the centre of the island at a distance of about fifty stadia, there was a mountain not very high on any side. In this mountain there dwelt one of the earth-born primeval men of that country, whose name was Evenor, and he had a wife named Leucippe, and they had an only daughter who was called Cleito.

The maiden had already reached womanhood, when her father and mother died. Poseidon fell in love with her and had intercourse with her, and breaking the ground, inclosed the hill in which she dwelt all round, making alternate zones of sea and land larger and smaller, encircling one another. There were two of land and three of water, which he turned as with a lathe, each having its circumference equidistant every way from the centre, so that no man could get to the island, for ships and voyages were not as yet. He himself, being a god, found no difficulty in making special arrangements for the centre island, bringing up two springs of water from beneath the earth, one of warm water and the other of cold, and making every variety of food to spring up abundantly from the soil.

He also begat and brought up five pairs of twin male children; and dividing the island of Atlantis into ten portions, he gave to the first-born of the eldest pair his mother's dwelling and the surrounding allotment, which was the largest and best, and made him king over the rest. The others he made princes, and gave them rule over many men, and a large territory. And he named them all; the eldest, who was the first king, he named Atlas, and after him the whole island and the ocean were called Atlantic.

To his twin brother, who was born after him, and obtained as his lot the extremity of the island towards the pillars of Heracles, facing the country which is now called the region of Gades in that part of the world, he gave the name which in the Hellenic language is Eumelus, in the language of the country which is named after him, Gadeirus. Of the second pair of twins he called one Ampheres, and the other Evaemon. To the elder of the third pair of twins he gave the name Mnescus, and Autochthon to the one who followed him. Of the fourth pair of twins he called the elder Elasippus, and the younger Mestor. And of the fifth pair he gave to the elder the name of Azaes, and to the younger that of Diaprepes. All these and their descendants for many generations were the inhabitants and rulers of divers islands in the open sea; and also, as has been already said, they held sway in our direction over the country within the pillars as far as Egypt and Tyrrhenia.

Now Atlas had a numerous and honourable family, and they retained the kingdom, the eldest son handing it on to his eldest for many generations. And they had such an amount of wealth as was never before possessed by kings and potentates, and is not likely ever to be again, and they were furnished with everything which they needed, both in the city and country. For because of the greatness of their empire many things were brought to them from foreign countries, and the island itself provided most of what was required by them for the uses of life.

In the first place, they dug out of the earth whatever was to be found there, solid as well as fusile, and that which is now only a name and was then something more than a name, orichalcum, was dug out of the earth in many parts of the island, being more precious in those days than anything except gold. There was an abundance of wood for carpenter's work, and sufficient maintenance for tame and wild animals. Moreover, there were a great number of elephants in the island. For as there was provision for all sorts of animals, both for those which live in lakes and marshes and rivers, and also for those which live in mountains and on plains, so there was for the animal which is the largest and most voracious of all.

Also whatever fragrant things there now are in the earth, whether roots, or herbage, or woods, or essences which distil from fruit and flower, grew and thrived in that land. Also the fruit which admits cultivation, both the dry sort, which is given us for nourishment and any other which we use for food – we call them all by the common name of pulse. And the fruits having a hard rind, affording drinks and meats and ointments, and good store of chestnuts and the like, which furnish pleasure and amusement, and are fruits which spoil with keeping. And the pleasant kinds of dessert, with which we console ourselves after dinner, when we are tired of eating – all these that sacred island which then beheld the light of the sun, brought forth fair and wondrous and in infinite abundance. With such blessings the earth freely furnished them.

Meanwhile they went on constructing their temples and palaces and harbours and docks. And they arranged the whole country in the following manner. First of all they bridged over the zones of sea which surrounded the ancient metropolis, making a road to and from the royal palace. And at the very beginning they built the palace in the habitation of the god and of their ancestors, which they continued to ornament in successive generations. Every king surpassed the one who went before him to the utmost of his power, until they made the building a marvel to behold for size and for beauty.

And beginning from the sea they bored a canal of three hundred feet in width and one hundred feet in depth and fifty stadia in length, which they carried through to the outermost zone. They made a passage from the sea up to this, which became a harbour, and left an opening sufficient to enable the largest vessels to find ingress. Moreover, they divided at the bridges the zones of land which parted the zones of sea, leaving room for a single trireme to pass out of one zone into another. And they covered over the channels so as to leave a way underneath for the ships; for the banks were raised considerably above the water.

Now the largest of the zones into which a passage was cut from the sea was three stadia in breadth, and the zone of land which came next of equal breadth; but the next two zones, the one of water, the other of land, were two stadia, and the one which surrounded the central island was a stadium only in width. The island in which the palace was situated had a diameter of five stadia. All this including the zones and the bridge, which was the sixth part of a stadium in width, they surrounded by a stone wall on every side, placing towers and gates on the bridges where the sea passed in.

The stone which was used in the work they quarried from underneath the centre island, and from underneath the zones, on the outer as well as the inner side. One kind was white, another black, and a third red, and as they quarried, they at the same time hollowed out docks double within, having roofs formed out of the native rock. Some of their buildings were simple, but in others they put together different stones, varying the colour to please the eye, and to be a natural source of delight. The entire circuit of the wall, which went round the outermost zone, they covered with a coating of brass, and the circuit of the next wall they coated with tin, and the third, which encompassed the citadel, flashed with the red light of orichalcum.

The palaces in the interior of the citadel were constructed on this wise:-In the centre was a holy temple dedicated to Cleito and Poseidon, which remained inaccessible, and was surrounded by an enclosure of gold. This was the spot where the family of the ten princes was conceived and saw the light, and thither the people annually brought the fruits of the earth in their season from all the ten portions, to be an offering to each of the ten. Here was Poseidon's own temple which was a stadium in length, and half a stadium in width, and of a proportionate height, having a strange barbaric appearance. All the outside of the temple, with the exception of the pinnacles, they covered with silver, and the pinnacles with gold. In the interior of the temple the roof was of ivory, curiously wrought everywhere with gold and silver and orichalcum; and all the other parts, the walls and pillars and floor, they coated with orichalcum.

In the temple they placed statues of gold: there was the god himself standing in a chariot – the charioteer of six winged horses – and of such a size that he touched the roof of the building with his head. Around him there were a hundred Nereids riding on dolphins, for such was thought to be the number of them by the men of those days. There were also in the interior of the temple other images which had been dedicated by private persons. And around the temple on the outside were placed statues of gold of all who had been numbered among the ten kings, both them and their wives, and there were many other great offerings of kings and of private persons, coming both from the city itself and from the foreign cities over which they held sway. There was an altar too, which in size and workmanship corresponded to this magnificence, and the palaces, in like manner, answered to the greatness of the kingdom and the glory of the temple.

In the next place, they had fountains, one of cold and another of hot water, in gracious plenty flowing; and they were wonderfully adapted for use by reason of the pleasantness and excellence of their waters. They constructed buildings about them and planted suitable trees. Also they made cisterns, some open to the heaven, others roofed over, to be used in winter as warm baths. There were the kings' baths, and the baths of private persons, which were kept apart; and there were separate baths for women, and for horses and cattle, and to each of them they gave as much adornment as was suitable.

Of the water which ran off they carried some to the grove of Poseidon, where were growing all manner of trees of wonderful height and beauty, owing to the excellence of the soil, while the remainder was conveyed by aqueducts along the bridges to the outer circles. And there were many temples built and dedicated to many gods; also gardens and places of exercise, some for men, and others for horses in both of the two islands formed by the zones. And in the centre of the larger of the two there was set apart a race-course of a stadium in width, and in length allowed to extend all round the island, for horses to race in.

Also there were guard-houses at intervals for the main body of guards, whilst the more trusted of them were appointed to keep watch in the lesser zone, which was nearer the Acropolis; while the most trusted of all had houses given them within the citadel, near the persons of the kings. The docks were full of triremes and naval stores, and all things were quite ready for use. Enough of the plan of the royal palace.

Leaving the palace and passing out across the three harbours, you came to a wall which began at the sea and went all round. This was everywhere distant fifty stadia from the largest zone or harbour, and enclosed the whole, the ends meeting at the mouth of the channel which led to the sea. The entire area was densely crowded with habitations; and the canal and the largest of the harbours were full of vessels and merchants coming from all parts, who, from their numbers, kept up a multitudinous sound of human voices, and din and clatter of all sorts night and day.

I have described the city and the environs of the ancient palace nearly in the words of Solon, and now I must endeavour to represent to you the nature and arrangement of the rest of the land. The whole country was said by him to be very lofty and precipitous on the side of the sea, but the country immediately about and surrounding the city was a level plain, itself surrounded by mountains which descended towards the sea; it was smooth and even, and of an oblong shape, extending in one direction three thousand stadia, but across the centre inland it was two thousand stadia. This part of the island looked towards the south, and was sheltered from the north. The surrounding mountains were celebrated for their number and size and beauty, far beyond any which still exist. They had in them also many wealthy villages of country folk, and rivers, and lakes, and meadows supplying food enough for every animal, wild or tame, and much wood of various sorts, abundant for each and every kind of work.

I will now describe the plain, as it was fashioned by nature and by the labours of many generations of kings through long ages. It was naturally for the most part rectangular and oblong, and where falling out of the straight line had been made regular by the surrounding ditch. The depth, and width, and length of this ditch were incredible, and gave the impression that a work of such extent, in addition to so many others, could never have been artificial. Nevertheless I must say what I was told. It was excavated to the depth of a hundred feet, and its breadth was a stadium everywhere; it was carried round the whole of the plain, and was ten thousand stadia in length. It received the streams which came down from the mountains, and winding round the plain and meeting at the city, was there let off into the sea.

Farther inland, likewise, straight canals of a hundred feet in width were cut from it through the plain, and again let off into the ditch leading to the sea. These canals were at intervals of a hundred stadia, and by them they brought down the wood from the mountains to the city, and conveyed the fruits of the earth in ships, cutting transverse passages from one canal into another, and to the city. Twice in the year they gathered the fruits of the earth – in winter having the benefit of the rains of heaven, and in summer the water which the land supplied, when they introduced streams from the canals.

As to the population, each of the lots in the plain had to find a leader for the men who were fit for military service. And the size of a lot was a square of ten stadia each way, and the total number of all the lots was sixty thousand. And of the inhabitants of the mountains and of the rest of the country there was also a vast multitude, which was distributed among the lots and had leaders assigned to them according to their districts and villages. The leader was required to furnish for the war the sixth portion of a war-chariot, so as to make up a total of ten thousand chariots. Also two horses and riders for them, and a pair of chariot-horses without a car, accompanied by a horseman who could fight on foot carrying a small shield, and having a charioteer who stood behind the man-at-arms to guide the two horses. Also, he was bound to furnish two heavy-armed soldiers, two archers, two slingers, three stone-shooters and three javelin-men, who were light-armed, and four sailors to make up the complement of twelve hundred ships. Such was the military order of the royal city – the order of the other nine governments varied, and it would be wearisome to recount their several differences.

As to offices and honours, the following was the arrangement from the first. Each of the ten kings in his own division and in his own city had the absolute control of the citizens, and, in most cases, of the laws, punishing and slaying whomsoever he would. Now the order of precedence among them and their mutual relations were regulated by the commands of Poseidon which the law had handed down. These were inscribed by the first kings on a pillar of orichalcum, which was situated in the middle of the island, at the temple of Poseidon, whither the kings were gathered together every fifth and every sixth year alternately, thus giving equal honour to the odd and to the even number.

And when they were gathered together they consulted about their common interests, and inquired if any one had transgressed in anything, and passed judgement. And before they passed judgement they gave their pledges to one another on this wise. There were bulls who had the range of the temple of Poseidon. And the ten kings, being left alone in the temple, after they had offered prayers to the god that they might capture the victim which was acceptable to him, hunted the bulls, without weapons, but with staves and nooses. And the bull which they caught they led up to the pillar and cut its throat over the top of it so that the blood fell upon the sacred inscription.

Now on the pillar, besides the laws, there was inscribed an oath invoking mighty curses on the disobedient. When therefore, after slaying the bull in the accustomed manner, they proceeded to burn its limbs, they filled a bowl of wine and cast in a clot of blood for each of them; the rest of the victim they put in the fire, after having purified the column all round. Then they drew from the bowl in golden cups, and pouring a libation on the fire, they swore that they would judge according to the laws on the pillar, and would punish him who in any point had already transgressed them. And that for the future they would not, if they could help, offend against the writing on the pillar, and would neither command others, nor obey any ruler who commanded them, to act otherwise than according to the laws of their father Poseidon.

This was the prayer which each of them offered up for himself and for his descendants, at the same time drinking and dedicating the cup out of which he drank in the temple of the god. And after they had supped and satisfied their needs, when darkness came on, and the fire about the sacrifice was cool, all of them put on most beautiful azure robes. And sitting on the ground, at night, over the embers of the sacrifices by which they had sworn, and extinguishing all the fire about the temple, they received and gave judgement. If any of them had an accusation to bring against any one; and when they had given judgement, at daybreak they wrote down their sentences on a golden tablet, and dedicated it together with their robes to be a memorial.

There were many special laws affecting the several kings inscribed about the temples; but the most important was the following: They were not to take up arms against one another. And they were all to come to the rescue if any one in any of their cities attempted to overthrow the royal house. Like their ancestors, they were to deliberate in common about war and other matters, giving the supremacy to the descendants of Atlas. And the king was not to have the power of life and death over any of his kinsmen unless he had the assent of the majority of the ten.

Such was the vast power which the god settled in the lost island of Atlantis.

[Author's note: This text has been edited slightly to break up overly-long sentences.]

INDEX